A Colorni-Hirschman International Institute 3

Dialogues

Eugenio Colorni and Altiero Spinelli

Dialogues

Edited by Luca Meldolesi
Translated from Italian by Michael Gilmartin

Bordighera Press

Library of Congress Control Number: 2020938869

Printed in the United States.

Published by
BORDIGHERA PRESS
John D. Calandra Italian American Institute
25 W. 43rd Street, 17th Floor
New York, NY 10036

A Colorni-Hirschman International Institute 3
ISBN 978-1-59954-176-1

TABLE OF CONTENTS

Introduction:
The Ventotene Dialogues[1]

On 22 August 2016, in a symbolic act (however fleeting) meant to expedite the navigation of the European caravel, the German chancellor, the French president and the Italian prime minister traveled to Ventotene to lay a wreath on the grave of Altiero Spinelli. It was precisely then that, as my own small contribution, I began writing this introduction. This was made possible by the availability of some texts of Altiero's from the period of his internment which had until then been "forgotten" (or nearly) by the critical press, as well as by my desire to better understand the genesis of the "Dialogues" and, indirectly, Eugenio Colorni's role in the process of constructing federalist policy and the Ventotene Manifesto. *It is thus an attempt to shed a little additional light (in a way that differs by design from many current reconstructions) on what happened at Ventotene between July 1939 and October 1941 in the now historic meetings involving Altiero Spinelli, Ernesto Rossi, Eugenio Colorni, and Ursula Hirschmann.*

1. In his 1984 autobiography — immersed in the tranquil joys of memory (as Manilo Rossi-Doria would have said[2]) — Altiero Spinelli reconstructed nearly every aspect of his dialogues with Eugenio Colorni at Ventotene[3]: "we spoke every day about all sorts of things — politics, non-Euclidean geometry, our fellow internees, what we had read, our personal lives, the great men of history — but I felt that he was always on the lookout for some hidden sore spot of mine, which he would then bring into the light, treated and healed [. . .]. I was fascinated by the almost infallible precision in the way he would discover the error in a logical argument, the dubious point behind an attitude, the rhetorical weight of an expression. The correction he proposed was not always acceptable, but he always touched points that were weak and therefore unsustainable.

---

[1]Thanks to Mario Quaranta and Nicoletta Stame for discussions and comments.
[2]Rossi-Doria 1991.
[3]Spinelli 1984, pp. 299–300.

Rather than passively allowing myself to be analyzed, I soon began to take the initiative — subjecting him to my own way of thinking but giving great weight to his judgments. If something held up under his scrutiny and won his approval I was reassured. But if he resisted, tore an idea down, or reacted ironically, for me this meant I hadn't properly thought something through, and it was back to the drawing board. I was grateful to him for this."

This was also how an important change took place in Spinelli's intellectual output. At one place in his diary, in an entry written on a train between Milan and Venice on 25 April 1953, Altiero said[4] that he had reread "with some curiosity" the letters kept by his parents that he had sent home during his 16 years of prison and internment. "What struck me most," he added, "was that up until Ventotene I had two completely different ways of writing. One was the way I write now, spare and clean and obviously aiming to understate any emotional motivation. [. . .] The second style was the one I used to express the thoughts that developed within me with the passage of time, with my readings and reflections. It was a contorted style, its strain reflected in the phrasing. It was the insufferable style of the writers who wrestled with Marxism, Crocianism, Hegelism — the style I do not like in Garosci, Valiani, Venturi. I wouldn't know how to write like that now because I am not able to think like that anymore. I had almost forgotten that for years this was my way of expressing myself [. . .] And yet it is not something I lost a little at a time, almost without realizing it. I have a strong memory of the circumstances in which I realized that it was false. In Ventotene in 1939 I began to weave a strange and extraordinary dialogue with Eugenio Colorni, one that went on for several years right up to his departure from the island. In part it was spoken and no trace remains except in my memory and in Ursula's — she was often present. But part of it was written. He and I, each on our own, continued our Socratic dialogue in the evenings [. . .]. I was the one who first wrote down one of these dialogues. When he read it — or rather listened to it, since I read that first one out loud to him and a few other people — he only remarked that: 'Up to a certain point

---

[4]Spinelli 1989, pp. 178–79.

it's very good and it's your own thinking; but after that it's nothing but that forced way of thinking that I consider false."

Writings and Metamorphoses
2. There is, then, in Altiero's writing style — and in his thinking style as well, an explicit break in continuity that can be detected *in corpore vili.* The first of the dialogues Spinelli refers to has a date (October 1939)[5] and a title (hardly unexpected): "Dialogue on the significance of systems."[6] Written in longhand (like the other "forgotten texts, of which we shall speak) on sheets duly stamped later with "Directorate Ventotene Internment Colony," it was deciphered (in large part) by Raffaella Cambiase, with the help of Vittoria Saulle and Giulia Vassallo, for the review *Eurostudium3w,* and has been available on line since 2007.[7] Skimming through it,

---

[5]This date alone clearly discredits Piero Graglia's statement (2010, p. 209 and ff.) that the friendship between Altiero, Ernesto, Eugenio, and Ursula was formed later, in the summer of 1940.

[6]Altiero's dialogues ("Dialogue on the significance of systems," "Contact in the night," [Ends and Means] and "Is what the gods want sacred or do the gods want what is sacred?"), the dialogues of Eugenio, Altiero and Giuliana Pozzo ("On Action"), that of Eugenio and Altiero ("On Success"), the first part of the "Dialogue on Detachment and death," written by Altiero along with his autograph note were checked against the originals kept in the Spinelli Fund at the Archives of the European Institute of Fiesole (Fi). Consulting these texts (not least to verify the contents of transcriptions from photocopies or microfiches) was an exciting experience because it brought us into direct contact with the universe of the Ventotene internees, and therefore with the world that produced the famous *Manifesto* — also kept in the Fund in its two versions, the one from Milan and the definitive one from Rome. The dialogues are written in a minute hand that uses every corner of the page, sometimes front and back — perhaps following instructions or perhaps to use less of the precious paper that was available. They form a crucial part of the educational endeavors, cultural and political, oral and written, that Eugenio, Altiero and other internees were undertaking on the island. Consultation of the documents takes place in a fabulous environment and the staff are very kind. Unfortunately, however, the cataloging and preservation system is rather antiquated, especially by comparison with the Mudd Library at Princeton where Albert Hirschman's papers can be consulted.

[7]It should be noted that the present research follows an inverse but complementary logic with respect to the work concerning Spinelli's philosophy animated by the group of young researchers (cited in the text) working with Prof. Francesco Gui. While that line of inquiry aims to highlight the upstream philosophical contributions to Altiero's federalist conversion, the present work intends to highlight the process of his intellectual reappraisal that preceded and accompanied the genesis of the *Manifesto.* Hence a different angle of interest in the texts of the period, leading to a focus on some writings rather than on others. And this, finally, opens the possibility of using some available transcripts of Spinelli's contributions for our own purposes, but also the need to painstakingly check them against the

you can even guess where, towards the middle of the text, Eugenio drew his dividing line between Altiero's positive argument and the "forced way of thinking" that Spinelli later abandoned.

"From that moment on," Altiero wrote on the same remarkable page, "I realized that I had to take care to express only my own thoughts and not to reformulate what I had learned but not digested in philosophical readings. I understood that you have to speak and write only the *clear* part of your thinking, leaving to ferment in silence anything rough or tense, or still under investigation. Writing is proclaiming an achievement. And since then I have not been able to write in the second style."

In any case, simply observing the texts available online leaves the impression that things are more complicated than Spinelli's conclusion makes them seem. In the first place, it is true that the "Dialogue on the significance of systems" represents a watershed. On one side are his previous writings (the letter to his brother Cerilo from 1935–36, "Rereading Croce's 'The Philosophy of the Spirit,'" May 1938 and "Some Observations Concerning 'Nature as History, not as History Written by Us. History and Prehistory,' also by Croce," June 1939), and on the other side those that followed. Understandably, however, an examination of these latter writings, especially those that spanned 1939–40, reveals the existence of a rather tormented process of transformation in thought and style. Because if it is true, as Altiero writes, that he did not lose his second style of writing (and thinking) little by little, almost without realizing it, it is also true that this abandonment could not have been instantaneous.

"Sometimes," Altiero records in his memoirs,[8] "one or the other of us, going over in the evening what we had said during the day, would continue the conversation by writing a dialogue in which the writer would have his say and would then imagine the other's replies. Sometimes there would be a further follow-up, written

---

original texts and take our own laborious turn at deciphering further writings of Altiero's.
[8]Spinelli 1984, p. 300. Obviously, the dialogues were written to be read and discussed between the two of them, not to be printed. This is something that has been kept in mind when making the decision to publish them. In other words, it is a good idea, along with looking at their intrinsic merits, to set them in the time and place where they were conceived and debated.

by the other, after which the dialogue would finish up in spoken form. Some of these written dialogues are in a sort of hodgepodge of things in my possession that I wrote during our confinement.[9] I don't believe I can say that any specific element in the thinking that has guided my actions since then comes from Colorni. But I do know for certain that my way of thinking would not be what it is if I had not had those two years — from my arrival at Ventotene in July of '39 until his departure for Melfi in October 1941 — of almost daily irreverent, inquiring and bracing dialogue with him."

And so we find in our hands an unexpected key to an issue we would like to unravel. Some of Altiero's writings, in fact, have Colornian arguments, or obviously were influenced by Eugenio — "Follow-up to 'Some observations about nature as history' etcetera" of November 1939, "Observations concerning an essay 'On the deception of words' written by Commodus" of December 1939, "Notes" of November-January 1939-40, "Contact in the night" of January 1940 — which, *ex ante* at least, we are unable to evaluate. This is because, in contrast to the first dialogue, we don't know Colorni's reactions on reading them, and also because Spinelli (as far as we know) did not look at them again. This too (and not only this, according to Francesco Gui,[10] judging from the lack of interest in Altiero's philosophical writings) was probably a source of some embarrassment among the critics, even those most explicitly "Spinellian,"[11] who in fact ignored them for many years.

3. We come briefly to the texts. "Dialogue on the significance of systems" (October 1939) takes on one of Colorni's classic war horses. It represents the start of what would become a custom, but its origin is "fortuitous, a chance conversation that was never even

---

[9]Presumably, Altiero is referring here to the first Spinelli Fund folder.

[10]Cf. Gui 2004.

[11]For example, Piero Graglia (in Spinelli 1993, p. 43, n. 30), referring to Altiero's dialogues ("repeatedly referred to and cited by their author, but without ever being made available in full") wrote that "even these writings are not considered publishable in the present collection, given their often intimate and personal nature." Instead Edmondo Paolini in his powerful 1996 volume of over six hundred pages of documentation and testimony limits himself to informing the reader (in a parenthesis in note 38 on p. 301) that Spinelli transcribed some of the dialogues with Colorni and other inmates in his Confinement Notebooks.

brought to a close." Spinelli continues that "it inspired me to set down my interlocutor's words in writing, for the purpose of clarification," in the form of a Socratic dialogue.[12] Thus this form was chosen by Spinelli and Eugenio liked it[13] — though the two protagonists, *Ceasar* (Colorni) and *Xavier* (Spinelli), would soon become, respectively, *Commodus* (the somewhat comical name of a Roman emperor: "commodious Commodus" he would be called at a certain point) and *Severus*.[14] The topic of the dialogue, as mentioned, is developed in an initially pleasing and precise way, at least to a Colornian ear, but it is subsequently lost in the philosophical currents.

Another of Altiero's texts, however — "Follow-up to 'Some observations about nature as history' etcetera" (November 1939) — begins as follows: "I was asked [evidently by Eugenio]: 'Doesn't it seem to you that the difference between philosophy and all the other sciences is this: that in all the sciences, knowing the subject matter means being able to reproduce it, or in more general terms to have its constituent elements available in order to establish how it will

---

[12]"Re-reading the first pages," adds Altiero, "I realized that they had incidentally taken the form of dialogue, and that is how I continued them."

[13]"The process of dialogue, like that of thought," explains Spinelli, "is such that it always returns to itself. It does not set a premise and then draw endless inferences. It instead poses a concept and always comes back to — modifying it every time, but always giving the concept in its entirety." As we shall see later on, this procedure lends itself to supporting (especially, I would say) Colorni's type of reasoning.

[14]It is easy enough, of course, to revisit these two emperors here, bearing in mind that Altiero had a better grounding than Eugenio in classical Latin and Greek, and that Eugenio, on the other hand, had a deeper vein of self-irony. Taken together, the two names Commodus and Severo evoke the transition point between the "age of equilibrium" and "the age of anxiety [or anguish]" of the Roman Empire — to cite two important recent exhibitions: AA. VV. 2012 and 2015. (Historically, Commodus was the restless son of the emperor-philosopher Marcus Aurelius. He succeeded his father at the age of 19 and was loved by the people and the army, but hated by the senate. He was considered the Roman Hercules, not least because he participated in gladiatorial combats, scandalizing the conformists. He had extravagant, megalomaniacal and absolutist tendencies of an orientalizing type. He was killed in a conspiracy and then rehabilitated by Septimius Severus who, after a brief interregnum, became emperor in his turn. As for Ritroso [Ernesto], there is apparently no classical reference: perhaps it expresses an aspect of Rossi's character in the sense that, as we shall see, he tended to be withdrawn. Finally, Ursula appears in the dialogues as Ulpia: probably Ulpia Severina, the wife of Aureliano, who at the death of her husband briefly exercised power — the only woman to do so in the imperial history of Rome.) The posthumous attribution of the title "Dialogues of Commodus" to these writings is inaccurate, if only because it refers to Colorni's contribution alone.

further develop, while for philosophy this kind of 'knowing' does not take place?" To answer this question, Altiero refers to "Some observations concerning 'Nature as history, not as history written by us. History and prehistory' by Croce" of June 1939 (and therefore before Spinelli's arrival at Ventotene), as well as to "Dialogue on the significance of systems" (cited above). From these writings he draws inspiration for his own presentation on intellect and philosophical reasoning, on death and on life.

In addition, "Appendix. Observations concerning an essay 'On the deception of words' written by Commodus" (December 1939) concerns an essay or chapter of Eugenio's (probably from the spring of 1939[15]) that has not survived, while "Notes" (November 1939–January 1940) also refers to words, as well as to mathematics, physics, etc., but with the aim of developing an independent philosophical treatment. Finally, after having in all probability discussed Eugenio's ideas (or even some texts) on love,[16] Altiero wrote "Contact in the night" (January 1940; cf. below), consisting of two parts:

---

[15]Actually, part of his argument was anticipated (in all probability) by Eugenio and Ursula in two letters on the deception of words, respectively of 6 and 25 May 1939. In the first of these, Eugenio wrote (among other things): "In conclusion, I will let you love your language, on the condition that you love it like Hölderlin and Nietzsche and George — in order to do it violence; not like Goethe and Mann, to submit to it. Please keep writing to me on this subject, because I'm openly stealing from you a chapter for my book, entitled 'the deceit of words.'" Then in the second letter, he clarifies: "Kant (the only philosopher I truly love) was brave enough to free himself from the myth of 'reality,' but not from the myth of 'words.' He had the courage to say that space, time, substance and causality do not represent anything real, but he did not have the courage to say that they are just tools, valuable only so long as they are useful. He said: we are bound to them, they constitute the necessary essence of our being, which is to say: they are not Reality (with a capital R), but they are 'Words' (capital W). Freeing oneself from philosophy (or at least from what has been called philosophy up to now) means freeing oneself from the capital letters, that is from the slavery of words. And to do this, to speak always in small letters, requires agility, ease, grace, modesty, good taste, simplicity, and honesty beyond compare." (Cf. Colorni 2016, chap. 3.)

[16]Such as the conclusions of "Philosophical criticism and theoretical physics" and/or "On the concept of 'love' (Colorni 2009, pp. 234–35 and 253–57), initially written (probably) in May-June 1939: cf., in this regard, Eugenio's letters to his wife Ursula of 27.5 and 10.6.1939: Colorni 2016, pp. 56 and 63–64. (But the versions of these two texts that have come down to us may also take into account the collective discussion of love which apparently occurred at the beginning of 1940. And the second text may have been written — or rewritten — ad hoc, since it was included in the "summaries" sent by Eugenio to Ludovico Geymonat in 1942 as an example of the themes to be addressed in his "Project for a scientific methodology review": Colorni 2009, pp. 176–79. Cf., concerning this, Quaranta 2011, p.128).

"I — Letter from Severus (A.S.) to Commodus (E.C.); II — Dialogue between Severus and Commodus." The first concerns psychoanalysis, love and (again) the deceptions of words and the intellect, and is followed by a brief dialogue and a final note on love.

Conclusion (albeit provisional): with surprising frequency, starting in the autumn of 1939, Altiero undertook to write texts, more or less in dialogue form, inspired by a theme often proposed by Eugenio and discussed with Eugenio. His aim was not so much to fully grasp what his friend meant or to thoroughly test the solutions he had offered in the discussion, but rather to utilize such occasions to express his own point of view and to make use of Eugenio's reactions. "The intellectual positions of my interlocutor," Altiero quite clearly pointed out, introducing "Dialogue on the significance of systems," "while seeming to me untenable, did not strike me as indifferent, or 'interesting' as we politely say of something that doesn't affect us; on the contrary, they met halfway with a number of my own thoughts. They helped me clarify these to myself. And this was basically the reason I wrote what follows."

4. This rather peculiar intellectual (and human) episode thus reflected the encounter between two thirty-year-olds (Altiero was two years older than Eugenio) endowed with strong personalities, but who were very different from one another.

Even "in the sadness of enforced inertia" (to use Colorni's expression[17]), they began to discover the possibility of a constellation of favorable circumstances (a win-win situation, as it would be called nowadays) for their respective cultural endeavors. Eugenio, engaged at the time in an extremely intense intellectual effort, took pleasure in the ongoing discussions with his friend (more than with the other internees) of this or that aspect of his arduous struggle against the philosophical illness; and in discovering along the way that the dialogue structure proposed by Spinelli allowed him to argue his positions in the most accessible and (at times) self-deprecating way. Altiero, on the other hand, realized that this openness on Eugenio's part was valuable for his own development — as a way

---

[17]Colorni, "Preface" to the Ventotene *Manifesto,* in Spinelli 1985, p. 195.

of arguing and testing certain of his conceptions, as well as reformulating his style of reasoning and expressing himself.

Both of them reacted against the oppressive conditions of "strict discipline" and personal isolation[18] they were in and benefited from the reciprocal intellectual interaction. But they were pursuing different goals. Eugenio, born a philosopher, intended to move forward in the process, already begun, of "unblocking" his (and others') thinking, which had notable consequences in so many fields, politics included.[19] Altiero, on the other hand, was a politician, initially trained in the communist ranks, who had studied philosophy in prison, on his own. He tried to react in his own way to Eugenio's reasoning, from the starting point of his own knowledge and experience, perhaps just to see how Eugenio would react. His aim was to emerge from his condition as an "amateur," and to improve his reasoning ability as much as possible, above all for political purposes.[20] He was more interested, one might say, in reshaping his way of thinking and expressing himself than in the actual content of any specific arguments — to the extent that, as we have seen, this was how he remembered this intellectual metamorphosis many years later — as a question (basically) of style.

On the one hand, however, it was true that this transformation was possible because, as Altiero's strictly philosophical writings show, he had already in a certain sense succeeded in coming to terms with "Marxism, Crocianism, Hegelism,"[21] so that now it was

---

[18]Ibid. Even from the other internees: for well-known objective reasons (such as Altiero's expulsion from the PCI), but for subjective ones as well (such as Eugenio's decision to live a secluded life — to avoid ideological discussions, to concentrate on studying, to support his numerous official requests with formally irreproachable behavior — cf. Gui 2010).

[19]Cf. Meldolesi 2017.

[20]In doing this, he never really tried to understand the genius of Eugenio; he was (and would remain) unable to fully understand it despite the friendship and collaboration between the two. For example, Spinelli (1984, p. 297) wrote about Colorni that "politics always interested him only to the extent that it was something he had to do, [which] at a rather superficial level always irritated him a bit, his true intellectual passions lying elsewhere": an ungenerous judgment, belied by the facts before and after Ventotene, and one which on the contrary betrays a certain rigidity of thought by comparison with the intellectual flexibility and versatility which, as we shall see, Eugenio demonstrated in abundance (cf. below, n. 91). Moreover, as known, this intellectual misunderstanding would be reflected, later on, in the "missed meeting" between Altiero Spinelli and Albert Hirschman.

[21]Gui 2004.

essentially a question of adapting the way he expressed himself to this "change of heart." On the other hand, however, as we have seen, this required a certain period of adjustment (however brief), so that in retrospect the texts appear, to today's reader at least, not as true contributions, but as writings that are sometimes success-ful, sometimes tormented; exercises interspersed with imaginative and evocative expressions that in any case let us glimpse the rea-soning of a new political Altiero — the one who shortly thereafter would take the field to great effect.[22]

This should not, however, in my opinion, lead to the hasty con-clusion, generally reached by the critics, that the writings of Eu-genio in the Ventotene dialogues should be summarily privileged and those of Altiero skipped over.[23] This if only for the reason that such an approach is the logical companion of its opposite,[24] gen-erally applied to the genesis of the *Manifesto,* which is to limit the discussion to the two actual drafters of the text — Altiero Spinelli and Ernesto Rossi (or even, often enough, just to the former!) — at the expense, obviously, of Eugenio Colorni.[25]

The purpose of these pages is to show, on the contrary, that to begin to understand what happened back then at Ventotene it is necessary (first and foremost) to put the respective worlds of Spinelli and Colorni, which so far have always been considered separately, in communication with one another. This leads to a twofold result: on the one hand to become (a bit more) aware of the consolidation and clarification of Eugenio's cognitive perspec-tive,[26] and on the other to grasp (better, compared with what has

---

[22]With the personal charm and the charismatic, messianic vision that we know. Perhaps this is why — because of the retrospective perception of the texts as (at least in part) outdated — neither Altiero nor the pro-European critics later felt the need . . . to go back to them.

[23]To the point of deciding to omit from the publication the first part of the "Dialogue on detachment and death" written by Spinelli: see Colorni 2009, p. 358 n.

[24]Also a questionable solution, to which the critics — be they long-winded or journalistic — generally accede.

[25]These are intellectual inclinations that obviously (it is hardly necessary to note this) re-flect as a whole the traditional division of labor between philosophers on the one hand, and political scientists (and historians) on the other.

[26]In fact (as the reader will have understood), the present work arises primarily from the need to place Colorni's dialogues in the environment where they originated in order to understand them better. Like the research on Eugenio's letters from prison and internment

been done up to now) the sense of the famous "political discovery" initially claimed by Ernesto (and Altiero) from which the *Manifesto* springs, and to which we must now briefly turn our attention.

Federalist Politics and Theoretical Balance

5. In fact, in the microcosm in which the Ventotene group lived in that fateful year of 1940, a second center of interest gradually took shape, inspired primarily by Ernesto Rossi, who had arrived on the island in October 1939 (that is, at the time of the first dialogue — Altiero's "On the significance of systems"). "He [Ernesto] said that he was born in the wrong century, because all his elective affinities were with the Enlightenment of the eighteenth century, especially English and French — he loved the clear speech, precise reasoning, and cult of rationality. I believe," Spinelli wrote[27] "that he dedicated himself to studying economics because in it he recognized the science which more than any other aimed to study the behavior of humans as rational beings. [. . .] Like me, he had quite a strong sense of the bottomless ocean of irrationality, brutality, stupidity, and ignorance [. . .]. But unlike me, he refused to try and listen to the chaos, to understand it and occasionally partly reduce it in that moment when a new cycle of rationality is born." The (somewhat elitist) "Jacobin spirit" that animated Ernesto is well known, along with the decisive role he had at Ventotene, not only in locating pioneering articles on Luigi Einaudi's federalism, but in the contact he had with Einaudi (Ernesto had been his assistant) and the acquisition (by this means) of some key texts "in the literature of English federalism, which flourished at the end of the 30s thanks to Lord Lothian" and of course by Lionel Robbins,[28]

---

and on the political writings that preceded it (in this series), this work also moves in the direction of bridging, as far as possible, the numerous "gaps" that still exist in the critical study and publication of the contributions of this author. Nevertheless, the truth is that we are still a long way from a complete and convincing edition of his extraordinary output.

[27]Spinelli 1984, p. 302.

[28]Texts that were "a revelation" to Altiero: cf. ibid., p. 307. According to the Appendix in Spinelli 1993, Altiero met (among others) Einaudi in 1920 and 1933, and Robbins in 1932, 1935, 1937 and 1940. In addition, in an interview (cf. Spinelli 1985, p. 202–03), Altiero recalled Friedrich Meineke's *Cosmopolitism and the National State* (1930) and Lionel Robbins's *The Economic Causes of the War* "which," he maintained, "I translated at Ventotene, and which the publisher Einaudi then published without my name."

and in the planning and actual writing of the *Manifesto*.

Much less well-known, on the other hand, is the picture of Ernesto that appears later in Altiero's diaries (13 April 1955):[29] "Strange man. It was Eugenio Colorni who gave the best description of him once at Ventotene. He is dynamic, active, always excited. He seems to be the personified expression of life and thought. In reality, he is a man who is afraid of life and of thought, because they carry in them the mystery of the future. He wants to be safe. Not to think of new things, but to repeat tirelessly, like a formula for a magic spell, the old things he already knows. He loves formally perfect logic because it contains nothing obscure or frightening. His work as a publicist is all about endlessly repeating a few clear and simple concepts [. . .] in the desperate hope that perhaps the world will adapt to them. But he doesn't like action aimed at bringing about this adaptation, because action is dangerous — it might fail — and he is afraid of failing. His infinite, puerile fear of life leads him to behave towards others like a child who wants to be loved. He rewards anyone who shows their love for him with excessive trust and admiration. In those who don't love him he forgives nothing. For him, federalism was one of his magic-rational formulas for spiritual security. To the extent that he tried to become a politician, he ceased to understand it. And since it is now a difficult policy, and offers no security at all, he gradually detaches himself from it."

Thus we find before us a personality very different from those of Altiero and Eugenio,[30] but one who nevertheless, together with them

---

[29]Spinelli 1989, p. 245. If I may be permitted a personal note, I would like to add that, duly adapted, Eugenio and Altiero's judgment of Ernesto has a more general meaning: in the first place, it illuminates a certain way of thinking widespread in post-war Italy in the secular culture as well as among post-war Italian economists of Salveminian origin, Paolo Sylos-Labini in particular.

[30]Note, in particular, Ernesto's downright paradoxical incomprehension of Eugenio's cognitive processes, as exhibited in the following words written in Colorni's honor (L'avvenire dei lavoratori, 15 July 1944; now in Rossi 1975, p. 189) : "Anyone who knew him as I did at that time [at Ventotene] could easily have come to the conclusion that Colorni was an intellectual absolutely incapable of practical action. He was continually in spiritual crisis. Every day he wanted to re-examine every problem over again, for the fear that his thinking would crystallize into well-defined categories, that it would settle into some comfortable system. It could be said that he loved the search for truth more than truth itself."

in the particular grim conditions of confinement, discovered con-
stellations of favorable circumstances to be set in motion in response
to developing events, and this with intelligent foresight and interest.

To say nothing, finally, of Ursula Hirschmann, rebellious, capable, generous, proud, determined[31] — whom destiny later kept
from completing her *Commemoration*,[32] and whose right to pass,
as she put it, from a decade of seeking "but never finding," to a period marked by "having found,"[33] has unfortunately been seasoned
with the pathological curiosity of die-hard Italian machismo.[34] Ursula immediately took on an organizational role involving contact
with the mainland that was decisive for the birth of Italian federalism, and — albeit at the price of considerable personal sacrifice —
she was later an ideal partner in Altiero Spinelli's long and difficult
European battle.

To conclude on this point, I am reminded of the ending of Albert Hirschman's *Journeys toward Progress*, where he explains that
achieving great changes sometimes requires that different abilities
and personalities be put to good use, as in the Risorgimento.[35] The
rationalism of Ernesto the economist has already been mentioned.
In addition, for Eugenio's "theory of discovery"[36] the federalist answer proposed in the Ventotene *Manifesto* was decisive — it was a
flag actually worth fighting for, and fiercely.[37] Altiero, once he had

---

[31]"A great heart," Albert Hirschman said to me of her one day, in private.

[32]Ursula Hirschmann 1974.

[33]Ibid., P. 3. In a short declaration of 1963 written in German and placed before the main text, Ursula wrote: "I am now fifty years old [. . .]. Over the last twenty years I have lived without asking myself questions, having found my raison d'être [. . .]. But between the ages of twenty and thirty I searched and searched without ever finding; and it was in those years that I met Eugenio and in part I shared his life."

[34]Already present, in my opinion, in the passage by Giorgio Braccialarghe cited by Altiero (1984, p. 300).

[35]"Of course," Albert explained (1963, p. 275), "these two tasks [plea bargaining and agi-tation] are so different that the best way to perform them is to entrust them to a plurality of main actors who feel totally independent of each other, as in the struggle for the unification of Italy, which was able to draw on the very different talents of Cavour, the head weaver, and of Mazzini and Garibaldi who covered the roles of conspirator and of agitator" — not to mention, I would add, Cattaneo: the great theorist of Italian and European federalism.

[36]According to which the key theses of the *Manifesto* were permitted to emerge because its advocates, with Altiero in the lead, had fought (as mentioned) against themselves, against their previous theoretical consciences, against their anthropomorphism.

[37]In fact, according to the testimony of Sirio Lentini, in the Roman resistance Eugenio

focused on his federalist objective, finally had the courage to pursue it relentlessly, to the point of receiving, as noted above, the reverent homage of the German Chancellor, the French President and the Italian Prime Minister. All this resulted from the raising of a crucial issue, which we cannot help but continue to explore — not least because it tends to reappear in other guises; and it will certainly come up again, many times, in the future.

6. And it is precisely in thinking about the future, and not only the present, that it is worthwhile to examine the Ventotene dialogues, certainly for their contribution to thinking and self-expression, but not only that — also to help us "learn to learn" from the evolving circumstances we find ourselves in (including those that are less than favorable),[38] and then, as we shall now see, to transform this process into one that is positive and collective.

At this point, a careful retrospective observation reveals that . . . and it is here that Eugenio steps before the class.[39]

A question immediately arises: how was Colorni able in these dialogues to write such memorable pages on so many apparently (but only apparently) dissimilar issues, using the theoretical investigations he was conducting as a basis, and measuring himself against current cultural trends, such as those of his main interlocutors — "Marxist, Crocian, Hegelian," in Altiero's case and English-rationalist in Ernesto's?

"was enthusiastic about his political struggle and the federalist idea" (cit. In Tedesco 2014, p. 150). Colorni fought for the unity of a federalist movement which was at the time animated by inevitably different cultural and political choices, faced as it was by the tendency to divide the world into spheres of influence that resulted in the cold war. He tried, Eugenio, to establish a sort of political partnership, even at a distance, with Altiero (to whom he had assigned the affectionate nickname of Pantagruel). And he maintained until the last, despite their differences, a relationship of friendship, esteem and active collaboration with Spinelli and with Rossi (Meldolesi 2017).

[38] I allude here to my *Learning to Learn* (2013) from Eugenio and Albert; and perhaps even more to my spontaneous reaction to the many (too many) young people who suffer from the difficulties they find themselves in. Take the example, I tell them, of the people in Trieste, Ventotene and the Roman resistance who were able to react with passion, but also with a grain of salt, to difficulties that were of an entirely different order!

[39] It is clear that Colorni, like many great innovators, suffered a great deal (too much!) due to the incredulity and misunderstanding of others, even those closest to him — with the exception, of course, of Albert Hirschman.

I would say it was by keeping faith with his research program; gradually exposing his friends to cultural and scientific themes that he considered relevant (but which would not alarm the camp authorities); utilizing the stimuli of their common discussions for his own purposes; and finally, resisting the passions — often pan-political, one might say — of his interlocutors. Which is to say, taking an interest in current events, of course, but energetically discussing the political situation, the war, the European federalist proposal, etc. *alongside* his own intellectual work — convinced as he was that progress there would *also* afford him a better understanding of these issues, much more so than vice versa.

Unfortunately, our present state of knowledge does not allow us to go much further in reconstructing the (individual and collective) trail of the little Ventotene group, nor to follow the successive lines of reasoning and argument of its members. We do not in fact know the calendar of the discussions and themes that were successively dealt with. Even the dating of the dialogues that have come down to us is unfortunately incomplete.

At the same time, to get an idea, albeit hypothetical and conjectural, of *what might have happened,* we can go back in our minds to Altiero's writings from the winter of 1939–40. As noted, these represent a sort of "intellectual apprenticeship" which found inspiration (sometimes) in this or that aspect of Eugenio's epistemology in order to present (and defend) some of Spinelli's own ideas. And yet, between the letter and the brief dialogue contained in "Contact in the night" (from January 1940) and Altiero's main dialogue from August 1941 which, as I will explain later, I gave a title ["Ends and Means"] there is a gap of a year and a half. Why?

To answer this, just imagine what the reaction of the protagonists would have been in the face of the terrible decline in the European political-military situation (the German blitzkrieg, Italy's entering the war, the invasion of France, etc.). Naturally, predictably, the group's daily political worries became increasingly overriding,[40] and each reacted in his own way: Altiero privileged

---

[40]At the same time, even in the spring-summer of 1940, despite the steady stream of dramatic news that reached the ears of the internees (however muted on Ventotene, a milita-

(not surprisingly) the political battle, while Eugenio was instead concerned, in spite of everything, to protect the continuity of his studies. This is also evident in the dialogue "On Action" (see below), written jointly in September-October of 1941,[41] in which Colorni has *Severus* say: "I really get irritated with speeches like the one *Commodus* made the other night when he was talking about next year as if he were going to be here forever"; to which *Commodus* replies, "for the last year and a half" (that is, since the start of the German "lightning war") *Severus* "has been jumping around on hot coals with one foot always off the ground, set to leave at a moment's notice."[42]

We know, of course, how things went after that:[43] the way the war was developing gradually pushed them, Ernesto and Altiero especially, to intensify the economic and political studies mentioned

---

rized islet cut off from the world), daily life in the "Confinement Colony" proceeded as usual, following its own pre-established rhythms. And even to our quartet, the beautiful season brought moments of serenity and even fun. Apart from the well-known daily events relating to the canteen, the chicken coop, the rabbits etc., I found interesting Ernesto's summer letters to his family (to which Piero Graglia — 2010, pp. 211–12 and 216 n. — has recently called attention). "I prefer to swim," Ernesto wrote to his mother, for example, "with S. [Spinelli], a boy who looks like the god Neptune — and with C. [Colorni], professor of philosophy. [. . .] Both these comrades of mine are very intelligent and well-read, and have a very lively curiosity concerning spiritual problems." And again: "tomorrow [August 12] we will have a swimming competition, with a bottle of *passito* as the prize."

[41] Bobbio (1975, p. 305, n.). The dialogue probably began in June of the same year, *Severus* according to a handwritten indication of Altiero Spinelli's in the original text.

[42] *Severus, Commodus* adds, doesn't study like he did before. "All he does is rehash reprimands and recriminations — dragging us all into endless discussions, which just between you and me are perfectly useless, since we already know each other's arguments. He overdoes it a bit, don't you think?" Of course, the one overdoing it here is *Commodus*, because he fails to come to grips with the political issues raised by *Severus*. But his argument is interesting precisely because it allows us to freeze this passage in a sort of snapshot. "Now the harm," adds Eugenio — *Commodus* "isn't so much in his doing this [that is, in dragging us into useless discussions] — it lies in the consequences it brings, and which it has on his friends. He was once the only person in this place [Ventotene] who was able to listen to others. In choosing his friends, he did not require that they agree with him. He asked only that they should be alive and have something to say." "Yes, yes, that's all well and good," answers *Severus*. "Those were fine things for quiet times [. . .]. Today I couldn't care less about this stuff. Now we've come to the crunch. *Commodus*: There — it's precisely this obsession with being at the crunch, when in actual fact there's nothing concrete that can be done. It wrecks the nerves."

[43] Even though, obviously, we cannot expect Eugenio and Altiero to have written about it openly in texts that would later be checked by the wary censorship of the "Confinement Colony Directorate."

above, which proved to be preparatory to the *Manifesto*. In fact, after the first dramatic impact, the increasing difficulties that the Axis armed forces began to encounter in their rapid expansion, along with the see-sawing trend of military operations on the chessboard of the war, could not but produce and then gradually feed the hope and the initiative of the anti-fascists — not least at Ventotene.

At the same time, spoken and written cultural dialogues also became a useful cover for their inevitably clandestine work-in-progress. The idea of a United States of Europe as a possible outcome of the war, initially proposed by Ernesto and Altiero (and then enthusiastically endorsed by Eugenio and Ursula) began to circulate freely and robustly in their little microcosm — to the extent that during the hard winter that followed, Altiero and Ernesto began preparing the draft of the first version of the *Manifesto*.

It was then, magically, that a theoretical subsoil that had been deeply explored and cultivated and a series of intense group political discussions gradually produced *Towards a Free and United Europe. A Manifesto* (this is the complete title). Written by Altiero and Ernesto in the first part of 1941, then corrected to take into account the group's discussions and the German aggression against the USSR, the *Manifesto* became a key political reference point for the group — and later for the Federalist Movement (founded in Milan in August 1943), after which, introduced and "edited" by Eugenio, it took its final form in Rome (in January 1944).

7. Now, if we consider Colorni's first dialogues (see below), written in a self-deprecating style while all this was going on and addressed to several others (in fact his fellow internees), we cannot avoid the notion that these extraordinarily dense pages contain in a nutshell several key results from his studies. First, there is a reckoning cast as a critique of philosophy and the physical-mathematical sciences from within the Italo-German culture of the time. It is a reckoning that in the end leads, as we shall see, to some important suggestions concerning escape routes.

This impression, which has been on my mind concerning the philosophical side for a long time, was recently confirmed for me (and completed) on the physical-mathematical side. I knew of course that in prison and under confinement Eugenio had utterly committed himself to the study of these disciplines. He had studied Perucca and other physics texts at length, and had then translated at Ventotene the first volume of a treatise by Bernhard Bavink: *Findings and Problems in the Natural Sciences. An Introduction to Natural Philosophy Today*[44] — as a way of learning the subject better, of course, but also (probably) to prepare an important cognitive tool in Italian for what he intended to undertake as the outcome of his studies. (I allude, of course, to the well-known "Project for a journal of scientific methodology,"[45] which was then taking shape in Colorni's mind).

But it was only recently that I really realized, so to speak, where Eugenio's reasoning was going when, following a lead from Mario Quaranta,[46] I opened *Natural Science on the Path of Religion* by this same Bernhard Bavink. "It is the outcome of numerous conferences," he explained (in the third person), "that the author held in various German cities shortly before the revolution of 1933 [the advent of Hitler, that is] on the theme: 'Modern physics and the conception of the world.' Interest proved to be such that it seemed appropriate to make the content of the conferences accessible to a larger audience in the form of a summary [. . .] *mainly dedicated to philosophers and especially theologians, and not to scientists.*"[47]

Now, religion aside,[48] this text, which Eugenio undoubtedly

---

[44]Bavink, 1947. The first volume of this treatise is divided into two parts. The first, "Matter and Force," includes: "The fundamental data of chemistry. Atoms and molecules. Meaning and value of physical hypotheses. The fundamentals of mechanics. Energy conservation and physics subdivisions. The kinetic theory of heat. The development of light theory. The electromagnetic theory of light. Relativity and the general field theory. Electronic theory (electrical atomism). The periodic system and isotopy. The phenomena of light emission and absorption. Quantum theory. Bohr's spectroscopy theory. Wave and quantum mechanics. The structure of molecules and crystals. Nuclear physics (chemistry). The constituent elements of matter. The concept of substance in contemporary physics. The problem of randomness. The cognitive process in physics." Finally, the text continues with a second part entitled "The earth and the universe."

[45]Now in Colorni 2009, pp. 176–79.

[46]Quaranta, 2011, p. 122.

[47]Preface to the Italian edition of 1942: Bavink, 1944, p. ix: emphasis added.

[48]Not least because, as we learn on p. x in a note from the translator (probably Colorni) *"in the last lines the author concludes by saying that* 'faith in God is not the result but the premise of this work.'"

knew and probably also translated,[49] includes in its index: "I. The mechanistic representation of the world [Galileo, Copernicus and Kepler]. II. The consequences of mechanistic views for the conception of the world. III. The decadence of the mechanistic conception of the world. IV. The failure of the mechanistic view of the world a) the development of the concept of substance in modern physics b) the causal problem."

This gives weight to a hypothesis that will seem reasonable, at least to anyone who knows Colorni's work. This is that since at that time in our part of the world there actually existed a dialogue between scientists and philosophers, Eugenio's enormous commitment to acquiring a command of the physical-mathematical sciences at Ventotene and his interest in the two texts by Bavink were in all probability accompanied in his mind by a theoretical (more or less explicit) fine tuning of the historical evolution of these sciences, a useful 'appendix' to the history of philosophy that Colorni had long been working on.

If this was indeed the case, then Eugenio's first two dialogues — "On reading philosophers" and "On finalism in the sciences" — would seem, as far as I can see, to reflect this double clarification. Undoubtedly, a true familiarity with the physical-mathematical sciences on the part of a young philosopher was far from usual (and still is — now even more than then). It repaid his dedicated course of study, but it also represented, in his eyes, the retrieval of a philosophical tradition going back to Kant, or even Descartes and Leibniz (his famous warhorse).[50] Especially since, surprisingly (at least for us laymen), among the scientists, as we have just seen, there was

---

[49]Quaranta 2011, pp. 116, 122. On the other hand, it is not difficult to understand why Eugenio, if he actually translated this volume (which I also think he did), preferred that his name not appear: Bavink (1944, see p. 24) had in fact come to an agreement with the regime.

[50]Cf., on this, Eugenio's letter to Ursula of 1 June 1939 (now in Colorni 2016, p. 56). "Descartes and Leibniz," he writes, "really did have something to say both in the field of science (one invented analytical geometry, the other infinitesimal calculus) and in scientific methodology. Only they preferred, for reasons of convenience, to express these things in the language then in use, the language of a theological-system. Therefore, to understand them it is necessary to "translate" from that systematic language to ours. Once this is done, theses and demonstrations that appear to be senseless games take on an important meaning, one that is in no way systematic.

a certain Bernhard Bavink, who had ventured into exploring *the reverse route* — that is to say an attempt to make certain aspects of the evolution of the physical-mathematical sciences understandable to philosophers and theologians, rather than to scientists.

Eugenio Colorni was clearly comfortable with all this — he appreciated the beauty and perhaps even the daring implicit in his intellectual exercise. And he sometimes tried (perhaps only in bursts) to communicate his intellectual enthusiasm for the subject to his interlocutors — even though it was obviously not an easy thing to put across to interned friends with quite different cultural backgrounds (and who had "calls of the wild" of their own).

Philosophers and Scientists

8. We now come to two texts (with the intention, to be clear, of bringing out a common thread in the problem we are considering here[51]). First of all, there is *Ritroso* (that is, Ernesto Rossi), who declares: "I am incapable of reading a philosophy book if I don't understand it completely." This is in fact how "On Reading Philosophers" begins.

Colorni's purpose is not so much to criticize Rossi's angle of vision[52] as to use it as a starting point (and then as a boundary). "And when I say understand it," continues *Ritroso*, the good economist (conversing, surprisingly, with a philosopher), "I mean grasping precisely the meaning of each word, and making sure that every word is always used with the same meaning, and that the reasoning is correct, and that the proofs don't contain appeals to principle. I don't know what to do with a book if I start to find this stuff."

Some skirmishes follow whose purpose, in my opinion, is to contextualize, but (please note) not refute, this beginning. *Commodus* (Eugenio) replies, asking, "Wasn't it you who insisted on the symbolic, allusive character of language, with its roots in the earliest customs of our childhood, these having been handed

---

[51]Of course this is *only one* of the possible readings of these two dialogues.

[52]As we shall see, the theoretical criticism only appears later, whereas here, in all likelihood, the psychological-introspective angle (later reported by Altiero: see above, sec. 5) is deliberately kept "under the radar."

down in turn starting from the (earliest) customs of humanity? Didn't you say that in the world of our senses it is impossible to distinguish anything that corresponds one hundred percent to a certain word [. . .]?" "I did say that, yes, and I still say it," *Ritroso* (Ernesto) replies, "But you were the one who insisted on the limits of precision, which are not the same in all types of reasoning, so that certain clarifications that make sense in one context are nothing but affectations in another."

Fair enough: we are not in a world of absolutes. But the point, in my opinion, is that the economist's need for exactness is useful to Colorni in explaining his radical critique of philosophy:[53] "Have you ever asked yourself," *Commodus* asks *Ritroso* a little later, "why philosophy abandoned the syllogistic method it used throughout the Medieval period, and the geometric method Spinoza used? These ought to be the safest methods for verifying a line of reasoning. They are the methods used today, with great success, in mathematics and all the exact sciences. But there was a certain moment when philosophy began to say that such methods were a type of 'empty formal logic,' and were inadequate for grasping 'the perennial becoming of life' and so on."[54]

This is the springboard of Eugenio's "philippic." Philosophers, he goes on to explain, were used to discussing the existence of God, the immortality of the soul, etc. They had established that proposed solutions "would be of value only when it was possible to enclose them in an impeccable series of syllogisms." But Kant, through "a procedure which in its turn cannot be called logical, but which rather reflects a reversal in point of view, a spiritual and moral inversion" analogous to Copernicus's swapping the earth and the sun, showed that "such syllogisms were badly set out," and that "syllogisms are not permissible in such arguments, because

---

[53]Cf. "The Philosophical Illness" (Colorni 2009, pp. 10–38).

[54]"And that moment," continues Colorni, "coincided with the period when light began to be shed on the very foundations of the syllogistic method, on the character of its postulates and initial definitions. Precisely at the time, that is, when the syllogistic method began to acquire clarity, thus becoming an increasingly useful tool for reasoning — at that very moment it was abandoned en bloc by philosophers."

the very bases for setting them are missing."[55]

The philosophers, however, rather than abandoning their line of work, chose to reshuffle the cards a bit. They created a new logic and changed the names of their fundamental themes: "they started talking about the Ego and the World, the Real and the Rational, the Entity and the Existent, Spirit and Matter, Subject and Object, *Sein* and *Dasein*." This way they continued to provide "apparently logical arguments for positions they held for completely different reasons."

Why? Why does this sort of "quid pro quo" between logic and themes continually recur? At this point, Colorni tries to penetrate the psychological process that supports these methods of reasoning. Like Poincaré, he maintains that logic is nothing but "the set of conditions that allow us to proceed with classification" and that the notable instinct to consider it, instead, the quintessence of reality comes in some obscure way from the depths of consciousness and from childhood.

"I think," he continues, "that a set of sensations comes to a child definitively bundled together [. . .] only when the child is able to identify it and recognize it by name. From that moment the name and the object become interchangeable; the child transposes onto the name a set of feelings that characterize the child's behavior in relation to the object, and in particular in relation to *objectivity* in general; that set of indistinct movements, that sense of experiencing an action that comes from the outside and of a possible reaction from our own body, generally accompanied by the notion of an object outside oneself [. . .].

Ritroso: But there is no scientific basis for any of this.

Commodus: I know; you took the words right out of my mouth."[56]

9. In any case, "On reading philosophers" (which I have inevitably dealt with in some detail) is only the "first act," one might say, of *Commodus's* dialogue with *Ritroso*. To get an overall sense of the rea-

---

[55]He showed "in short, that these arguments are not the object of logical reasoning." "The same arguments are summarized here that lie behind the two theoretical pieces [by Colorni] *Philosophical Criticism and Theoretical Physics* and *Philosophy and Science*" (Cerchiai, in Colorni 2009, p. 290, n.)

[56]It is just a "vague and confused impression of mine" referring to psychoanalytic research.

soning we need to venture further[57] into "On finalism in the sciences." As *Commodus* declares, "I believe that you [*Ritroso*, economist, rationalist — he doesn't say it; the reader is left to guess] say things that are much less obvious and much more subversive than they seem at first glance. I think, that is, if you went into the very heart of the scientific edifice [something that *Ritroso* (Ernesto) evidently does not intend to do], you would find it much more difficult to get rid of these finalistic and metaphysical residues [not specified], than you think where you are now, stating the principle from the outside." The theme of finalism, which blossomed in the first dialogue "in the intimate relationship [in childhood] which links naming to objectifying," is thus revisited (by adults) as a well-known tendency, one recognized by *Ritroso*: but only from the outside of scientific edifice.

"If people as experienced and savvy as Poincaré and Duhem couldn't manage it [breaking loose from finalism]," *Commodus* (Eugenio) continues, "it isn't because of an oversight or a residue of sentimentality in their personality, it's the blind alley they're in, where their reasoning gets all tangled up and which they can't escape from without invoking the harmony of nature, or of a geometrizing God or who knows what else? Is it possible to avoid this blind alley? I think it is, although it is anything but simple, and up to now as far as I know it has never been managed successfully."

This already gives us enough to set out the most challenging part of Colorni's reasoning. "These transcendent and finalist principles," he adds, "are not only a construction of philosophers who contemplated the edifice of the natural sciences from the outside, [. . .] they are essentially the foundations on which the experimental sciences themselves built their edifice. Eliminating them means subverting the edifice of the natural sciences from top to bottom."

This is in fact the rationale behind what would shortly become the noted Colornian epistemological program.[58] Eugenio argues that it is essential to work on concrete scientific problems, "noting

---

[57]Note in this regard that the first dialogue ends, not coincidentally, with three ellipses and that the second begins with a response by *Commodus* to a question of *Ritroso's* that is not in the text — as if to say: you connect them.

[58]Which would give rise, among other things, to the 1942 "Project for a Journal of Scientific Methodology" (Colorni 2009, pp. 177–79).

the benefit to science itself from the elimination of its metaphysical-finalist substrate. I do not think there is any argument more
effective for a methodological criterion than a factual demonstration of its utility."

Eugenio came back many times to this point[59] and tried right
to the end,[60] without success, to find a way to trigger the epochal
transformation he thought was necessary. It was an attempt that
even today remains as an important marker on the arduous path
of knowledge.[61] The remainder of the dialogue, along with other
contributions of the period, can be read as a simple argumenta-
tion (and conclusion) of this thesis with regard to physics, punc-
tuated with numerous examples (which, for reasons of space, we
must pass over). Colorni thinks, basically, that Poincaré's critique
of the principles of physics and Einstein's theory of relativity have
opened an important breach in the old structure. And also that,
beginning with the debate this unleashed, it would be possible to
revisit and develop the gnoseological program of Immanuel Kant.

"The fact is," Colorni argues at a certain point, "you want to
spread among young people the idea of proper scientific thinking,
kidding yourself that it is unprejudiced and anti-metaphysical. I
think [on the other hand] that finalism and a certain form of transcendence today find their main support in the physical sciences."
"I do not see," Ritroso replies, "that it's really necessary to subvert all
of science [. . .]. You could even concede the use of all metaphysical
and transcendent concepts, as long as you remained aware that this

---

[59]Even twice in this same dialogue, in addition to the instance just mentioned.

[60]Testimony of Guido Piovene, "Il Tempo," 7 giugno 1944: now in Gerbi 1999, p. 297.

[61]A competent and balanced exposition on this may be found in Quaranta (2011). It is by
no means settled, however, whether Eugenio's rather exuberant, not to say impetuous way
(including investing his own subconscious without reserve) is the most advisable road to
hoped-for discoveries. This is a question that inevitably concerns character, along with
the fact that fortunately there is no one single road to discovery — there are many. Each
researcher must understand which of them are the most promising (and most suited to their
own characteristics). On the one hand, it is essential to free the mind, and "never lose sight
of Colorni's lesson," as Hirschman once told me; but on the other — and this is for us
ordinary mortals — it is necessary to apply our capacity for open-mindedness with saintly
patience and to process the results (not least through a high level of self-reflection) — an
exercise that often requires remarkable serenity of mind. This too, if I am not mistaken,
was from the beginning a source of Albert's refusal (more tacit than explicit) to follow
Eugenio in the complex and turbulent intricacies of personal introspection.

use was purely conventional and symbolic, and preceded it with an initial disclaimer, an *as if* — in the sense that [obviously, for an economist] given certain assumptions, it follows that. . . etc. etc. "I disagree." Colorni comes back. "There are ideas which, once they are known to be conventions and not *realities*, can never again be used in the sense they had before. This anti-finalist correction is not a side issue for science, but deeply affects what science is." "Finally!" I exclaimed to myself when I read this passage. The intellectual contrast between Colorni and Rossi has come out into the light of day. So much so that, after having covered several pages with examples from physics, Eugenio concludes: "You [*Ritrosio*] think that anti-finalist claims are in the mainstream of classical experimental science and the scientific positivism of the last century. I think instead that they are in an important branch off this stream, a branch that is now threatening to replace the mainstream itself, and was set in motion by Poincaré and Mach (if not by precursors), taking their inspiration less from Spencer and Comte than from Kant."[62]

10. Unfortunately, we do not know the exact date of the discussion, presumably a lively one, that followed *Commodus's* (Eugenio's) presentation of these two dialogues to the Ventotene group. We may suppose, however, that Colorni's enthusiasm and effervescence on that occasion, in publicly revealing in words and writing part of the results of the extraordinary theoretical fervor that gripped him at the time, did not help him make himself understood. *Ritroso* (Ernesto) in all probability did not understand even the terms of the question — such was his misunderstanding of Eugenio's way of thinking[63] (and such were the typical characteristics of his education in economics, which I would call, speaking from experience,

---

[62]"I also think," the passage goes on, "that if anti-finalism is to be taken to its logical consequences and concrete results, we must abandon the classical conception of science as an abstract and symbolic expression of experimental facts (the idea that these facts can always be traced back to some order and harmony), and instead develop the conception of science as the logical deduction of consequences implicit in the initial assumption of some definitions suggested and recommended (but not imposed) by experience — that is, by the behavior of our senses when exposed to external stimuli."

[63]Cf. above, n. 30.

"a hard initiation").[64] It is also possible that Colorni's intention in writing the two dialogues might (in a certain sense) have been to get the message to someone else; in other words that he was aiming for a breakthrough mainly with Altiero. In any case, the evidence indicates that the operation did not succeed. Two new dialogues, in fact, probably sprang from the discussion, and it is to these that we now turn our attention: one by Spinelli from August 1941 which in view of its content I have called ["Ends and means"]; and the other, deservedly famous, by Colorni — "On anthropomorphism in the sciences" — addressed directly to *Severus* (Altiero).[65]

Now all we have to do is insert Spinelli's ["Ends and Means"] after "On Reading Philosophers" and "On Finalism in the Sciences," and before "On Anthropomorphism in the Sciences" to realize that it represents what might be called the key tile in the mosaic, the missing link that should be placed just there, right where it belongs.[66]

A glance at the piece reveals that it is set in the middle of the story, where *Commodus* (Eugenio) has led us with his reasoning on philosophers and scientists. And at the same time, a comparison of Altiero's dialogue with the opening of "On anthropomorphism in the sciences," shows that the latter, as we shall see,[67] in fact makes reference to the former.

In any case, moving ahead in ["Ends and Means"], it also seems clear that *Severus's* (Altiero's) purpose is different from *Commodus's* (Eugenio's). In this dialogue, the reasoning gravitates toward the ends, while the means become tools, manipulations, mechanisms and mechanizations — terms that in themselves show how Spinelli saw the natural sciences from the outside (and perhaps from a visu-

---

[64]In the sense that those who have really struggled to acquire this mindset (by means of what Colorni himself — in the second fragment of the Appendix to "On psychologism in economics," which the reader will encounter later — called "a long and silent apprenticeship") will then steer away from any possibility of having to question it again (Hirschman 1970, pp. 92–98). Eugenio and Altiero's psychological criticisms recalled above should be added to this typical condition: cf. sec. 5.

[65]Erroneously attributed to 1938 by the journal *Sigma*, which published it for the first time in 1947, this famous dialogue was also written (in all probability) in 1940–41.

[66]Which can only be done today, and which therefore inevitably says a lot (incidentally) about the limits of the now historical editing of these texts — starting in the immediate post-war period.

[67]See below, sec. 11.

al angle that still hasn't completely come to terms with what Bavink called "the classic mechanistic representation of the world"). He doesn't (usually) engage directly with physicists and their discoveries — as Colorni tries to do. His text instead reflects an interest and background in thought and action that cannot be boiled down to the simple split between philosopher and scientist. Between these two intellectual types politics emerges gradually — and with it, the dissimilarity between the intellectual politician (Altiero) and the political intellectual (Eugenio).

There is in fact a concluding section in this dialogue that succeeds with a pinch of irony in conveying the climate of the discussions at the time along with some critical comments which, typically, are addressed to Eugenio. "I really admire the way you talk one minute 'in a scientific setting' and the next in some other," *Severus* in fact claims, addressing himself to *Commodus*. "You who mock Crocian schematizations! By now I am perfectly aware that when it comes to anything but science you want to be soft, a listener, artistic, carefree, not boxed in, and so on. But you view all this as a sort of divine leisure that you allow yourself. In serious things, in physics and other things as well, you need security — you need to go into battle well-armored, and the harder the armor is, the more rigid, secure and forbidding, the safer you feel. You are afraid of getting hurt. All this talk of mine — you can take it as the doubtful head-scratching of someone who doesn't believe in these sharp divisions, this world where the precise and secure are strictly distinct from the insecure, the sensitive. Probably, and I hope so for your sake, this artificial toughness of yours will be very useful in physics, and then everything will be fine and all the rest will be forgivable."

Anthropomorphism and Its Surroundings

11. Reading this passage one wonders what important "leveraging" role it had in suggesting some of Colorni's lines of argument in "On anthropomorphism in the sciences."

Here, in fact, we arrive at the point of contact between the two dialogues. Skimming through Spinelli's, one easily sees that in the final part it is about life, about the possible "destruction of the other's goal of winning," about "chopping a living dog into two dead ones," about conciliation, history, politics, biology, etc. And how, on the other hand, does "On anthropomorphism in the sciences" begin? Like this: "*Commodus* (to *Severus*): I will suppress the anger that your confused and bombastic talk makes me feel, first of all to point out that you have not even offered the beginning of a discussion of the two main points of our conversation — namely, 1) whether there is a *qualitative* difference between biology and physics; and in particular whether the fact that two half dogs are not equal to one whole one might be compared to the fact that two atoms of hydrogen and one of oxygen are not a water molecule. 2) What the characteristics of *historical knowledge* are and whether it has anything to do with scientific-natural knowledge; our having agreed that saying that historical knowledge is *freighted with the future* and the other kind isn't, even if it were true (which it is not), would not mean nearly enough."

In short, the two texts are closely connected. And the reader might conclude that nevertheless this is a dialogue between deaf people in which each has his own ax to grind. But such is not the case (or perhaps not entirely). Because actually it is Altiero's dialogue that ends up sparking the important, wide-ranging, well-argued dialogue "On anthropomorphism in the sciences" (which I will refer to below). It is as if Eugenio had thought: if that's how things are, I have no choice but to explain myself from the heart — clearly, contentiously, explicitly.

"Your method is this," *Commodus* tells *Severus* a bit later:[68] 1) Reduce what I say to trivial paradoxes; 2) Counter them with trivial truths; and 3) Nobly profess disgust with both positions. [. . .] I never said that life *doesn't exist*. Nor do I deny that there may be forces that we cannot grasp. I say only that if they cannot be grasped, then we cannot say anything at all, and that we can only say something about them if and to the extent that they can be. And if they can be grasped it means that they fit into our patterns of regularity, prediction and rebuilding. And once they have fit into these patterns, they are in our power."

---

[68]Also, he admits a bit later, "to show that his own polemical weapons are just as sharp."

This discussion of history and the natural sciences thus marks the starting point of Eugenio's line of reasoning that distinguishes between predictable and unpredictable events. "This word *prediction*," he explains, in a barely veiled attack on mechanistic conceptions, "does not necessarily indicate something mechanical or narrow. It can be viewed as something embodied in the very nature of man; an agility of movement, a control of the situation, a precision of reflexes that makes an action safe and fruitful. But reduced to its most intimate essence, it will still be that faculty of being able to see, to the greatest extent possible, that given certain facts about the present and the past, certain others will occur in the future."

"What you are doing, if I understand correctly," Colorni has *Severus* say later, "is waging a campaign against anthropomorphism, [which you see] as the number one enemy of science [. . .]. To the extent that man is so in love with himself that he sees in himself the supreme purpose of the world, or a world made in his own image and likeness, to that extent science does not progress. And this anthropomorphism is often so subtle and inadvertent that it is difficult to flush out." "Ultimately," says *Curiosus,*[69] "all you're trying to say is that everything we know we have reduced to our own image and likeness." "You are both right [. . .]," *Commodus* replies, "*Curiosus's* kind of anthropomorphism exists, of course, but it is something that is experienced, not desired. It is the recognition of a fact — that we are unable to get outside ourselves; for us, knowing can only be in the form of learning — which amounts to reshaping [what we intend to learn] to fit our grasping organs."[70] "And from the time this restriction was discovered, twenty-five centuries ago, human thought has done nothing but struggle to get out of it [. . .] *escape from it.* [. . .] Every time you want to escape from *man as the measure of all things* and try to discover the conformation of the actual *laws of reality,* you can't help but imagine in a more or less

---

[69]A third interlocutor who has not been identified.

[70]"And when we recognize once and for all [. . .]," writes Eugenio a little further on, "that there is no getting outside ourselves, and that everything we take in will always be affected by our grasping organs; [this] may teach us to keep the organs relaxed, soft, without preconceived form, ready to adapt themselves so as to engulf any stimulus that touches their semi-fluid suckers."

sophisticated way, that these supposed *laws* include a set of *tendencies, purposes, and harmonies*, etc. that come from the world of our own desires and feelings. This is the anthropomorphism that I maintain is damaging to science[71] and, I would say, all knowledge."

12. "Supposing while not conceding," *Severus* then argues, "that you could eliminate anthropomorphism in reckoning with the external world, there is at least one field from which you cannot eliminate it — the case where the object of your consideration is a person, or other people." *Commodus* replies that "If the object I am studying[72] resembles me to a T, clearly I have to attribute to that object everything I attribute to myself — namely, goals, volition, free will, etc."

Eugenio decides at this point to remove a thorn (and more than one) from his side. The question, he declares, does not concern "the battle," "going back and forth trying to get the upper hand (something you [*Severus* (Altiero)] are fanatical about)."[73] And further on: "I don't much care for your description of the two men trying to overpower each other and taking turns *using* each other. The way you experience contact with another man as a collision, a struggle, an effort to overwhelm or not to be overwhelmed is to me the worst aspect of everything you do and think. For you a relationship with another hub of life is always in some way a need

---

[71]Whose autonomy, moreover, Colorni does not respect, so that he writes: "Actually, I think autonomy is the main disease of philosophy, and perhaps of the sciences as well. [. . .] I would, if anything, reject autonomy or, more modestly, take seriously discoveries made by thinking," wherever they occur. Is this not a fundamental root of Albert Hirschman's "trespassing" (1981), and "crossing boundaries" (1998)?

[72]With a pinch of self-evident irony.

[73]What I call a living being," Altiero has *Commodus* say in ["Ends and Means"], "is something that does not submit to me, something I cannot use — something, that is, that I do not know. [. . .] If dominating you were a purpose of little importance, I would be able to give up knowing you and using you. If, on the other hand, manipulating you motivates me, for whatever reason, then I will go about devising means that will allow me to get hold of you — that is to say, understand what it is that makes you tick." *Severus*: "Then there will be a fight between us, because I too, o Zarathustra, have my own goals to achieve, and I am quite willing just to treat you scientifically as an instrument. And I am afraid you will never be able to know my goals well enough to master them because in the course of the fight I will continually change them, keeping in mind, dominant over all the others, one purpose only — to defeat you, to make you my instrument, and even if you come to discover this you will not be able to use it because it is perfectly antithetical to what you want. In fact, you want me to stop having the arrogant desire to use you, and instead you let me do it."

for self-assertion. *Severus*: [. . .] I took that example, but I could just as well have taken some other one. *Commodus*: But to me it's interesting that you took that one. The tongue probes where the tooth is sore. And I think the topic will be very useful to us."

First of all, because it allows Altiero's argument to be overturned: "What I mean," Eugenio concludes, "is that the true manner of emotional attachment to other people is to let them exist, not to transform them the way I want, but to enjoy their being different from me. That is what I call loving and understanding another person."[74] From here it is possible to derive "a series of precepts and metaphors, which I leave to you [*Severus*] to work out as an exercise."[75]

It is as if Colorni realized at a certain point that in the past he had been a bit too indulgent with Spinelli. As if he realized he had (implicitly) allowed him to entertain some misconceptions — perhaps in order to facilitate the "intellectual improvement" his friend had been engaged in. Nevertheless, generous by nature (and vocation) Eugenio doesn't set about exposing these contradictions point by point. It is enough to call attention to an aspect of Altiero's argument that he "doesn't much care for."

This aspect is also aptly chosen from another viewpoint. It al-

---

[74]This is the companion to the "prediction" discussed above. With respect to other people, Eugenio had clarified a little earlier, "we are equipped with special intake organs, quite different from those that bring scientific knowledge — that predict, that is — but which nevertheless allow us to derive from their use a level of satisfaction at least as great as prediction would provide. They are what I would call, in a word, organs of *loving*. In using this word I mean something very wide-ranging, a generic affective attitude that includes things like hate, fear, hope, desire, pleasure, pain, etc. It is these organs of attachment that we use on objects that resemble ourselves." And again: "Loving in the true and non-degenerate sense of the word means seeing your own object of love as supremely other and therefore always new, always a mystery, every time met with surprise as if for the first time: in a word, unforeseen and alive. And this once again is by analogy with ourselves: because what we love best in ourselves, what we consider most intimately ours, is our freedom of will — the intimate and essential possibility in us that we can be different every time from what would have been predictable."

[75]"Not 'don't do unto others as you wouldn't have them to do unto you' but 'do unto others what others would like done to them.' Not 'to know others look inside yourself'; but 'to know others, look at others.' And notice what they have that is theirs and is peculiar, different from you. Don't look for points of contact, least common denominators, universal categories, etc. Try to learn their language without always using yours as a basis of comparison. And so on."

most seems, in fact, as if Colorni is saying that the fact that the intellectual politician (Altiero) sees life as a matter of self-assertion with respect to others[76] should not stop the political intellectual (himself) from developing a broader and more convincing point of view — one that enjoys diversity. Or rather, in today's parlance, that responds to it (and to fragmentation) with respect, consideration and empathy[77] — that is, the point of view of universal brotherhood. This is a theme which, in his effort to define their respective points of view, Colorni revisits several times in his dialogues;[78] and which in a certain sense touches on the general inspiration of his work — that underlying insight which at times escapes the reader intent on following Colorni's arguments; but precisely because of this . . . we must not allow it to slip through our fingers.

13. Solomonic conclusion. "We can label as science," *Commodus* affirms, "any and all activities involving research and knowledge that try to construct, by any means (mechanical, mathematical, statistical, probabilistic, philosophical, etc.), systems of predictability. We can refer to finalistic activities as those in which an emotional element comes in, directed toward other people, ourselves, past and future generations or what have you [. . .]. Depending on how you define history and philosophy, for example,

---

[76]"Between you and me in this situation we've got ourselves into," he had Altiero say to *Severus* (to himself, that is) in ["Ends and Means"], "there are now two alternatives. One is that one of us manages to destroy the other's will to win — and I do mean *destroy* and not simply *understand*, since understanding it serves no purpose as long as it remains inexorably antithetical to the other's desire to win. [. . .] The other alternative is that each of the two adversaries recognizes in the other a hub of activities that achieve purposes, and they make peace. On what basis? Surely on the only basis possible, which is to establish a certain coordination in their purposes. Each recognizes in the other a certain positive rather than simply negative determination, and the word 'life' which seemed to indicate the unknown, now indicates a well-known thing [. . .]; it indicates another self."

[77]A truly unexpected point of contact with the last works of Clifford Geertz, partner of Albrt Hirschman during the Princeton years (Geertz 1999, Meldolesi 2016a and b).

[78]Cf., for example, what Colorni has *Commodus* say a bit earlier: "I often think this meanness is basically necessary if you want to build something. It is the tribute you pay to *getting things done*. People who do things are necessarily more aggressive, less open, less available, and less free than those who do not. They must to a certain extent become deaf and blind to what lies outside what they are doing, which they must love a love that is exclusive, concentrated, selfish, and mean." See also the jointly written dialogue "On Action."

you can think of them as related to the natural sciences or to art or to something else. And to set this or that definition, therefore, is the same as saying that a certain activity must be carried out in this or that way."

"History, it seems to me," Commodus continues a bit later,[79] "can mean three different things: [. . .] Analyzing events for the purpose of establishing in them systems of *constants*, laws that repeat, relations of causes and effects that, as they say, *account for* what has taken place. This way of thinking is more or less consciously scientific — aimed, that is, at establishing a system of predictability"; "though very different from science in appearance, is in many ways related to it." Furthermore, the second way of doing history is also "very similar to science, but does not identify with it. It is the simple search for the facts that have occurred, and the objective assessment of them. The procedure in this type of history is very similar to that of the experimental sciences — it sets great store by precision and objectivity. But it is missing that push toward the future, the inductive element and the formulation of laws." "The third way, finally, is the good and true and right one, the one in which you [*Severus*] bask and revel — true history as experienced, living and working history, in which the past is your past, and precisely for this reason it is articulated toward the future, not as a prediction, but as a tendency, a push, a positioning of ends. The history that is Life.[80]

Severus: I don't see what there is to make fun of.

Commodus: Neither do I, really. But still," he adds (clearly al-

---

[79]Having stated that "one of the results of this discussion might be understanding more clearly what we mean by history. *Severus*: [. . .] For the last century and a half it's all that's been talked about. *Commodus*: Well, I don't know anything about it, or else I've forgotten all this research you're talking about. And I haven't read Croce's latest book *History as Thought and Action*. So I risk either talking nonsense or saying things everyone knows. But I would say them with a certain naivety," "free of systematic preconceptions," "without being overwhelmed by traditional models." Note here the typical search by Colorni for a fresh, direct, perhaps naive, innocent approach, free from pre-established intellectual cages, and thus such that it can then be verified, corrected, and made to evolve further (perhaps with a good dose of ingenuity).

[80]Cerchiai has observed (in Colorni 2009, pp. 316–17, n.) that this is a simple transposition of a well-known passage from *Teoria e storia della storiografia* [Theory and History of Historiography] by Benedetto Croce.

luding to Croce's historicism, which then held sway), "I have an urge to make fun of it, maybe because of the obstinacy and violence you put into your love of history, which is to me, as always, a bit suspect. I sense behind it personal ties and grudges; I can see you holding on by inertia to the road once taken, wanting at every turn to convince yourself that it is still the best — the most just and glorious." — instead of continually challenging it, which would be the advisable course. . . ."[81]

Is that all? It is not. In conclusion, Eugenio produces a para-scientific (and ironic) "marvel" according to which, since some traits in the population of southern Calabria are apparently similar to the global average for the same traits, the statistics for married Calabrian men with offspring should allow the identification of a new universal constant that would point to a certain finalism within nature. . . . This is a deliberately spurious pseudo-scientific conjuring trick that allows him to introduce one last argument into the text.

"**Ritroso** [Ernesto]: Don't be offended by my question, but how long have you been doing science?

Commodus: Around two years.

Ritroso: Then you won't mind if, just to clarify my ideas about scientific principles, I consult people who have been at it a bit longer.

Commodus: [. . .] It seems to me, *Ritroso,* that you are too attached to professional authority. Are you so sure that going to an official school and reading a lot of papers and having long experience with the tools of the trade are absolutely necessary conditions for understanding something about the basic principles of a science?

Ritroso: Frankly, yes, I do believe it, petty and pedantic as it may seem. [. . .]

---

[81]The observation, *Commodus* specifies, "is not directed at the thing itself, but at the way you practice it." In fact, he clarifies a bit later, "this last way of doing history, seeing it as humanity's past, in which our own past is implanted, clearly does not include prediction, but it does to a very large extent include affection (in the broad sense of the word). In short, it is a question of setting goals, of initiating actions dictated by feelings and relationships that exist between us and ourselves, and between us and other people, present and past. History allows us to expand this affection and these relationships, to extend them to what was and to what is to come, to have feelings and sketch out actions in the context of a broader horizon, one which potentially embraces the totality of our fellow beings."

Commodus: [. . .] I wanted to make an observation, limiting myself to physics, that I think may be allowed even though I've had only two years experience. And that is that belonging to the professional category of physicist entails such close contact with physics and such direct dealings with specific moment-by-moment problems of research that there is scant possibility to re-examine initial problems and fundamental principles." From here, predictably, the line of reasoning returns to the necessity of reconsidering such problems and principles.

"**Ritroso:** That may be the case in physics. But in economics?

"In economics, my friend," **Commodus** concludes (with something between irony and ridicule), "I'm ready to concede that everything is as going as well as it could possibly go."[82]

Conclusion

14. The confrontation via dialogue, oral and/or written, between Altiero, Eugenio, Ernesto, Ursula (and others) was thus fair but "vigorous." You might say that it "baptized" in a scientific key a tiny political-cultural discussion community which even today remains surprisingly and unexpectedly important.

Altiero challenged Eugenio on his own turf and provoked a proud, rich and creative piece of fine tuning. Ernesto, thought present, played a more modest role. Ursula, the letters make clear, had (up to a certain point) intense dialogues with Eugenio. And the very fact that these "fine things for quiet times,"[83] as Altiero put it (with a dash of irony), allowed the participants to "have their say" (clearly, explicitly) while fully respecting each others' ideas is undoubtedly a surprising result, which also suggests a subsequent weakening of reciprocal polemical vigor — due if nothing else to the decrease in the material left to argue about . . .

In fact, it is enough to scroll through some of the jointly written texts from the last Ventotene period, such as "On action" and "On success" to realize that now the tone is more relaxed, some-

---

[82]Cf. below, the *Appendix* to this introduction.
[83]Cf. above, n. 42.

times even jocular.[84] ("When I was an adolescent," he wrote in an illuminating passage [at least for anyone who knows his 'cult' essay, "The Philosophical Illness"], "I had three older cousins [Enrico, Enzo and Emilio Sereni], who made it their task to remind me at every turn how far I was from the ideal of virtue and morality that they perfectly represented. I feel now as if I've returned to that time; only there is just one cousin now [Altiero], but doing the work of three. And with this difference as well: at that time I felt guilty all the time and took my cousins' admonitions very seriously; now I couldn't care less").

These dialogues probably reflect the effects that the evolution of the political situation and the development of the federalist position itself had on the functioning of the group, which now appears more solid and cohesive. And the fact that these dialogues were written jointly (with the handwriting sometimes changing on the same sheet) perhaps represents an important clue. In fact, someone writing in an often penetrating and ironic way may refer to other people's points of view — while keeping intact (it goes without saying) his or her own theoretical, cultural, political, preferences. It is as if the dialogue itself, its pattern repeated many times, had by then served its pedagogical function — it had taught them to discuss and learn reciprocally, from each other. The dialogues reflect a better (but nevertheless mobile) balance between great freedom of thought and collective commitment[85] — what the Ventotene group, in its various manifestations, would later succeed in repeating on

---

[84]The dialogue "On Action" was written by Altiero (*Severus*), Eugenio (*Commodus*), and Giuliana Pozzi (*Genevieve*); while "On Success" and "On Detachment and Death" were written by Altiero (*Severus*) and Eugenio (*Commodus*). Ursula (*Ulpia*) and Manlio Rossi-Doria (*Modesto*) also figure in the second part of this last dialogue, written by Eugenio at Melfi. In a first phase, as we have seen, the dialogues had (indirectly) a leading role in opening the way to a new political position, while subsequently this relationship was in a certain sense reversed, because this new position actually favored cultural discussion and the drafting of dialogues. It is in any case true that the theoretical and political discussions at Ventotene remained very much alive in Eugenio's memory, since he was able to write on 2 May 1943 (now in Colorni 2017, p. 146), in concluding his last wishes: "I don't care about being cited or publicly remembered. The only thing dear to me is the thought that for a while I will still be part of my friends' conversations — conversations which were perhaps the purest joy of my life."

[85]A new "miracle" akin to what occurred, according to Albert Hirschman (1990, pp. xxix–xxxi) at Trieste in 1937–38 among those around Eugenio Colorni.

the mainland, in launching the Federalist Movement and in the Resistance. They are dialogues which, in spite of the difficulties of the time (and of what followed), one may still read with pleasure today, drawn in by the various voices and points of view. . . And then, as for the dialogue "On detachment and death" — we know that "it actually took place in a very unusual environment" (Ventotene) and that it was then written up by the two friends[86] (first by Altiero at Ventotene[87] and then on the mainland by Eugenio) after two years of intense and fruitful collaboration and theoretical-practical construction. It is a dialogue that unfolds in an unavoidably sad atmosphere — because of both the separation (painful in itself), and the content (and perhaps the presentiment) that the dialogue gradually reveals and develops. But it is dominated by a calm, interconnected and affectionate sort of reasoning — by their need to understand each other, to reduce the distance between them, while acknowledging their well-known differences; almost as if to prepare the transformation of these differences in a way that would enrich the common initiative soon to be actually undertaken. As a

---

[86]More precisely, a first handwritten draft of the opening written by Altiero entitled "Dialogue of Detachment" is from September 1941 and is accompanied by an October note addressed to Eugenio (see below, in the appendix to the text) which begins as follows: "This sketch of a dialogue, which I jotted down last month following your observation at the beginning and then didn't go on to finish, I give to you to read as is. It ran aground because of what almost always happens with me — after a few pages I'm no longer satisfied and I start over. I'm giving it to you to read all the same because there is a certain symbolism [. . .]. Our friendship began with a dialogue [see above, sec. 2]. Now its initial period is ending with [. . .] a dialogue on detachment." In Melfi, Eugenio then decided to go on and complete the dialogue, admirably involving Ursula (*Ulpia*) and Manlio Rossi Doria (*Modesto*). In fact, in the Spinelli archive there is a typed definitive version of the dialogue, entitled "Dialogue on detachment and death," now available online (see, above, sec. 2). It is published below — in place of the dialogue "On death," which appeared in Colorni 1975 and 2009 — with some modifications. In fact, in addition to numerous small corrections suggested by a comparison of the various available texts, an examination of the original draft of the first part of the dialogue written by Altiero showed that a page was skipped (or lost) in the machine transcription. It has therefore been retrieved from the manuscript and reinserted into the dialogue.

[87]Note in this regard the confidence of Altiero's argument in this text — especially compared with the uncertainties in the writings from before the "Colorni cure." After Eugenio left, Altiero wrote a dialogue in May 1943 between Jacolo (Alberto Jacometti) and Sancho (himself), entitled "Is what the gods want sacred or do the gods want what is sacred? (Socrates)" which investigates why among men there are those who work for the collective good: see below.

joint venture by the two protagonists, this dialogue is in my opinion the most successful.

To give an idea of it, we need only mention the relationship between the seeker who receives and the politician who gives. "The receiver," says *Severus* at the end of his analysis, "is a microcosm, the center of harmonization of the gifts he receives, and it is natural that the giver seems to him abnormal. This latter [. . .] is part of the cosmos, and his work is directed towards it to make it richer."

"Your interest," *Commodus* (Eugenio) finally replies to *Severus* and *Modesto* (Manlio Rossi-Doria), "is too passionate and personal, and leads you to work too hard preparing to do things yourselves, and not hard enough on seeing to it that they get done at all. I, on the other hand, precisely because my interest is more lukewarm and reactive, don't dwell so much on action aimed at creating a certain state of affairs, as on the state of affairs itself; I am so well aware of the difficulties that I am ready to accept that it will come about through the work and the efforts of someone else. This is, I recognize, the attitude more of a spectator than an actor; but actors perform for the spectators, after all, and it is not a bad idea that they should sometimes listen to their audience's opinions."[88]

15. We must not, however, be deceived by this conclusion, or more generally by the somewhat resigned tone, even at the political level, of the text. "Only Eugenio knew how to both say and do," Albert Hirschman told me.[89] He respected professional politicians, but he did not always agree with their actual behavior. He believed that study and action could be alternated, and that one could (should) feed the other, and vice versa.[90]

---

[88] And Eugenio has *Ulpia* (Ursula) say to *Severus* and *Commodus*: "Here are two gentlemen, both dominated by the fear of dying, who are doing their best to pretend that death doesn't exist. One sweats and struggles to build something that allows him to say 'Not everything dies'; the other creates a moral attitude, a personality, whose essence is in the satisfaction of not trembling. And might there not be a third solution: to embrace it, the fear?"

[89] Private conversation in the summer of 2000. It is probably the greatest eulogy for Eugenio that could be imagined.

[90] On a large and small scale, and in theory and daily routine. During the Trieste years, for example, Colorni had a typical mode of expression: "Are you anti-fascist? And what are you doing against fascism? Nothing? Then you are not anti-fascist!"

"It might seem strange," recalled Paolo Pavone, then a young socialist and for a brief period Eugenio's comrade in the Roman Resistance, "that at the same time that he was distributing underground newspapers and preparing an insurrection, he was also debating weighty problems that have burdened humanity for centuries. But in fact this was one of the uplifting characteristics of that situation, and the fascination Colorni held for two young people like Lopresti and me came precisely from our seeing him as the symbol of that fusion."[91]

If we didn't wonder what all this meant from a political point of view we would be falling into the usual trap of the division of intellectual labor (in this case reinforced by conditions at the Ventotene Confinement Colony) between philosophers and political scientists. As against this obsolete model, Eugenio believed that avoiding blunders required the continual questioning of ideas in the light of an evolving situation, that the situation was in fact always changing, and that adaptation to it required using the various possibilities contained in the situation itself, rather than being concerned with probable trends or imagined implications. He believed that reasonable doubt, not ideological security, was the proper stimulus for action; that openness to the unexpected was essential, as was identifying and fighting against one's own psychological obstacles; that we need to reflect on what surprises us rather than simply pressing ahead; that valid and convincing leadership is actually possible and must be demonstrated in the field, and so on.

Now if, with all this in mind, we pass through the famous pillars of Hercules that, despite Eugenio, today separate political action and theoretical reasoning (even — we might add — in discussions of Colorni's own work) we will be somewhat surprised to come across the criticism of two of Spinelli's psychological attitudes — the "Pantagruelian attitude" and the "sin of 'ideology'" — contained in a letter of Eugenio's from May 1943 that recalls the

---

[91]Pavone 2010, p. 206. "I remember Angelo [Colorni]," said Giuliano Vassalli (2004, p. 40), "— this great scientist, this great scholar, this great freedom fighter — also as an exquisitely political man, exceptionally good not only at political activity and propaganda, but also, while only slightly older than we were, at teaching us."

dialogue for four hands mentioned above.

The Pantagruelian attitude, he writes, "is the one you (Altiero) described in your 'dialogue on detachment' [. . .]. It is an attitude I deeply admire and sympathize with (which I set out in a 'dialogue on death' that I never sent you). It is one of the most exalted and generous of human dispositions. At the same time, it is by no means the attitude of a modern politician — that is of someone who wants to achieve certain ends. It is the attitude of the promoter, the teacher, someone who radiates warmth, someone who need only present himself to be followed."[92]

Doesn't this passage perhaps give the impression of a sudden inversion of roles, a sort of head-to-tail flip in Eugenio's reasoning? Why didn't he send his friend Altiero his "dialogue on death"? Perhaps because — I would surmise — he was by then thinking of once again prioritizing action, thus launching his "courageous phase."[93]

It is then understandable how, through this metamorphosis, Colorni bounces with agility from one end to the other of his theoretical-practical "keyboard." His philosophical-scientific reasoning, which frees the mind and pushes it onto the road to discovery, also allows him to look at reality with ingenuous, innocent, and therefore unprejudiced eyes[94] and to commit himself accordingly to the search, even hypothetical and conjectural, for escape routes and initiatives that fit with it — to commit himself, in a word, to its possibilism.[95]

---

[92]"That some politicians have been like this," the passage continues (Colorni 2017, p. 148) "is unarguable. But will tomorrow's political struggle really present itself in these terms? Will the masses really orient themselves toward a political position of this type?" These are questions that in any case do not rule out taking direct action. Indeed, it would be Eugenio who was totally committed to the Roman Resistance, convinced as he was that the federalist idea of a united Europe, by then brought into the light of day, needed to be validated in the practical politics of the time. It is thus clear how and why, in contrast with any predetermined position, the versatility and flexibility of his thinking in the face of the developing (objective and subjective) situation led Colorni to advocate continually shifting angles on the same theme — politics.

[93]Tedesco 2014, p. 171. Eugenio's last wishes (mentioned above, n. 84) are from 2 May 1943.

[94]Like those of his students in Trieste: Colorni 2017, p. 101 and 109. Cf. also, above, n. 79.

[95]Meldolesi 2017. The failure to understand this key point (let it be said in parentheses) has prevented the critics (see for example Graglia 1993, pp. 189–90) from penetrating the actual theoretical function of this important text. Instead, their focus is on the political proposal, which later proved to be ineffective, but which Colorni himself would certainly have updated and gradually transformed, something he had actually begun to do before his death.

Moreover, if we look at all this in the light of the texts we have considered up to now, what becomes clear is that Colorni had an inspiration that was different from Spinelli's, one linked to the theme of love.[96] Eugenio certainly does not deny the existence of abuses of power in politics (how could he?). He only suggests that in taking concrete action and in its teleological projection such behavior may be mollified and mastered by action at the level of empathy — affective action; and, vice versa, that only love opens a valid perspective on politics. This is also how, in the Roman Resistance, Colorni — in the apt expression of Giuliano Vassalli and taken up by Daniele Pasquinucci and Francesco Gui[97] — was able to serve as "at once a critic and a linchpin" with a gift for both "balance and foresight" (a role he filled in the Federalist Movement as well).

"Dear Leo [Solari]," writes Luisa Villani, Eugenio's last partner, in a note from 24 January 1979,[98] "instead of making a photocopy, I've had the page with my notes [on Colorni] typed up. Take them for what they are, some hasty notes that attempt to highlight some very hastily conceived links, and have no pretensions to logic — [they are] merely intuitive."[99]

---

[96]"I would just urge them," Eugenio wrote in his last wishes (now in Colorni 2017, p. 143), referring to his "little ones" (Silvia, Renata and Eva, the three daughters he had with Ursula), "to consider love as the most serious and important thing in life; the thing that brings us close to another being, forgetting ourselves and wanting that person to live in their own essence, so very different from us. I would urge them not to squander their feelings, not to mistake superficial and passing excitement for love. These same wishes go to my wife, whom I bless along with our three little ones, hoping with all my heart that she finds the serene happiness that my incapable, unhappy, desperate love was never able to give her."

[97]"From the papers of the regime," wrote Gui, who worked in the documents section of the Central Archive of the Fascist State (2010, p. 296), "Colorni's political and intellectual portrait emerges strengthened in its precocious, steadfast, balanced, original, as well as courageous and farsighted configuration [. . .]. Though convinced of the need for collaboration among all the forces opposed to the regime, and even while committed to militancy alongside the other components of the liberation struggle — the communists first and foremost — the professor remained entirely alien to the logic of those who saw the USSR as the country leading the world revolution [. . .]."

[98]Discovered personally in September 2016 in the Solari fund, deposited at Solari's request at the Nenni Foundation in Rome.

[99]It is probably an old page of handwritten notes of Luisa's from 'back in the day,' which Leo had requested a photocopy of, and which she instead sent from Milan typed and accompanied by this note. It is known that Luisa Villani and Leo Solari collaborated daily (and dangerously) with Eugenio in 1943–44; so it did not surprise me that the testimony on

Thus, commenting on a concluding passage on love in "Philosophical Criticism and Theoretical Physics" (analogous to those we have seen above in the dialogue "On Anthropomorphism in the Sciences,")[100] Luisa wondered whether "the Europeanism of E. [Eugenio] C. [Colorni] does not have its beginning in this sphere of his experience." Her answer was as follows:

"He abhors a federation formed for economic and political purposes, put together through the diplomacy of states. Rather, he sees a federation in terms of the socialist movement — that is, born of the people. And it is therefore revolutionary (just as he abhors arranged marriages, or unions without love, in which the other person tends to be exploited and diminished).

War and resistance are opportunities — they must be followed by a re-foundation — which involves a revolution.

But it is no accident that he says that the romantic era of mass revolutions has ended. And so . . . ?

In this passage on love[101] we see the principle that the revolution the resistance should foment is based on.

Man must open up to a search for the different, the unique, the new.

A people must seek in another people the different, the unique, the new.

The other who is difficult to understand requires a healthy dose of detachment, attention to detail . . . and love.

And as soon as he pronounces the word he relates it to the forms and lines of development it takes in modern culture, and he

---

the theoretical foundations and on the federalist spirit of Colorni contained in these notes in effect emitted . . . a fragrance of fresh laundry.

[100]Cf. above, sec. 12. The passage is the following: "the way it has been configured in our society — that is, as a complex, sentimental, emotional relationship involving habits and personal interests between two beings who consider themselves moral and spiritual equals — love perhaps represents for a modern man the most direct, scorching experience of 'the existence of another person,' a person who is often very different from him in character, likes and dislikes, habits and childhood memories. To allow her to exist by his side, indeed to desire her existence more than his own, not trying to absorb her precisely because of her peculiarities, to penetrate that soul with the respect due to a delicate and unknown thing whose balance and harmony might be upset by a rough or abrupt gesture. . . ." Luisa refers in particular to the final proposition (truncated) that begins with "penetrate."

[101]See preceding note.

indicates it as the spiritual form which best expresses the attitude that allows man to master processes and openness to others. These latter are sought not in the strict laws of reason but (in the sphere of relations with other people, in the moral sphere) in what distinguishes, in the renunciation of anthropomorphism, in respect for the other, etc. etc. On this he bases the Federation of peoples."

Appendix: "On Psychologism in Economics" and Economics[102]

It is not difficult to imagine why Eugenio undertook to write "On psychologism in economics" during (presumably) the last phase of his internment at Ventotene. On one hand, there was the desire to pursue the debate with Ernesto Rossi[103] (the text seems to take up the argument at the point where Colorni had left it in "On anthropomorphism in the sciences": cf., above, sec. 13), and on the other, the need to furnish the debate in the Ventotene microcosm with an example of his own ideas that was different from the "already used" example of the physical sciences and mathematics.[104]

But getting down to the actual writing was evidently anything but simple for Colorni (his acquaintances notwithstanding: Albert Hirschman in Trieste and Ernesto Rossi at Ventotene). Also because (apart from what he had "picked up" from the discussions) Eugenio, in the prohibitive conditions of confinement, actually tackled the subject with the single volume of economics in his possession: *An Essay on the Nature and Significance of Economic Science*, by Lionel Robbins from 1932. Whence came "On Psychologism," a repetitive unfinished text with a line of argument that is not always easy to follow, which Norberto Bobbio included with Colorni's dialogues in 1975, mostly for the sake of completeness.[105]

---

[102]The writer is, by chance, an economist who (to return to some of the arguments mentioned above: see n. 64 and sec. 13) has attended more than one official school, read numerous economics treatises, and therefore has a longstanding familiarity with the tools of the trade; indeed — he had an initiation so harsh that he was forced to work hard . . . to emancipate himself from it. This appendix, among many other things, helps us understand why.

[103]It is in fact probable that in writing this Eugenio intended to bring *Ritroso* (who is portrayed) "out of his hole." See below, n. 106.

[104]It can be deduced, for example, from his "I advise you not to embark on a discussion on this subject; [experience and the rigidity of a body]" as Colorni has *Severus* (Altiero) tell *Ritroso* (Ernesto) at a certain point, "otherwise you won't come out of it without having first had to sit through the entirety of special relativity."

[105]"I see the following pages," wrote Norberto Bobbio (1975, p. 283), "as a fourth 'dialogue of Commodus,' although less elaborate than the previous ones; in fact the characters are the same, and this seems to be indirectly announced at the end of the third dialogue ["On anthropomorphism in the sciences"]. Unpublished. The typescript is entitled: 'Is it possible to build an economic science independent of psychological and sociological premises?' But it is not clear if it refers to an unfinished dialogue or only to the first pages" — this perplexity (more than for the reason he gives) says a lot about the understanding of the nature of the problems on the part of the one who expressed it.

In my opinion, however, it takes on far greater importance —
in terms of meaning and implications — in the light of the discovery of three related and previously unpublished fragments (see
below in the appendix to the dialogue)[106] and in the light of recent
developments in the discipline of economics. To clarify this conviction, I will recall in a nutshell some key points underlying Eugenio's
reasoning — so as to focus on them from this double point of view.

In the first place, Colorni knew a lot more about psychology
than economics. It is known that along with the natural sciences,
psychology was his preferred field of study during the last years of
his life. It therefore makes sense that, as the title of the dialogue
shows, he concentrated on this aspect of the question in an effort
to clear himself a path in the theoretical bunker of neoclassical
economics; and it makes sense in particular that he attacks the pretense of economics to build a science (therefore capable of prediction) without heeding the content of scales of preference.

Eugenio's intention is to show that economics cannot disso-
ciate itself from philosophy. This leads him to argue that demand
curve results in fact apply to the average, but not to the individual,
whose behavior may well well be different from what the theory
would predict. In other words, the Colornian refutation of the key
assumption (*homo economicus*) supporting the shape of demand
curves with respect to price is arrived at through a simple transition from macro to micro.

In Colorni's view this is a severe blow to the scientific pretensions of economics.

But does it also mean, one wonders, that the fact that much

---

[106]I thank Geri Cerchiai for the archival indications for these fragments. The second,
"Commodus to Ritroso" was published by Cerchiai in Eugenio Colorni *Five Methodological Writings* (2016a), while I found the first "Ritroso to Commodus" and the third, "Fight,
but listen!" in the archives of the Dept. of physics of the La Sapienza University of Rome.
These fragments are probably the result of the immediate use at Ventotene of the unfinished
dialogue. This in the sense that, as far as I can understand, Eugenio's "On psychologism
in economics" provoked a rapid and rather "professional" response from Ernesto; Colorni
thought to answer him in kind, but then he thought better of it: he accepted Rossi's criticism and he managed in the end to explain himself better; once Ernesto and Eugenio had
clarified things on an added sheet. Thus the unfinished dialogue and the three fragments
actually constitute a textual unit to be interpreted as a whole.

human behavior is not covered by the theory should simply lead to the theory's abandonment? This is not Eugenio's intention. On the contrary, by analogy with the evolution of the physical-mathematical sciences, he thinks that changing the basic categories can save the technical-scientific nature of the discipline and at the same time make it correspond more closely to reality — prefiguring the reasoning of Albert Hirschman, who not by chance gave the title *Come complicare l'economia* [*How Economics Should be Complicated* (1988)] to a recapitulating anthology of his works.

But perhaps we can go further. It is possible that in his enthusiasm Colorni cultivated the hope that freeing the discipline from some of the anthropomorphic constraints that had been imposed on it would allow it to take flight, a bit like what happened in physics with Albert Einstein.[107] Now, reasoning with the benefit of hindsight, it seems to me that this is not exactly how things went. Undoubtedly, in the last decades there has been a great reworking of the discipline that has taken into account a multitude of impulses and behaviors — that is to say passions and not only interests — a process that started thirty to forty years after Eugenio's dialogue (and which in retrospect clearly shows his extraordinary foresight).

But more than representing a leap forward at the interpretive and normative level, this led to the somewhat unexpected outcome of "relocating" a discipline in the making. On the one hand, as some critics claim (Krugman, Rodrick), it turned economics into "an endless theory of models," each corresponding to (and therefore usable in) specific conditions; so that the economic and statistical sciences today have become a highly specialized field that continually poses the problem of its application — in the

---

[107]He writes for example that if we realize that "initial definitions in economics are marked by extremely elementary psychological principles — obvious, self-evident, but still psychological — [. . .] then when we find ourselves faced with a phenomenon that stems from more complicated psychological factors, we will be tempted to verify it with the tools already in our possession as economists. Or rather, we can modify our tools (that is, our definitions and initial postulates) in the light of the new phenomenon and obtain new laws, perhaps more limited than the previous ones, but such that thanks to them the great calculating machine that we have available in economic science is not simply thrown out. Something similar is happening in physics with the introduction of non-Euclidean geometry, etc. And the benefits are immense."

sense that the statistician, the economist, the econometrician, the applied economist and so on must each develop a rather particular concrete sensitivity and be familiar with the situation to which they refer before proposing their own medicines. . . .[108]

On the other hand, and not least because of this, economics (like philosophy, political ideology, etc.) has reduced its level of generalization[109] and abandoned its claim to be all-encompassing — an undoubtedly desirable result, but one (often) not desired by economists — a sort of unintended consequence of their actions. Thus a collective space has been created — like that of the "Interpretive Social Science" of Albert Hirschman and Clifford Geertz — in which economics cannot be absent, but in which, at the same time, it is no longer "dominant" in an imperialist way.

Conclusion: as demonstrated by the three fragments published below in the appendix to "On psychologism in economics" (and especially the second, the very important "Commodus to Ritroso"), Eugenio had his own particular way (from inside, but from outside as well) of "assaulting" the old ways of thinking — in philosophy, politics, the natural sciences, psychology and economics. Neither in word nor deed would he accept preconceptions or boundaries. He had a special knack for discovering numerous different ave-

---

[108]Colorni had advised the discipline of economics to "revise its original definitions [. . .] even at the cost of causing the collapse of all the most celebrated laws and the most unshakable principles"; and to that end he had suggested taking inspiration from physics. "Physicists," he explained, "have always been concerned that their definitions should be such that the reality of experience can be entirely contained in them, and to arrive at definitions that adapt in the most precise way to the essential characteristics of what we see, touch, measure and experience. They are ready to abandon the most stable laws — concepts that had until now been the safest; notions of equality, simultaneity, space, and causality; laws concerning the conservation of energy, etc. Indeed, they exhibit a certain arrogance, a sort of iconoclastic ardor that urges them forward even in the face of some conceptual cornerstone, as long as they can fit their science to the concrete reality of the events that take place." Economics today is certainly not in a comparable condition, although the hope remains that economists will be gripped in their turn by the same "arrogance" — both in the construction of models appropriate to needs, and in the wise choice of their prescriptions. This last aspect is, in reality, particularly difficult for economists because it involves wide-ranging knowledge and investigations of faceless subjects generally distant from their mindset.

[109]As Colorni had foreseen: see, above, n. 107; but for the reasons mentioned in the previous note, this has not yet been sufficient to produce the desirable (and desired) "immense advantages."

nues, theoretical and practical, both ways out and ways forward. Many others undoubtedly exist and are continuously being recreated — solutions which, to be identified and put into practice, await the outcome of our struggle with ourselves, against our anthropomorphism and (Albert Hirschman would add) against our poverty of imagination.

But however inspired we may be by a passion for change, it must be recognized that such change is difficult; it occurs through tortuous, partial, and unexpected processes and requires a daily effort — not only from us but over several generations. There is still, for us and for everyone — and this is the moral of the story — a theoretical-practical world that we must learn to conquer: without rest, without end. . . .

Luca Meldolesi

Bibliography

AA.VV. (2004) *Eugenio Colorni 1944-2004. Dalla guerra alla Costituzione europea.* Proceedings of the debate of 18 May. Ed. Maria Pia Bombaca. Rome: Municipality of Rome III.

AA.VV. (2010) *Eugenio Colorni dall'antifascismo all'europeismo socialista e federalista.* Ed. Maurizio Degl'Innocenti. Manduria-Bari-Roma: Lacaita.

AA.VV. (2011) *Eugenio Colorni e la cultura italiana tra le due guerre.* Ed. Geri Cerchiai and Giovanni Rota. Manduria-Bari-Roma: Lacaita.

AA.VV. (2011a) *Eugenio Colorni federalista.* Ed. Fabio Zucca. Manduria- Bari-Roma: Lacaita.

AA.VV. (2012) *L'età dell'equilibrio (Traiano, Adriano, Antonino Pio, Marco Aurelio 98–180 d.C.).* Ed. E. La Rocca, C. Parisi Presicce, and A. Lo Monaco. Roma: Musei Capitolini.

AA.VV. (2015) *L'età dell'angoscia. Da Commodo a Diocleziano 180–305 d. C.* Ed. E. La Rocca, C. Parisi Presicce, and A. Lo Monaco. Roma: Musei Capitolini.

Albertini, M. (1979; 2nd ed. 1993) *Il federalismo. Antologia e definizioni.* Bologna: Il Mulino.

Bavink, B. (1944) *La scienza naturale sulla via della religione.* Torino: Einaudi.

____. (1947) *Risultati e problemi delle scienze naturali. Introduzione alla filosofia naturale dei nostri giorni.* Vol. 1. Trans. Eugenio Colorni. Firenze: Sansoni.

Bobbio, N. (1975) "Introduzione" and editing of Colorni, E. *Scritti,* cit.

Cerchiai, G. (2009) "Introduzione" and notes for Colorni, E. *La malattia,* cit.

____. (2016) *Cinque scritti metodologici di Eugenio Colorni nelle carte di Vittorio Somenzi.* Laboratorio Ispf Rivista elettronica di testi, saggi e strumenti, xiii.

Colorni, E. (1944) "Prefazione," to Spinelli, A. and Rossi, E., *Problemi della Federazione* cit.; now in Spinelli, A. *Il progetto,* cit., 1998.

____. (1975) *Scritti.* Ed. N. Bobbio. Firenze: La Nuova Italia.

____. (1980) "Pagine di Eugenio Colorni." In Solari, L., *Eugenio Colorni,* cit.

____. (1998) *Il coraggio dell'innocenza.* Ed. L. Meldolesi. Napoli: La Città del Sole.

____. (2009) *La malattia della metafisica. Scritti filosofici e autobiografici.* Ed. G. Cerchiai. Torino: Einaudi.

____. (2016) *Microfondamenta.* Ed. Luca Meldolesi. Soveria Mannelli: Rubbettino.

____. (2016a) "Cinque scritti metodologici," in G. Cerchiai, cit.

____. (2017) *La scoperta del possibile. Scritti politici.* Ed. Luca Meldolesi. Soveria Mannelli: Rubbettino.

Croce, B. (1917) *Teoria e storia della storiografia;* new ed. 1989 ed. G. Galasso. Milano: Adelphi.

____. (1938) *La storia come pensiero e come azione.* Bari: Laterza.

Einaudi, L. [Junius] (1920) *Lettere politiche.* Bari: Laterza.

____. (1933) *La condotta economica e gli effetti sociali della guerra italiana.* Bari: Laterza.

Geertz, C. (1999) *Mondo globale, mondi locali. Cultura e politica alla fine del ventesimo secolo.* Bologna: Il Mulino.

Gerbi, S. (1999) *Tempi di malafede. Una storia italiana tra fascismo e dopoguerra Guido Piovene ed Eugenio Colorni.* Torino: Einaudi.

Graglia, P. S. (1993) "Introduzione" and editing of Spinelli, A., *Machiavelli*, cit.

____. (2010) "Colorni, Spinelli e il federalismo europeo." AA. VV., *Eugenio Colorni*, cit.

Gui, F. (2004) "Da Ventotene alla Costituzione europea. Speculazione filosofica e azione politica in Altiero Spinelli." AA.VV. *La Cultura europea, la Costituzione dell'Unione e la sussidiarietà dopo la riforma del Titolo V della Costituzione italiana*. Roma: IISS.

____. (2010) "Colorni 'elemento di contestazione e di cerniera' nei documenti dell'Archivio centrale dello stato." AA.VV. *Eugenio Colorni dall'antifascismo*, cit.

Hirschman, A. O. (1963) *Journeys toward Progress. Studies of Economic Policy-Making in Latin America*. New York: Twentieth Century Fund.

____. (1970) *Exit, Voice, and Loyalty: Responses to Decline in Firms, Organizations and States*. Cambridge, MA: Harvard UP.

____. (1981) *Essays in Trespassing: Economics to Politics and Beyond*. Cambridge, UK: Cambridge UP.

____. (1988) *Come complicare l'economia*. Bologna: Il Mulino. [English trans.: *How Economics Should Be Complicated*. New York: Peter Lang, 2020.]

____. (1990) *Tre continenti. Economia politica e sviluppo della democrazia in Europa, Stati Uniti e America Latina*. Ed. L. Meldolesi. Torino: Einaudi.

____. (1998) *Crossing Boundaries. Selected Writings*. New York: Zone.

Hirschmann, U. (1974) *Rievocazione incompiuta*, mimeo.

____. (1993) *Noi senzapatria*. Bologna: Il Mulino.

Meinecke, F. (1930) *Cosmopolitismo e stato nazionale*. 2 Vols. Firenze: La Nuova Italia.

Meldolesi, L. (2013) *Imparare ad imparare. Saggi di incontro e di passione all'origine di una possibile metamorfosi*. Soveria Mannelli: Rubbettino.

____. (2014) *L'ultimo Hirschman e l'Europa*. Soveria Mannelli: Rubbettino.

____. (2016) *Rammendare il mondo*. Soveria Mannelli: Rubbettino.

____. (2016a) *Intransigenze, Mediterraneo e democrazia*. Soveria Mannelli: Rubbettino.

____. (2017) "Introduzione" to Colorni E. *La scoperta*, cit.

Pavone, C. (2004) "Intervento." AA.VV. *Eugenio Colorni 1944–2004*, cit.

____. (2010) "L'incontro con Colorni." AA. VV. *Eugenio Colorni dall'antifascismo*, cit.

Paolini, E. (1996) *Altiero Spinelli. Dalla lotta antifascista alla battaglia per la Federazione europea. 1920–1948: documenti e testimonianze*. Bologna: Il Mulino.

Quaranta, M. (2011) "La 'scoperta' di Eugenio Colorni nelle riviste del secondo dopoguerra. Gli scritti sulla relatività." AA. VV. *Eugenio Colorni e la cultura*, cit.

Robbins, L. (1932) *An Essay on the Nature and Significance of Economic Science*. London: Macmillan.

____. (1935) *Di chi la colpa della grande crisi? E la via d'uscita* Ed. S. Feanaltea. Torino: Einaudi.

____. (1937) *Economic Planning and International Order*, London: Macmillan.

____. (1940) *The Economic Causes of the War*. London: Macmillan.

Rossi, E. (1944) "Eugenio Colorni." *L'Avvenire dei lavoratori* 15 luglio; now in E. Rossi, *Un democratico*, cit., 1975.

____. (1975) *Un democratico ribelle*. Ed. Giuseppe Armani. Parma: Guanda.

___ and Spinelli, A. (1944) *Problemi della Federazione europea.* Ed. E. Colorni. Roma.

Rossi-Doria, M. (1991) *La gioia tranquilla del ricordo.* Bologna: Il Mulino.

Solari, L. (1980) *Eugenio Colorni. Ieri e sempre.* Venezia: Marsilio.

___. (2004) "La lezione di Angelo." AA.VV. *Eugenio Colorni 1944–2004,* cit.

Spinelli, A. (1984) *Come ho tentato di diventare saggio. I. Io, Ulisse.* Bologna: Il Mulino.

___. (1985) *Il progetto europeo.* Bologna: Il Mulino.

___. (1989) *Diario europeo 1948/1969.* Bologna: Il Mulino.

___. (1993) *Machiavelli nel secolo XX. Scritti del confino e della clandestinità.* Ed. Piero Graglia. Bologna: Il Mulino.

___. (2007) "Scritti filosofici." *Eurostudium 3w.*

___ and Rossi, E. (1944) *Problemi della Federazione europea.* Ed. Eugenio Colorni. Roma.

Tedesco, A. (2014) *Il partigiano Colorni e il grande sogno europeo.* Roma: Editori Riuniti.

Vassalli, G. (2004) "Intervento." AA.VV. *Eugenio Colorni 1944–2004,* cit.

___. (2010) "Ricordo di Angelo (Eugenio Colorni e la Resistenza romana)." AA. VV. *Eugenio Colorni dall'antifascismo,* cit.

1. Altiero Spinelli: Dialogue on the Significance of Systems[1]

Preliminary Note

The following pages have an entirely fortuitous origin. A casual conversation that was not even completed led me to write out my companion's thinking for the purpose of clarification. Rereading the first pages to a friend, I realized that without my intending it they had been written in the form of dialogue, and that was how I then continued it.

The dialogue form has the advantage of staying close to the thought process itself, which performs internal dialogues rather than monologues.[2] It has the obvious defect of alluding to many more things than it explains. But it would be absurd to want to explain everything, as will indeed be evident in the pages that follow. The dialogue process, like thinking, always doubles back on itself. It does not set a premise and endlessly draw inferences from it, but rather lays out a concept and keeps coming back to it, modifying it each time but always stating the whole concept. This inevitably produces repetition. A clever pen might avoid making the dialogues boring. Perhaps I haven't succeeded in this, but I never set out to write something entertaining.

The intellectual positions of my interlocutor, while seeming to me untenable, did not strike me as indifferent, or 'interesting' as we politely say of something that doesn't affect us; on the contrary, they met me halfway in a number of my own thoughts. They helped me clarify these to myself. And this was basically the reason I wrote what follows.

---

[1]Checked by Nicoletta Stame on 18.11.2016 against the autograph text kept in the Spinelli Fund at the archives of the European University Institute at Fiesole. The marginal notes that could be deciphered, which were all in the same hand, probably that of Manlio Rossi-Doria [MR-D], have been transcribed in footnotes next to the point where they had been placed in the text. Caesar is Colorni and Xavier is Spinelli [editor's note].
[2]When it performs monologues it's chanting the mass, not thinking [MR-D].

CAESAR: A system is supposed to be a key that provides an answer to all the problems that actually confront us or that could confront us. It claims to provide a concept or a set of concepts that constitute the essence of reality, and under which we should be able to subsume every particular object of our minds in an infinite series of judgments. The task of philosophy would then be to enumerate such concepts or categories. This is what the whole of philosophy comes down to and substantially always has.

But a system is an illusion, and moreover an illusion that is sterile. It is an arbitrary generalization from a particular experience. It is a generalization about what the system itself contains, because its content is limited to the problems that concern a single philosopher, who never notices the vast numbers of other problems that lie outside his system. It's a generalization that is even more gravely arbitrary when it comes to its own form, since its requirement of completeness doesn't correspond to anything real, but only answers our own need for peace and security, our desire to feel we're standing on solid ground where we can dispel the darkness around us.

But in reality this firmness is relative and temporary, and the light from it doesn't reach beyond a certain perimeter.

Once we realize that this need itself doesn't correspond to anything real, but only comes from our fears, there's no longer any reason to try and satisfy it. A child afraid to go into a dark room just wants to feel the security of his mother's hand. Having recognized that the origin of the fear is nothing but a fantasy, the child will reach for the light switch to see what he was looking for.

Once we recognize the fictitious nature of any system, or of any list of ultimate truths or categories, there is no point in launching yet another quest for a new one when we should just be looking at the specific organizational arrangements that for the moment interest us and that we hope will be useful. In doing this, however, we always need to keep in mind that: 1) an arrangement will not apply to *all* problems, only those that gave rise to it; 2) its value should be measured by its utility rather than some groundless truth criterion. Such an arrangement cannot be given an a priori justification. To do so would be the same as saying that it contained its own raison d'être and was self-sufficient — in other words that it was an actual system. Every organizational arrangement is a risk, a tentative foray on the part of the organizer. If it yields results, these are its justification. It has proved useful. If nothing comes of it, it has not. In any case it was never self-sufficient, *hortus clausus,* and was never either true or false unless, following Goethe, we mean that it was *fruchtbar . . . ist, allein ist wahr.*[3]

Finally, a system cannot tolerate another system right next to it; it has to either repudiate it — declare it false — or absorb it into itself, considering it a momentary, necessarily abstract manifestation of itself. An organizational arrangement, on the other hand, will accommodate an infinity of other extraneous and even contradictory arrangements — contradictory, it must be said, only to insistently systematic eyes, but in reality simply different.

The life of the mind, once liberated from the oppressive nightmare of the system, becomes very free and immoderate, and above all more fertile. Without this prejudice it can deal with anything. It can fearlessly bring down any idol that it realizes is or has become sterile, empty of inventions or discoveries.

This position is of course a renunciation, an abandonment of the dream of completeness, but proper reflection reveals this as the abandonment of a ghost, a nightmare, because systems have never been anything else but the suppression of the teeming life of the spirit, not a liberation.

XAVIER: In this way you say goodbye forever to all systems (I note in passing that the polemic against systems was led in Italy by Croce himself who, unaware of the contradiction, was the creator of an extremely rigid system). But you haven't said goodbye to the system-organizing activity of the mind. What does this consist of? Or, to say the same thing, what is the value of it?

CAESAR: But now I claim the right to refuse to consider this question. We have just seen that there is in fact nothing else but single arrangements. The only answer might therefore be: I will concern myself with this or that actual individual accommodation, not with this system-organizing activity.

---

[3]Only what is fruitful is true [MR-D].

XAVIER: An answer like that could only come from someone with no connection to the anti-system argument outlined above. For such people the question might as well be in Chinese, not worth answering — or even better, they wouldn't know how to answer it. But the duty to face it and solve it is inescapable now that the controversy has been set in motion. Once that happened we moved outside the particular workings of *this* arrangement and expressed a judgment about the *significance* of arrangements generally. In the argument itself you are answering the question, and it isn't acceptable now to stop the answer halfway, since this would mean being satisfied with a concept that is crippled.

CAESAR: But I am satisfied with it.

XAVIER: If you were satisfied you wouldn't be in a position to challenge others to be more precise. But I don't believe you are satisfied. It's no accident that you come back so relentlessly to this problem. If you were satisfied the discussion might just as well end here. If it continues, there must still be something, whatever it is, that you feel needs to be clarified.

So we have seen that for any specific arrangement we can reject as inconsistent the question of its truth (truth in this case referring to the self-justification that the arrangement itself ought to contain). A justification is rightly required for the things it produces since it is only for these that the arrangement was devised. This was in fact its criterion of utility.

The question before us now is: What is the arrangement? It has no apparently useful purpose. In which case the question is pointless! You cannot even say it's because it was imposed by necessity. Organizational arrangements were outside the criterion of true and false. This question is in turn outside the criterion of useful and useless.[4]

CAESAR: Here again I insist on the criterion of utility. It is not important to me to look into what the arrangement is, what its value is. A world may arrive in which it is of no use at all. But here,

---

[4]I don't understand the question. In giving arrangements a utilitarian purpose has C. not already implicitly replied that the utility of systematic activity helps us in the world, helps us master the forces that we find in it, thus increasing our power? [MR-D.]

in our world it yielded results, and what results! So I stick with it without pointlessly inquiring into its value.

XAVIER: Pointing to results, not to this or that result but to overall results — in a word, pointing to progress — you have once again resorted to a new term that is no longer specific, as were all the constituent elements of individual arrangements.[5] Progress might be a great thing or it might be an empty shadow. We have not taken a step forward. Until we understand what progress is we will know nothing whatever about the value of the instrument that produced it.

Here we are in entirely new territory. From a world of details that no single organizational arrangement could get us out of (since even the possible and necessary generalizations were nothing but details) we suddenly find ourselves transported into the world of the universal, the ultimate foundation or essence, if you like, of that mass of details.[6]

CAESAR: Universal — particular! How powerful the closed circle complex is, and how difficult it is to truly get rid of it and not just talk about it! We're right back in the world of systems we thought we had left behind once and for all. It's not enough to have renounced completeness using reasoning. Reasoning is a simple exhibitor of psychic impulses that go much deeper. If the desire for completeness is not eradicated there, reason will always be ready with syllogisms that can make it reappear anywhere. We need to know how to get rid of it emotionally, to escape feeling the need for it any longer. This is the only way the demon of philosophy will be killed.

XAVIER: And truly, it appears to you as a demon, philosophy, and you hurl yourself against it as if it were a personal enemy that must be destroyed if you are to gain your freedom.

CAESAR: This is what I have actually had to do. For a long time I was ensnared in Italian idealist philosophy, Croce especially. All mental activity was directed toward better defining the categories of the spirit — whether there were 3 or 4 of them or more or less, whether they were this or that, whether they were connected

[5] Why jump to this vague concept? I don't see the need [MR-D].
[6] I do not see myself in any way compelled to enter a metaphysical world [MR-D].

according to the dialectic of opposition or distinction, whether and how everything was spirit, and so on. It was real scholasticism. Thinking amounted to dawdling around in a void. — Then I noticed that this formalism was leaving out a mass of interesting things — ignoring them completely. Philosophical reasoning never got anyone anywhere. There were more things in the world than philosophy ever suspected. What I needed was to embark on a specific course of study, since only specific studies serve a useful purpose. Before that I was just making grand useless gestures in a vacuum. This was philosophy! And you want to lead me back to all that ineffectual running around, showing me that it's necessary? No thank you. It isn't necessary, and I am truly happy to be free of it. And besides, hasn't it always been like this? Humanity took steps forward only when it freed itself from the scholastics. Look at the example of Galileo, of Kant. Today a new scholasticism oppresses us. Anyone who is happy can stay, but it's a sterile happiness.

XAVIER: A psychoanalyst would deduce from the eloquent passion of your raging against philosophy how harsh your imprisonment was and still is. People don't rage so fiercely against an enemy they no longer fear. Even psychoanalysis itself should have taught you that in the case of an impulse flung out so violently simply dismissing it is not the same as overcoming it. Indeed, it continues to operate just the same, even in your present state of denial. And this twisted reappearance of it is a general illness. You are ill with philosophobia, and the reason is that you are basically infected with philosophilia. In order to truly free yourself from this torture, I believe that it is actually the path of psychoanalysis that you need to follow — as a way of re-introducing your own spiritual processes to your consciousness, becoming aware of every phase of them and of their genesis. In this way it may be possible to escape once and for all from this dilemma that now seems insurmountable: system and anti-system.

CAESAR: I am not at all ill with philosophobia. Actually, I can even admit to practicing philosophy myself when I work on my theoretical physics problems, and this is also true in the case of aesthetics. It's just that I don't do my work with the presumption of philosophers who think they can get to the bottom of the universe, when even they are just working on specific problems. Why should their work be worth more than mine? As you see, this is not an illness — indeed, I am quite calm and serene, and my only response to philosophical hubris is an ironic sneer.

So I don't understand where you could be going with this re-examination of the process of liberation from the system ghost. From conversations I've had with a number of people I am inclined to suspect that you want to surreptitiously reintroduce your own philosophical baggage yet again. But please, go ahead — I'll be interested to see what pops up.

XAVIER: In the first place, let's examine the position of someone in relation to the philosophical system they are thinking about. Whatever this system is, it seems to me safe to say that the thinker is in the same position as an architect in front of a building. The building is not the architect, it is another thing. And the architect has a certain number of tools — material and mental — that can be used to carry out the construction. We thus have three things that are distinct from one another: the architect, the tools, the building.

CAESAR: I suppose you are aware that no principled objection can be made in the case of the tools. All tools are good, *as long as* by means of them the building emerges. And the building itself is made for some purpose — that is, it must have some use, maybe even to produce enjoyment, but a purpose nevertheless. It is not an end in itself.

XAVIER: My point exactly. In philosophy we have the thinker, the thinker's tools, and the system. Three distinct entities. The thinker, once the creation is done, can disappear; having no further function beyond that of demiurge. The tools of the mind are necessary for the creation of the system. (In Croce, for example, the tool is the anti-positivist polemic).[7] Once the system has been created they are also of no further use. Archaeological curiosity may lead to an investigation of how the system was constructed. But this really is only simple curiosity. The stones of the pyramids stand on their own in such a way as to create the pyramids themselves without

---

[7]Analogies are always dangerous. The anti-positivist polemic was if anything the occasion, but never the tool. The thinker's tools are categories, syllogisms, etc. [MR-D.]

recourse to the scaffolding and winches and shoulders of slaves by which they were built. The tools of the thinker are nothing more than a temporary dialectic (in the Platonic sense of this term) for bringing about the construction of the system. This then is made in such a way that the individual parts of it are connected to each other by logical links — that is, by links such that you *must* pass from one part to the next,[8] and then to the third, and so on, until you return to the first, which is what for example Croce calls ideal history. This logic is different from the above dialectic, which proceeded from a need for a system to its realization. This other proceeds from one moment to the next within a given system.

What tools should the thinker use? Any tool,[9] clearly, that will be useful in bringing about what is needed. They are tools, and it is not possible to demand from them any other value besides instrumental. Brilliant thinkers will use tools that their own genius leads them to invent. Foolish ones will clumsily mishandle the finest and most ingenious tools.

CAESAR: Excellent. This is exactly what I maintain. And the system itself has also been built for some purpose. It also has an instrumental value. Croce, for example, offers his system as a "work tool."

XAVIER: The construction of the system is certainly carried out for a purpose. In general I think our answer should be that the impulse to create a philosophical system is due to this: of everything that comprises our knowledge, nothing shows stability. We look at something and it unravels. The full becomes empty, the empty full; the good evil and the evil good, the beautiful ugly and the ugly beautiful. Everything flows and changes. Yet behind this perpetual alteration we try to find something stable that the alteration proceeds from.

CAESAR: Might it not be a vain search for something that doesn't exist?

XAVIER: It might be. It's not that we look for it because ob-

---

[8]What does that *must* mean? Why this circle, necessarily? Because otherwise the philosopher wouldn't be able to relax in the illusion of the absolute? I don't understand. Why given? [MR-D.]

[9]Not everyone has this tendency. Those who do end up in religion or idealism [MR-D].

jects make us somehow understand that it's there; indeed, as far as they are concerned, they make us understand that it is not. We look for it because we can't do without it.[10] And we cannot do without it because we are not simply a flow of feelings. If that were the case we really wouldn't see any problem — we would just flow. But we reflect on the flow. We ask ourselves what it is.[11] The "what is it" reduces the flow to appearances. Consciousness is nothing but this problem. It is this problematic position that really makes the flow flow. It's only because there is a need for non-alteration that there is any awareness of this flow. On the other hand nor would simple non-alteration give rise to any problem or any consciousness. It is impossible that consciousness either just stands still or just flows. Standing still on its own is equivalent to flowing on its own. Each refers to the other. It does not matter to us now that the search for permanence may perhaps be in vain. It is a search we pursue due to the simple fact of being conscious, of thinking.

The "what is this flow" degrades the flow until it gives the appearance of something else and elevates the answer to a conception of this something else, of[12] the permanent substratum of that appearance, which is therefore no longer flow and appearance, but the essence of that appearance. — This concept is the system.[13]

CAESAR: This need to look for the stable behind the unstable is not an original quality of the conscience, it's a psychic complex that has an empirical origin that is traceable using appropriate psychoanalytic tools.[14]

XAVIER: No. It's not a *complex* — a *quality*, that is, that consciousness *has* and that it might well not have. This need is consciousness itself. When you talk about qualities or complexes of the psyche (here the same as consciousness), you're talking about

---

[10]I do without it [MR-D].

[11]But the reflection itself is a continuous flow. The question "what is this flow?" is ambiguous. I ask myself how the flow happens, and I try to respond with as accurate a description as possible. I do not seek the deep cause for flowing because, for me, it makes no sense. What did X. mean when he wrote "Consciousness is nothing but this problem"? Damn dialectics! [MR-D.]

[12]*Of* or *to*? [MR-D.]

[13]I don't know what to do with it [MR-D].

[14]I don't understand how Caesar could have taken psychoanalysis seriously [MR-D].

something that is incidental to it, and not what it is. You may not be satisfied with what I have told you consciousness is, and you may try and define it differently, but if you do you should be aware that you will have to completely eliminate complexes and any other incidental qualities from your exposition, since the problem of definition will only arise *after* they are eliminated.[15]

CAESAR: For now, by all means go ahead with your reasoning, since as far as I can see it will end up proving my point all by itself.

XAVIER: I think so too. A system is thus the exposition of the permanent in the flow. Precisely because it is permanent, it is supported by a line of logic that leads from element to element and never leaves the system itself, a line that constitutes a closed circle.[16] — Once the system has been worked out, it is believable that the key to the flow has finally been found or — identical here — the key to the universe. A sense of satisfaction fills the philosopher at last. The question: "what is the flow" has been answered. He can now abandon the dialectic that led to the construction of the system and can enclose himself there, to refine and perfect the edifice. There is also the work of application, but this basically comes down to a pastime, since it is known a priori that the application will succeed. Through such applications the philosopher will give a nod to the world, and will then intone:

Der Anblick gibt den Engeln Stärke[17]
Und alle deine hohen Werke
Sind herrlich wie am ersten Tage[18]

---

[15]Isn't it possible that after you identify all its qualities as incidental there will nothing left? Continuously, X. reasons as if it were indisputable that there are essences of things that must lie behind their appearance. A metaphysical mentality [MR-D].

[16]The Catholic catechism is also a closed circle, nor does it seem to me any less valid in satisfying the demands of completeness than philosophical systems. "Who created us?" God. "Why did he create us?" "To love him in this world and then go and serve him in heaven." They are meaningless questions and answers, but they give hundreds of millions of people the illusion of having anchored the fragile boat of their life to the rock of the absolute [MR-D].

[17]Sight gives the angels strength.

[18]And all your high works / Are as glorious as on the first day.

The work that will really matter now will only be formalistic. It is no longer invention, passing from not knowing to knowing,[19] but just bringing some light to elements that had previously been left in the dark but were undoubtedly already present in the system itself, or correcting small details neglected in the initial fervor of construction. And while the original philosopher, at least while constructing, was responding or trying to respond to a real worry, and not just to a desire for formal order, his disciple (or the philosopher himself, as his own disciple) has no problem that goes beyond this formal order, having arrived at the building not through personal labor (or dialectic) but through being led there by the hand, by the master of the house (or a servant). The disciple will act within this circle and play around with logical moves to make sure the machinery is working properly.

This work, carried out by angels who roam happily in creation, is in the long run a very boring job.

Der Philosoph, der tritt herein und beweist Euch, es müßt so sein:
Das Erst'wär so, das Zweite so;
und darum das Dritt', und Vierte so;
und wenn das Erst'und Zweite nicht wär; das Dritt'und Viert'wär
nimmermehr.
Das preisen die Schüler allerorten, sind aber keine Weber
geworden.[20]

CAESAR: Just what I think.

XAVIER: If we want to escape from this miserable rat's death, I think we need to ask ourselves *why* this happens. If we don't ask ourselves this, if we limit ourselves to noting that this is the case, noting it perhaps because we ourselves spent a long time wandering around in those empty rooms, and having felt a profound nau-

---

[19]Nice to know [MR-D].

[20]The philosopher comes forward / To show you that it must be like this. / Since the first one was like this and the second one is too, / the third one and the fourth are like this. / And if the first and the second were not, / Likewise the third and fourth would not be either. / Students praise him everywhere, / but they have not become weavers.

sea at seeing that there is no trace of actual life in them, that they offer no way of satisfying the thousand questions that life presents to us, that even in the absence of such questions we cannot even find an outlet for the mental energy that resists lingering perpetually on what we already know, dismantling and reassembling the clockworks of the system, and looks instead for something new — if, I say, we limit ourselves to simply noting this, and draw the conclusion that since there are no exit doors we must jump out the window, we will certainly be making a fine leap of liberation, but perhaps we will not be really free, because in reality the system is not outside us, like the edifice — it is within our own minds. It is not as easy as jumping out of some window if we're still carrying the system with us.[21]

CAESAR: How?

XAVIER: Like this: we've noticed that the system, once in place, doesn't answer the questions it is asked, but only those that it asks itself — it claims, that is, to be universal (universal here meaning responsive to all questions) when in reality it isn't.

So we tell ourselves that we might as well give up building a system that makes that claim, and just build more modest ones with an arbitrary door that lets us in and out whenever we want, without acrobatics or metaphors, which[22] are based on arbitrary definitions whose arbitrariness we are fully aware of. With them we can claim to reach only some particular goal.

CAESAR: This is precisely what I say we have to do.

XAVIER: But in the meantime we still have something of a bad conscience.[23] We know by now that this system (Croce's, let's say), or these n systems we have noted, have this defect of pseudo-universality, but for all we know there might be some other one, unknown to us and maybe to anyone, that doesn't have it and actually is universal. Do we shrug our shoulders and declare that we don't want anything to do with it? We're dealing here with a ghost that we can't manage to get rid of.[24] Every specific cut-rate

---

[21]Only metaphysicians have this edifice — a clot in the brain [MR-D].

[22]I limit myself to this [MR-D].

[23]Not at all [MR-D].

[24]It's a ghost that has never bothered me [MR-D].

system (or accommodation, if you prefer) that we set about building, precisely because it comes with a declaration that it does not mean to be universal, is essentially declaring: *I am not and do not want to be* what deep down you expect me to be.[25] Every arrangement or accommodation (since it is to this that we have reduced the previous pompous systems) has the diabolical temptation to turn into a System; it is, if not an imitator of God, certainly an imitator of Systematos, which we must continually remind to get down from its high horse, the way Pangloss (eternal Pangloss who is in each of us) had to be reminded to work in the garden. So many times, for example, in the middle of defining some physics concept I've heard you say, without anybody asking, "this is a very useful definition, *I don't mean from a philosophical point of view, which wouldn't matter much,* but for science." Ouch! Who raised the ghost of philosophy? It was there, right on the face of that same beloved scientific definition, that you saw flashes that brought to your mind the abhorred philosophical definition, and you had to ward it off with the ritual exorcism:

Incubus! Incubus!
Triff hervor und mach den Schluss![26]

Every specific accommodation arises from a need that is no different from the need that gives rise to the System — the need, that is, to give some consistency to what is apparently inconsistent. And as long as we go on setting ideal points that we arbitrarily declare to be fixed when we know perfectly well that they aren't — system fever will prod and sting us[27] again and again, because arbitrariness cannot satisfy a consciousness in search of a point that is really fixed, that we must necessarily declare to be fixed. The arbitrary arrangement is itself part of the flow, and consciousness is instead the need to determine what is beyond the flow.[28] Have we become skeptical about

---

[25]I don't expect anything but useful results [MR-D].
[26]Nightmare! Nightmare! / Come out and let's get this over with!
[27]Not me [MR-D].
[28]I'm not satisfied with this definition [MR-D].

whether this is possible? It doesn't matter. The goad is always there just the same, and it creates a state of permanent dissatisfaction.

Anyone whose first mental weapons, and this seems to be your case, were forged exclusively in the context of systematic formalism, may at first be happy to have broken out of that prison. In the time available he refined his instruments of reasoning, and now he is eager to employ them in more lively ways. He has discovered that the important thing is not the constructed system, but he is nevertheless still convinced that systems must be built, that there is nothing else for the mind to do. Logical formalism is in his blood. He throws himself into this or that argument, *quaerens quem devoret,* taking delight, that is, in building . . . systems, albeit on the cheap. Topics are for him basically of little importance. Even today, while tackling the theory of relativity, he thinks that at a certain point he'll ditch it and turn to something else. The absence of "presumption," the "lightness," is due basically to the fact that there is no serious involvement with the topic. This is no more than a pleasant occasion to sharpen up his ingenuity — which is entirely formalistic and therefore indifferent to substance.

And yet even this is unsatisfying. The elimination of the philosophical System has created a void that begs to be filled. And he fills it with the concept of utility, of fertility, which is what remains when everything is reduced to the level of tools. But the concepts of utility and fertility are neither useful nor fertile — they have no exploitable value. What are they but the fixed points the conscious mind was seeking that make sense of the seething spirit?[29] And yet, if on the one hand this central concept attracts our attention, imposing itself in an absolute way since it occupies this central place as the prime mover of everything, on the other hand we are afraid to pin it down, since we feel that we would be falling back into the vicious circle of creating a philosophical system. When I have properly defined this concept I will have obtained the wonderful result that all specific research will have been devalued. The concept will have explained everything and killed everything at the same time, since there is life only in specific research, while

---

[29]And why not? For me, all concepts have an instrumental value with respect to living [MR-D].

here there is nothing but empty conceptual formalism.[30]

We are in an odd situation. I need the concept of utility so I can orient everything around it, and on the other hand I can't get close enough to actually define it without making everything else pointless. The much vaunted liberation has turned into a torment. We desire and at the same time detest this search for the principle of everything. As Catullus says:

> Odi et amo. Quare id faciam fortasse requiris.
> Nescio, sed fieri sentio et excrucior.[31]

But in reality we now know that the reason lies in the fact that we never really broke free of the spirit of the system. We had indeed shaken off a particular philosophical system, but we never actually left the territory of systems research and development.

CAESAR: I'm not quite sure what you mean. Explain further.

XAVIER: Weren't we perhaps, like the infamous philosophers, also looking for the fixed points in the flow, the forms or categories — the atoms of thought, as you once put it — that would tell us what the meaning of the flow is, what the essence is behind the appearance?

CAESAR: With different expectations. But yes, like the philosophers we were also looking for this.[32]

XAVIER: The different expectations no longer matter, because we have seen that this search for essence has within itself a tendency to arrive at the determination of the ultimate essence — to pass, that is, from provisional and incomplete arrangements to a definitive and complete system.[33]

Before going on I would like to note, even at the cost of repeating myself, the point at which we have arrived:

1) The activity of making systems (culminating in the philosophical System) is a necessity of consciousness. It cannot be defined as an incidental quality (that is, by methods of investigation

---

[30]I don't entirely get this [MR-D].

[31]I hate and I love. Why do I do this, perhaps you ask. I do not know, but it happens and it is torture.

[32]Here Caesar plays the part of Socrates's interlocutor in his Platonic dialogues. Too easy [MR-D].

[33]No [MR-D].

consisting of psychological analysis, which examines what conscience has and not what it is), and therefore it cannot be eliminated. 2) If this activity trips us up in contradictions, as it seems
to be doing now, the explanation again cannot be sought using
more or less psychoanalytic methods, because the contradictions
come from a place that has nothing, absolutely nothing to do with
psychological processes. It is, one might say,[34] the mind battling
against itself, and not against its own incidental habits. A way out
will or will not be found, but if it is it will only be by way of thinking.[35] 3) And in any case not by following the path of analytical
thinking and formal logic. This has proved worthwhile, as we have
seen, only in determining the connections among the various
parts of an elegant and established system. Faced with contradictions it is unable to choose between one term and another. And
if we find ourselves facing a contradiction such that one term not
only negates but at the same time affirms another,[36] it will be mute
and powerless. Don't you think?

CAESAR: Yes, I would think so.

XAVIER: We actually already find ourselves facing such a
contradiction. Consciousness is as we have seen a living contradiction. And this is only insofar as it strives to stop what cannot be
stopped. And the solution was not choosing between "going with
the flow" and syllogizing in a chain of fixed concepts, but rather establishing a link between the two irreconcilable terms, such
that the flow is derived from the fixed points.[37] Consciousness at
the same time denies and establishes variation in the essence and
change from this into that.

But this solution nevertheless puts us once again in a strange
situation. An arrangement in fact tends toward becoming a system,
toward closing itself within itself and becoming all encompassing
and self-sufficient, and until it does it will not leave us in peace. But
while it is becoming these things it lets go of the actual flow and

---

[34]The sort of expression I distrust because it can mask emptiness [MR-D].
[35]Aren't the ways of psychoanalysis ways of thinking? [MR-D.]
[36]These are things that I don't understand [MR-D].
[37]Too abstruse for me [MR-D].

turns into a formal mechanism of abstract concepts — it dries up. So that as soon as a system is made it needs to be thrown away and another made . . . ad infinitum. The history of human thought is peppered with endless sequences of systems, approximately classifiable, like so many skins that the mind has periodically had to shed. These systems seemed definitive and complete every time, but in reality they were always temporary and incomplete, just simple arrangements. In fact, they were only ever applicable to certain more or less extended groups that were in any case always clearly delimited in terms of conscious experiences, and they expressed the essence of these.[38] The limitation of these experiences, however, became the limitation of the essence itself. Closed up within themselves, such systems had nothing to say about all the possible experiences that had not contributed to shaping them. If in the course of time they have more or less managed to let some of these in, it is because they increasingly take from these new experiences only those aspects that are old and already known to the system maker, and not the new ones. These latter always end up looking irretrievably rebellious, hence the necessity for new systems.

You noted, and you think it's a great conquest, that the system degrades into a simple arrangement. But you must see that things also go the other way — an arrangement upgrades itself into a philosophical system.

We have called consciousness the living contrast of reflecting on the flow. This superior phase, in which we determine the fixed points in the flow and these in their turn escape us, we can call — with the old German philosophers — the intellect. The intellect is the categorization, the shaping of the system. It too is a living contradiction.[39] And here again it is by no means the case that because it is a contradiction it can be eliminated. Indeed, it is because it is a contradiction that we have to live with it. It's elimination would mean falling back into a state of simple consciousness, but this, inasmuch as it entails reflecting on the flow of sensation, necessarily regenerates the positions of the intellect.

---

[38]Damn the word essence [MR-D].
[39]A characteristically philosophical mode of reasoning [MR-D].

CAESAR: There is no other way to escape the contradictions of the intellect except to jump now and again back into the spontaneity of life or to return, as you say, to a pure state of consciousness in order to climb back up the steep arid slope of intellectual work.

XAVIER: It's a kind of labor of Sisyphus, since there seems to be no escape route. We all have our pain, and if you wanted to define yours, you would have to call it the pain of being pure intellect, the desire and at the same time the desperation that come with never being able to be anything but intellect. You want to degrade[40] the results of this as temporary, arbitrary, not real, mere instruments — and yet you feel bound to this work of determining abstract concepts as if by an unbreakable chain.[41]

CAESAR: But come on — since you say it's a necessary position, you too have to admit that it's impossible to escape from it. Or is it? And if so, how?

XAVIER: Before we get into this question I would like to look at an example that I think will help us find a way out of this desperate situation.

To survive, every human society needs some kind of organization. While this is being created it gives the appearance of being able to satisfy all the society's needs. It is precisely for this purpose in fact that it is desired. And yet the social group itself can never manage to live in the organization created.[42] It feels like an ever more stifling encumbrance weighing it down. And from one, two, and then a thousand sides the work of modification, correction and finally destruction begins. But the purpose of this is never, as the anarchists dream, to eliminate any organization at all, but rather to replace one with another. A perpetual restlessness agitates us. Is it a useful restlessness in that it prevents us from rotting in stasis? And why after all should this inertia be bad? Or is it perhaps useless, because it just moves us from one illusion to another? And why should this mad flight in pursuit of a ghost be bad? In reality,

---

[40]It doesn't degrade them [MR-D].

[41]This is not a chain. It is the recognition of the value of such central concepts in contributing to a greater probability of success with respect to proposed purposes [MR-D].

[42]Because society itself is not a static thing. The makeup of a society is like the clothing that has to be replaced as a child grows [MR-D].

this restlessness is neither useful nor useless — it is beyond good and evil, it is necessary, it is life itself. And yet when needs are being carefully analyzed, and the causes — in vulgar parlance — of a given historical process are under study, it is not included. Just as it isn't included in a careful analysis of the organizational forms a society aimed for — in a study, that is, of the so-called operational ideals of a given historical process.[43] It is included only when it is conceived as an actual autonomous process in which needs[44] and ideals are only features, albeit necessary ones. The driving engine, and with it all the movement taking place, is political activity — not needs, nor the law nor constitutions. But political activity is not a third term that is added to the other two; it is their very existence. If we take needs, we see that they strive to organize themselves.[45] If we take the organization we see that it strives to let needs express themselves. The one appeals to the other. But even here there is resistance since needs split an organization and the latter, in its turn, suffocates needs. The solution is in political activity, which achieves both and alters both. Order and disorder at the same time.[46] And you cannot even say that political activity is arbitrary, reformulating it from the ground up as a third entity that will amateurishly draw on these or those needs and build this or that organization. It is arbitrary only in its words and gestures, in propaganda that uses this or that language, in its appeal to this or that sentiment — but not in its substance. The tools are arbitrary, and the only criterion for their use is whether they work, but not the needs and the organization, which are the constituent factors, the substance, the thing itself. Don't you think?

CAESAR: Yes. That's right.[47]

XAVIER: But let us try to conceive political activity not as we have just described it — that is, as an autonomous process — but rather as an effective third term that has before it needs awaiting satisfaction, and works to build an organization which is also, in its

---

[43]This case seems to me to be included in the previous one [MR-D].
[44]I don't understand [MR-D].
[45]Political language. Needs and organizations do not strive. I don't understand [MR-D].
[46]Unity — distinction!!! [MR-D.]
[47]Lucky him [MR-D].

turn, separate from it — a goal not yet reached, but something to be achieved one day, and once and for all. In such a case, shouldn't we judge the activity with criteria of utility — in such a way, that is, that if the organization achieved is good, that is if it satisfies many important needs, it will justify the activity, and if it satisfies few or no needs it will be its downfall?

CAESAR: Clearly that is how it should be judged.

XAVIER: But since there will be no organization, whatever it may claim, that meets all needs, shouldn't political activity be considered as a tool that gives only partial solutions, and not, as it boasts, complete and definitive ones?

CAESAR: Yes.

XAVIER: But we have just seen that political activity is not the external mediator between needs and the organization, but rather the process itself of organizing needs, and that the criterion of utility, which was valid as long as we considered the three as abstract features,[48] no longer tells us anything now that we know that none of them exists as a means for achieving the others. The organization of needs is not an end of something else, it is an end in itself. Isn't this the way things are in politics?

CAESAR: Yes, exactly like that, I would say.[49]

XAVIER: So, getting back to our problem, we said that in philosophy we had the thinker, the instruments of thought, and the system as three entities, distinct and separable from one another. We left it like this: To make sense out of the chaos of sensory experience the thinker has to construct a system, and makes use of certain tools for this purpose. The sensory chaos might be called the primordial data. The need for order is an entirely subjective need of the thinker, who can therefore arbitrarily set about putting in order this or that area of the chaos. The utility of the tools derives solely from the utility of the system they serve to create. The value of the system itself lies exclusively in the satisfaction it provides to the subjective and arbitrarily determined need of the thinker. These were the terms of our problem, weren't they?

---

[48]Don't like it [MR-D].
[49]Happy man [MR-D].

CAESAR: They were, yes.

XAVIER: And it seemed so natural that they should look like this! And yet here again we have been the victims of a bad joke, and it looks like they have appeared in a false light, as terms that are distinct and independent, when in reality they are not. In fact, we had seen, had we not, that the flow of consciousness necessarily requires fixed points — arrangements?

CAESAR: Yes.

XAVIER: So in that case, we're not dealing with the external intervention of a third party (the thinker). The thinker is nothing but this self-organization of the flow of sensations, the essentializing of appearances.[50]

CAESAR: So it would seem.

XAVIER: So even here the criterion of utility fails, or is at least reduced to a second-order criterion. It might for example be more useful in theoretical physics to postulate a constant speed of light, rather than the rigid body handed down to us from an earlier theory. Things are more simply represented this way, and more manageable — we can perhaps eliminate some pitfalls. In short, it might be to our advantage to get rid of some old habits. In this case the criterion of utility is without doubt valid. But in physics, theory is neither useful nor useless — it is not formulated for some extrinsic purpose but is rather the process of organization of physical experience, which is a necessity of consciousness.[51]

And arbitrariness basically coincides with utility, since if something is only useful or useless, we can always take it or leave it depending on whether we come across something else still more or still less useful. So even arbitrariness, I say, fits into that same restricted sphere in which the criterion of utility is valid.

CAESAR: And so if it isn't utility, what is the criterion that supports this process? Truth, perhaps?

XAVIER: What is this criterion of truth?

CAESAR: This is where I wanted you to go. The criterion of truth is absurd. What would be true, if such a thing were ever at-

---

[50]No [MR-D].
[51]No [MR-D].

tainable, would be the complex of concepts comprising the ultimate, complete and definitive Philosophical System. But it is unattainable. On the other hand, even if it could one day be reached, until we possess it we do not know what is true and we cannot use it as a criterion for seeking itself.[52]

XAVIER: Perfectly right.

CAESAR: So giving up the criteria of truth and utility, which I had clung onto out of necessity, you are left even more uncertain than you criticize me for being.

XAVIER: Let's think again whether it might not be possible to escape from the minefield we've got ourselves into. Why is it that we would call this ultimate and definitive System, if it were ever found, *true*?

CAESAR: Because in such a case we would have to declare that what it affirms *is,* unequivocally *IS.* Not just that it seems to be to us, in which case it might be just a Veil of Maya. It is, of necessity. We would be compelled to recognize it.[53]

XAVIER: So the criterion of truth, if it ever existed, would be the criterion of necessary existence?

CAESAR: Yes.[54]

XAVIER: But in that case it's clear that a criterion of this kind cannot be applied to the products of the intellect in themselves, which at most have a perfect internal coherence that is completely formal and has nothing to do with the "is."

CAESAR: Then we agree.

XAVIER: No. The conclusion of what we have said is that the truth of this essence that is *given* once and for all is empty. It is necessary, and as such *is* certainly true, as we can now say of the search itself.[55]

Indeed it is not a search — one that aims, that is, to discover

---

[52]There is a Platonic dialogue that says the same thing. I don't remember which [MR-D].

[53]If Caesar is still using these terms it means he hasn't yet freed himself from metaphysics. What the devil does that IS mean? [MR-D.]

[54]Bravo! [MR-D.]

[55]Given the aforementioned truth criterion, X. would be right. But I don't know why he should call truth the necessary attribute of a subject. To create confusion and then demonstrate whatever he wants [MR-D].

something that already exists, because the essence is not a previously existing thing to be discovered, but rather is placed, created by the mind itself. The truth is thus the activity of consciousness itself.[56] We have come a long way in search of a fixed point outside ourselves, and as it turned out we ourselves are the fixed point. Flow and system, chaos and cosmos are the features of consciousness, and not things that stand in front of it.

This fixed point is not, like the essence we were seeking before, something that should calm us — it is anxiety itself. It doesn't devalue the particular because it lives on it. It doesn't let us relax in a system because it creates and destroys systems. And it is not a system — just as no living philosophy has ever been a system. It has at most *had* systems.

Now this is where philosophy is, and not in the formal logic of a system. Attacking philosophy, you were actually pursuing a ghost.

CAESAR: I want to admit you are right. There is still my original objection — What is the use of all this? The conclusion we've reached is this: that the truth is the work, the specific endeavor of organizing — scientific, political or however else you want to define it. You might as well work, like *Candide,* but of course in your own particular garden.

XAVIER: In fact, philosophy is not something useful in the sense that it serves some ulterior purpose. We don't do philosophy for pleasure but rather out of necessity. Simply working or organizing makes us feel the contradictory nature of the terms opposing us, like destiny weighing us down, infecting all of our work with nothingness, and making it appear arbitrary and insipid — useful as far as it goes, but useless basically. To use Barth's apt image, it puts all our detailed work in brackets and places before us a minus sign. We need to move beyond this contradiction, and the only way to overcome it is not, as we have seen, to ignore it, but to understand that it is the leavening agent in our work itself.

We do philosophy[57] to understand the meaning of life. And we cannot renounce understanding, renunciation itself being an

---

[56]Muddlers; damn the philosophers [MR-D].
[57]Poetic language [MR-D].

attempt to understand, an attempt which is nevertheless unsatisfactory.

All specific arrangements (which now also include the lists of philosophical categories) derive their value from philosophizing.[58] We therefore need to understand them historically, and therefore we must proceed in each case to identify them, knowing that the truth, our reassurance, is not in them, in the circle that is closed or only apparently open or closed, but rather in the self-propelled[59] basic motor that is the restlessness itself.

And there is one last observation I would like to make: Philosophy cannot establish a priori what work we should dedicate ourselves to. When questioned on this it is mute, useless, if you will. It provides the answer to another question: What is the meaning of the work I am doing? — Philosophizing, reflecting on the meaning of work will reveal this but will at the same time change the work itself into something more serious, more profound.[60] But if I am basically indifferent to what work I do — if I work, that is, as a pastime or out of curiosity, if my life is as light as a feather in the wind, it certainly won't be philosophy that gives it substance. Indeed, my philosophy will be the philosophy of curiosity, of the meandering feather. Philosophy does not produce a solution to whatever problem is posed; it is not an oracle open to anyone and nor is it a mill where you put in wheat and out comes flour — it is life itself reflecting on itself. This is the profound meaning of Kant's claim that you cannot teach someone how to do philosophy. — This observation is almost trivial for someone who has approached philosophy starting with the problems of life; but it certainly must instead be a laborious conquest for students of philosophy, who have to assemble and disassemble systems at a time in their lives when there is as yet no serious problem of life that leads them to philosophize.

And so you see that what you called the presumption of philosophers — actually plain speaking and not just professorial arrogance — was in reality far more than a residue of forgotten psycho-

---

[58]So all arrangements, even the stupidest and most absurd, have the same value [MR-D].
[59]Self-propelled? [MR-D.]
[60]I don't think so [MR-D].

analytic complexes. It was instead simply the sense of seriousness which can and indeed must be there, even when the tone is less than serious. And that vaunted lightness, when it is not an attempt to philosophize and therefore not light at all, as in your case — when instead it is real lightness, is something even its bearer is unaware of, and it appears in the eyes of someone who doesn't have it in a truly unflattering light, more like the insipid pap of the Gospels, which ought to be chucked out and trampled.

CAESAR: At this point, even though there's still a lot to say, we're both tired and we can put it off to another occasion.

October 1939

2. Altiero Spinelli: Contact in the Night

1. Letter from Severus (A.S.) to Commodus (E.C.)[1]

Psychological mechanisms and habits are the framework upon which our mental lives take shape. The set of all these mechanisms comprises what we call character. Character is therefore not only the complex of so-called moral habits, but of all of them. The Oedipus complex, or any other idiosyncrasy, be it racial, national, class-based or individual, is a feature of character.

Habits constitute the strength of individuals, because it is through them that they are able to build a sturdy underlying structure and thus free themselves from a whole series of acts, reducing them to mechanical gestures and reactions that are automatic. If moment by moment we had to re-engage with all our attitudes toward the whole universe, we would be forever at the starting line, in a dreamy, foggy state, perpetually tangled up and stumbling over ourselves. But for the individual, habits are also a prison. They do not in fact arise as a solid pedestal from which the soul can soar; they do not breathe harmony and perfection in every respect. They arise from the need for defense against the turbulence of life, and because of this they often arise very unreasonably indeed, so that as they settle in to the point of becoming idiosyncrasies (habits whose starting point we no longer even remember), they mostly constitute an impediment to more unrestricted action. Thus we very often become prisoners in our own castle.

The study of habits, conscious and unconscious, is therefore extremely important. It is the study of our psychic anatomy; our strengths and weaknesses. Weaknesses, incidentally, that can be corrected, since by actually studying the genesis of habits we glimpse the possibility of no longer being their prisoners. Character is a skeleton. If the skeleton is internal, then we are vertebrates

---

[1] Checked by Nicoletta Stame on 29.11.2016 against the autograph text kept in the Spinelli Fund at the Archives of the European University Institute at Fiesole (editor's note).

and habits are a strength in that they do not prevent us from making contact, through our soft skin, with the things that surround us. If the skeleton is external we are crustaceans and habits are our weakness, as they preclude our making soft contact. The ideal would be to transform the human crustacean not into a human mollusk, but into a vertebrate — if possible not a pachyderm.

What you propose and what you reproach the idealists for never having done, is no less than to study these psychic mechanisms. Study them to expose the sensitive flesh.

The aim is to achieve contact with others, to gain access, that is, to the immediate knowledge that lies beyond that crust.

Now this entire armory of mechanisms is the product of the intellect. From the very elementary psychic systems discovered by psychoanalysis up to the most complex scientific, philosophical and ethical systems — all this is the work of the intellect. You would like to mark out the limits of all this in order to be able to look beyond, to really know the other. The other you are looking for is another person, man or woman. . . .

What are we looking for in the other? Here is another individual like me, strong in skeleton and weak under the shell. What we gather from the other is not character, not the intellectual element. Indeed, character is precisely what we want to put aside. Character is what separates us from one another. What we are looking for lies behind the negating, distinguishing power of the intellect. It is the "contact in the night" — the "divine otherness" of Lawrence, what Hegel calls substantial life. This immediate knowledge, not without reason, has been identified in love, without which a person is a *kýmbalon àlalázon*.[2] Love is Pandean communion. Even St. Paul in his hymn to love is Dionysian and pantheist. And Lawrence is right in saying that when it comes to love, everyone has the absolute "belief in the blood, the flesh, as being wiser than the intellect."[3]

Contact in the night is the cancellation of cold individuality —

---

[2] Clashing cymbal.

[3] I put Lawrence next to St. Paul smiling at the juxtaposition. However, I am aware that this is not so paradoxical. Even St. Paul deeply loves the flesh and wants it resurrected and sanctified. And even Lawrence hopes for the resurrection of the flesh. Only the body can really love.

that is, of distinction. You say: I want to discover the other, what it is that's different from me, but up to now I've only looked for what is like me. – But note that the other is other only by virtue of individuality. Eliminating this brings a sense of Pandean communion but not a sense of otherness. The otherness exists while there is mystical tension, and not in the realized mystical union. In this the I and the you are left behind.

Love is always directed toward concrete flesh and bone people; and it is in fact no accident that Christianity, putting αγάπη [agápe, love] at the center of its religiosity, gives the flesh such a broad and fundamental place in its mystery. (God had to become Jesus to love and be loved, the dead will rise again, and so on.) — Thus, love is always directed towards an individual. But what it reaches is not the individual but rather the common substance behind all individuals. Underlying the doctrine of love there is always pantheism, the Pandean sensibility. To stay with St. Paul for a moment we see that for him the realization of love and the realization of pantheism coincide, and entail the elimination of the contrast between God and "the world." So that God is everything in everything.

You don't trust this conclusion. You think that up to now what we've had is religious mysticism with God as its object, and that what we need is atheist mysticism with humanity as its object. Consider, though, that the first of these is not directed at God, indeed it is pantheistic, and that this new mysticism of yours doesn't stop at the individual but rather looks at what is behind, and all it finds there is the mysterious god Pan. The idea of God and of the individual are both products of the intellect, of Mephistopheles. Behind Mephisto there are the Mothers, the "contact in the night." Love is identical to the Pandean sensibility.

Immediate knowledge or love is not taught — contradiction precludes it. We can evoke it with allegories, artistic performance, or suggestive words if it is dormant, but we can make it understood only to those who already have it. Just as you can't explain lovemaking to a eunuch.

You can express your own sense of love by letting whoever has an ear for it listen, but you can't teach it. Teaching, in fact, means making distinctions, analyzing, syllogizing — that is, putting the intellect to work. But how can the intellect arrive at a determination of what love is? It will try to identify psychological mechanisms and habits, seeking to understand how they arose and to what end the individual consciously or unconsciously puts them to use. Finding distinction, mediation and consistency everywhere, it will arrive at the ultimate denial of itself, giving a judgment of love that is totally negative. Love is not any of this — in fact with respect to all this it is the opposite. Get rid of all this scaffolding, and if there is a heart-beat beneath it, if you are not a whitewashed tomb yourself, you will discover what love is.[4]

Love and intellect would seem then be the two fundamental forms of our being. Through the intellect we separate ourselves from the original substance we arose from and try to subordinate everything to ourselves. Through love we are reunited with it. The intellect directs the other towards me and drowns the other in me. Love directs me toward the other and drowns me in the other.

It's either one or the other. With different feelings at different times this theme of the alternation of the human spirit has been pondered or sung a thousand times.

Beyond Lawrence, I recall how Leopardi and Jacobi shrank from Spinoza's cold intellect and invoked immediate knowledge, which is in fact the context of love.

But is it also true that there is nothing but this alternative, that we are either in the realm of the intellect or of love? – Ouch! Intellect and love are surreptitiously becoming two categories. – And it couldn't be otherwise, as long as we give the floor to the *ur-teilende Kraft*[5] of the intellect, which always determines and fixes static categories. The intellect will reach a level of self-denial such that it recognizes the superiority of love, but this will involve subjecting love to the cold breath of the analyst who examines this and that, setting limits and drying things out so that they fit into categories.

This is substantially the road you intend to follow in your essay

---

[4]Every time immediate knowledge is placed next to the intellect the main task of the intellect becomes cathartic. For example, for Croce the Spirit is something immediate, and consequently his philosophy no longer looks like cleaning the temple to clear the way for the unhindered advance of the goddess.

[5]Dividing power.

on the deceptive quality of words. The great deception is the intellect — the light that will not allow you to experience the deep and mighty darkness that words can only vaguely convey. Moved by experience, which has shown you how radically different from the intellect love is, you are preparing to communicate the discovery to others.

But I think you need to understand clearly that you cannot go down the road of either the hymn to love or of intellectual categorization, because the former is nothing but the immediate expression of immediate knowledge, and the latter is the external anatomy of the same immediate knowledge, a list of judgments that tell you this is that or this is not that, but never tell you anything at all about this or that. Intellectual labor is a process of mediation that always presupposes something immediate, a datum on which the mediation can work.

The road we do take must be one in which the immediate generates by itself and in itself its own mediation and distinctions. The object of our investigation must be a living concept and not a dead one that we anatomize.

If we go this way, though, we find ourselves on the other side of the distinction between intellect and love. We no longer have an either/or situation, nor do we have static categories. Substantial life or divine otherness is no longer the yearned-for destination, the point of liberation from the captivity of the intellect, but is rather the starting point from which the differentiating and individualizing work of the intellect arises. Which taken abstractly in itself is the static opposite of love, but which in reality is the means by which mystical love becomes rational love — that is, love that no longer drowns in the divine otherness, but can coexist with other individuals it has acquired an understanding of, and consists not of darkness alone, but of darkness striving to become light.

What you want to achieve, the understanding of an individual, is unattainable via the mystical route of renouncing the intellect, since what you reach is not the individual, but the naked substance that lies behind all individuals. Instead, such understanding is achievable only if this substance has transformed itself (I say transformed *itself* and not *has been* transformed by our intellect) into ego — that is, if it has run the thorny gauntlet of the intellect.

If the problem of words is re-examined from this point of view it will be seen for example that the chapter on deception has to be followed by one on disillusionment, since words are a deception (and a means of separation) when they are intellectual words, when they are judgmental, but they are a disillusionment when they transform judgment into exposition, into a narrative of origins.

Disillusionment — which means presupposing the deception, the distinctions, the fixed points without which the description can never get started, but which the description itself must drop when on its own. This is moreover implicit in your requirement that words should not be eliminated, but rather translated, so that you still have words, but they are no longer what they were.

Another example: reasoning is intellectually a means of conquering other minds. After having defined it in this way, you are naturally forced to condemn it for violence and fraud. But who, except in mathematics, is convinced by reasoning? To my knowledge, nobody.

Becoming convinced means establishing a certain pre-reasoning communion that prepares us to understand the meaning of the reasoning. Should this be considered superfluous in the case of someone who is already fundamentally convinced? On the contrary, once this happens reasoning is no longer a means of doing violence and convincing someone your own methods are right — it has now become the means for that conviction to manifest itself, to show that it actually exists. So it is no longer superfluous, but is instead the original conviction becoming or striving to become aware of itself, to escape from its own immediacy. This is reasoning no longer seen in its immediate aspect as a pedagogical tool, but "translated" — that is, understood as what it is really intended to be.

If you look at a thinker's system you realize after a while that without exception what he meant was different from what he actually said. The system looks like a fraud! What was left unsaid was the thinker's original belief. But if we can just manage to make contact with this, the thinker immediately appears alive to us, close to us. We understand what he meant, and even after centuries we will help him say what he himself could not say.

I could give more examples covering a great variety of cases.

But I want to limit myself to drawing a methodological conclusion.

Dividing life into two distinct faculties is easier, more comfortable, apparently more paradoxical but actually more banal than understanding it in its unity. Not in its primordial unity of substance or darkness or whatever you want to call it, but unity that is spread between the distinct faculties and then drops them in its private moments, renewing and transforming itself in the process.

This way is the more difficult, because it requires letting go of ourselves, trusting that we will find ourselves again, albeit transformed. People are generally afraid of letting go of themselves because they are afraid of getting lost. And even when they mark out a distinct area for letting themselves go right next to the area where they have to be careful and control themselves, they are still afraid of getting lost. Contact with the night or with the Mothers will always be a plunge, intoxicating and brief, but we always quickly come back up from it to icy but safe Mephistopheles, who gave us the key so we could get there, but who did not go with us.

Even this method of letting go of yourself, confident that you will find yourself again, if ossified into an intellectual rule, can become an anchor we drop for fear of getting lost. This fear is so great that we resort to anything to save ourselves, even to accepting the advice not to save ourselves. But the good news is that this advice, if understood in this way, will be given but not applied. We can fool ourselves that we can skip the worrying experience of letting go (Lao-tze's doing without doing), since we know that we will find ourselves again. But since none of us knows in advance how to go about finding ourselves, no one can forgo the experience and still be under any illusion that we know what is there on the opposite shore.

Now it's still not quite clear to me whether this is exactly what you call the way of love or auscultation, and which I rather prefer, with Hegel, to call reason — to distinguish it from the mystical way of immediate knowledge, which is simply antithetical to the intellectual determination of categories and judgments.

Note. I don't know if you realize that the problems that occur to you are similar to those that presented themselves to Schelling and Hegel after Fichte — no longer seeking to understand the framework of the spirit, but rather its genesis, its experience. Jacobi decided suddenly to abandon the path of intellect and plunge into that of immediate knowledge. Schelling wanted the intellect to travel the whole road to self-destruction in the absolute, "where all cows are black." Hegel, with considerable courage not always matched by coherence, wanted the spirit to abandon itself in order to find itself again.

I have long been aware that Italian philosophy, with Croce and Gentile, has in its own way retraced not the path of Hegel, as it claims, but that of Fichte.[6] No wonder problems crop up today that are all but identical (there is no longer the heavy burden of German logic and theology) to those of Schelling and Hegel. Today we can study Hegel without needing to become Hegelians anymore. We study him as a friend and not as a teacher.

January 1940

II. Dialogue between Severus and Commodus[7]

SEVERUS: It's not that I want to reduce others to one. And neither does Lawrence.

The gamekeeper's attitude towards Lady Chatterley is as you describe: one of understanding, compassion, and self-abnegation in front of the other. Artistically as well, the gamekeeper is a pale figure in front of Connie. The center of the novel is the woman, and the divine intoxication of the senses described is female and not male. Not even Lawrence, I repeat, *wants* to reduce the other to oneself.

What you don't want to understand is that this reducing happens by itself, without anyone wanting it to. In Lawrence's novel there is no apparent trace of this reduction. Lawrence's awareness of it is something I gathered from Huxley and to me it is an indication Lawrence's profundity.

In short, it isn't enough to say: I *want* to devote myself to the

[6]Hegel's simplification in the Kantian sense had already been begun by Spaventa.
[7]Checked by Luca Meldolesi on 18.11.2016 against the autograph text kept in the Spinelli Fund at the Archives of the European University Institute at Fiesole.

other, but that's all — I don't want to be shipwrecked in this sea. The shipwreck happens by itself and you just have to go with it. You have to let yourself go in actual fact when you find yourself in this situation, and you have to let yourself go in your mind when you think of it. You mustn't be afraid of the unintended consequences. They are the most important ones.

COMMODUS: If this is really the way things are, then what I have said loses all its freshness. . . .

SEVERUS: To hell with freshness.

COMMODUS: And if I don't know how to live in relation to someone else, I will never understand that person, not ever. I know where I'll end up — at that divine otherness, that substance common to everyone, including me; I will still be alone with myself, a closed monad — the very stage I wanted to escape from.

SEVERUS: Actually, if you *want* to escape from it, you never will. I want to embarrass you, if I can. You want a love that demands no recompense; that accepts reciprocation with ever renewed gratitude. You want the ego to completely humble itself, to the point even of rejecting the maxim 'love your neighbor as yourself' because in it the ego still looms. You *want* to make yourself small. But, as you say yourself, all this devotion is also dictated by a motive of self-preservation. You fear that the other might be disgusted with your ego; you are afraid of being abandoned. It is this fear of losing yourself that makes you recoil before the darkness that Lawrence shows us.

In my opinion, aggrandizing the other is just as frightening as aggrandizing yourself. You must heroically not give a damn about yourself or the other. This is the only way you will find both again. And not in the darkness of contact in the night.

And it's not as if this is big news. It is what's always done, more consciously or less. The problem is to be able to realize it, to do it consciously and therefore better.

January 1940

For each individual, events occur in his own image — an aphorism that is somewhat disturbing because it seems paradoxical and thus meaningless (Since the contact between the individual and the event is random, how could any pre-established harmony exist between them?); and nonetheless, in thinking about it and referring to our own experience, we are forced to recognize that it is much more profoundly true than it appears to be at first sight.

Events are without doubt infinitely multicolored, and for each of us they just happen the way they happen, but every event in fact has a thousand different faces. I have a tendency always to notice one aspect in particular. I am well aware that there are others, and indeed I calmly proceed to deal with them and resolve them. But the aspect that strikes me is in fact not one of those that I know how to manage and resolve; it is something I have to endure; something that calls not for action, but for passion. There is an insurmountable barrier of powerlessness that makes me stop and look on, inert and suffering, instead of moving against the hostile severity of the event. Acting in fact means entering into communion with the event and ensuring that it is no longer a thing looming over us, but something we can work together with. Enduring means having fate hanging over you. Now this fate is not really in the event, which in itself, unless it is a piece that fits a puzzle, is a random occurrence — it is instead due to the fact that the individual is in some way [prisoner: crossed out and replaced by] paralyzed and unable to recognize the opportunity and make something of it. And this inability is because the individual doesn't want to. To function he should

1940

3. Eugenio Colorni:
On Reading Philosophers[1]

RITROSO: I am incapable of reading a philosophy book if I don't understand it completely. And when I say understand it, I mean grasping precisely the meaning of each word, and making sure that every word is always used with the same meaning, and that the reasoning is correct, and that the proofs don't contain appeals to principle. I don't know what to do with a book if I start to find this stuff.

COMMODUS: Wasn't it you who insisted on the symbolic, allusive character of language, with its roots in the earliest customs of our childhood, these having been handed down in turn starting from the (earliest) customs of humanity? Didn't you say that in the world of our senses it is impossible to distinguish anything that corresponds one hundred percent to a certain word; and that when you say "the cat eats the mouse," you don't know, at the end of the day, what it means?

RITROSO: I did say that, yes, and I still say it. But you were the one who insisted on the limits of precision, which are not the same in all types of reasoning — this means that certain clarifications that make sense in one context are nothing but affectations in another. When I speak of precision in philosophical definitions, I'm naturally talking about the sort of precision you can reasonably expect in a conversation of this kind, but without which it's not even worth trying to follow the thread of the argument.

COMMODUS: What makes you so sure there are arguments in philosophy books?

RITROSO: Don't start with the usual paradoxes. They don't affect me anymore. Actually, they never have.

COMMODUS: Have you ever asked yourself why philosophy abandoned the syllogistic method it used throughout the Medieval period, and the geometric method Spinoza used? These ought

---

[1]In *Sigma*, I, I (1947), pp. 40–43 (editor's note).

to be the safest methods for verifying a line of reasoning. They are the methods used today, with great success, in mathematics and all the exact sciences. But there was a certain moment when philosophy began to say that such methods were a type of 'empty formal logic,' and were inadequate for grasping 'the perpetual becoming of life' and so on. And this moment coincided with the period when light began to be shed on the foundations underlying the syllogistic method, on the nature of its postulates and initial definitions. The exact moment, that is, when the syllogistic method began to acquire some clarity and become an increasingly useful reasoning tool — right then, it was abandoned by the philosophers en masse. Why?

The reason, it seems to me, is not very palatable. Philosophers are people committed to crusading for some of their own personal concerns, which are when it comes down to it always the same; once they were called "existence of God," "immortality of the soul," etc. Today they are called "spirituality of being," "autonomy of moral laws" or something else. They are, I repeat, personal affairs; needs, requirements, trends, and stimuli that arise in an obscure way from the depths of consciousness and from childhood up-bringing — things only very advanced psychology might be able to clarify a bit for us. (Don't make that sulky face — I said psychology, not psychoanalysis).

Nevertheless, philosophy has committed itself to the solutions to these problems that it has arrived at through reasoning. There are many ways of promoting an idea: through arguments and suggestions that affect feelings, adopting a utilitarian perspective, inculcating fear. Philosophy has not chosen any of these tools, and has instead chosen reason. It established that whatever solution it produced for the problems of the origin of things and of chance and necessity would be valid only when it was possible to enclose them in an impeccable series of syllogisms. It's a promotion like any other. An established thesis is accepted because it is firmly chained to everything else, because of the completeness of the cycle it belongs to. When the philosophers were able to demonstrate "formally," through syllogisms, the existence of God and the immortality of the soul, they believed they had reached the apex of their aspirations.

Now it happens that a more thorough examination of the actual foundations of the processes of logic and reasoning led to the conclusion that the syllogisms themselves were badly set up. Indeed, we have become convinced that syllogisms are not permissible in such arguments, because the very bases for setting them are missing. In short, we recognize that such arguments are not the subject of reasoning. Kant arrived at this — and he got there through a procedure which in its turn cannot be called logical, but which rather reflects a reversal in point of view, a spiritual and moral inversion by which, for example, a Copernicus came to suspect that it would be easier to describe things putting the sun instead of the earth at the center.

In any case, Kant presented the thing with so much evidence and persuasion that nobody who came after him could help but acknowledge it, least of all the philosophers, whom he was addressing especially.

After such a discovery there should have been nothing left for the philosophers but to give up their favorite arguments, or else to acknowledge them openly as personal matters, absolved of any objective truth criteria or demonstration. But to do this would have meant giving up their livelihood, so rather than do this they chose to reshuffle the cards a bit. They created a new logic that they held up as true in opposition to the old one, which they now scornfully called formal (and frankly I have never understood in what sense this new method can label itself logical). They even changed the names of their fundamental themes, and instead of God and the soul they started talking about the Ego and the World, the Real and the Rational, the Entity and the Existent, Spirit and Matter, Subject and Object, *Sein* and *Dasein*. This way they were able to carry on undisturbed with their trade, and even as they venerated Kant as their master, they were able to behave as if his teaching had never happened — that is, to go on giving seemingly logical explanations for positions they held for entirely different reasons. Bradley, an English philosopher you might like, said, "Philosophy is a way of finding complicated and difficult reasons that prove things we knew in the first place."

Now, before responding to the objection I can already see

forming on your lips, I think it would be interesting to study the psychological procedure by which this method of reasoning might acquire a certain persuasiveness, so that it could be invoked whenever you want to be sure your feet are planted on solid reality. The thing seems so plain to us today as to almost not need explaining; but the fact is it is not. Essentially, logic is nothing but the set of conditions that allow us to proceed with classification (cf. Poincaré, *Dernières Pensées*, p. 102)[2]. What creates this instinct in each of us to consider it instead the quintessence of reality?

I think that among the mysteries of childhood there is a deep and obscure relation between naming and objectifying. I think that a set of sensations comes to a child in a definitive bundle but that the child assigns it this unity and permanence of identity only when he or she is able to identify it and recognize it by name. From that moment the name and the object become interchangeable; the child transposes onto the name a set of feelings that characterize the child's behavior in relation to the object, and in particular in relation to *objectivity* in general; that set of sketchy movements, that sense of experiencing an action that comes from the outside and of a possible reaction from one's own body, generally accompanied by the notion of an object outside oneself, which constitute such a great part of the set of stimuli and reactions that comprise our feelings towards reality. . . .

RITROSO: But there is no scientific basis for any of this.

COMMODUS: I know; you took the words right out of my mouth. All this is nothing more than a vague and confused impression of mine, and not based on any concrete study. And I don't believe that concrete studies exist in this field that are not psychoanalytic.

RITROSO: But those are not concrete studies.

COMMODUS: Perhaps, but I think the reasons you criticize them are even less concrete. And besides, is it a requirement that in every conversation we should be supported by "concrete studies based on science"? I will give you my impression, if you will allow me, and you can treat it as such. Psychoanalysis is a science at a stage more or less like that of astronomy before Copernicus

---

[2]H. Poincaré, *Dirnières Pensées*. Paris: Flammarion, 1917 (editor's note).

or alchemy before chemistry. In a vague and mythical way, full of prejudice and too-quick generalizations, it has identified relations and relationships that were previously unobserved. It has sketched out a semblance of a research method — one that is so uncertain and unreliable that half the time its results are the opposite of what was wanted. But we are moving in a completely unknown field, and the material that is coming to light is so interesting that to reject it only because it has not yet been organized according to the golden standards of the scientific method seems to me the height of professorial philistinism.

But let us close this parenthesis. If I am not mistaken, you were in agreement about the intimate connection between naming and objectifying. Now I think that precisely as a function of this intimate relationship, it must have happened that when philosophical reflection began to reveal to people that the data of the senses could in no way guarantee any correspondence with reality, they turned to. . . .

4. Eugenio Colorni: On Finalism in the Sciences[1]

COMMODUS (*responding to Ritroso*): You are absolutely right and I see it just the way you do. Only I think you say things that are much less obvious and much more subversive than they seem at first glance. I think, that is, if you went into the very heart of the scientific edifice, you would find it much more difficult to get rid of these finalist and metaphysical remnants than you think, standing where you are now and stating the principle from the outside. If people as experienced and savvy as Poincaré and Duhem couldn't manage it, it isn't because of an oversight or a residue of sentimentality in their personality, it's the blind alley they're in where their reasoning gets all tangled up — a place they can't escape from without invoking the harmony of nature, or a geometrizing God or who knows what else? Is it possible to avoid this blind alley? I think it is, although it is anything but simple, and up to now as far as I know it has never been managed successfully.

The fact is that these transcendent and finalist principles are not just a construction of philosophers contemplating the edifice of the natural sciences from the outside and admiring its order and architecture. On the contrary, they are the actual foundations of an edifice built by the experimental sciences themselves. Eliminating them means subverting the structure of the natural sciences from top to bottom. In my opinion this is not only possible but needs to be done — it would make the edifice of the sciences much more satisfying and logical; but the essential thing is not so much to advocate these principles as to apply them directly to concrete scientific problems, noting the benefit to science itself from the elimination of its metaphysical-finalist substrate. I don't think there is any more effective argument in favor of a methodological criterion than a factual demonstration of its utility.

It may seem strange that even the physical sciences are imbued

---

[1] In *Sigma*, I, I (1947), pp. 44–51 (editor's note).

with transcendent and finalist assumptions, but it is not for this reason any less true. Just think of the very concept of the "constancy of the laws of nature" and of the various *principles* of inertia, energy conservation, minimum action, etc. which are actually stated and used as a synthesis of the harmony of the universe. Consider that Newton built his theory based on the concept of absolute movement and absolute time; and now that these concepts have collapsed in the face of a simple logical examination, Newton's theory has also collapsed. (This is a typical example of the incalculable consequences that the application of a rigorous and unprejudiced logical method can have on the very structure of physical laws.)

Today we no longer believe in absolute movement, but we believe in *universal* constants, a concept that carries with it a mountain of finalism. And yet without it, all of modern (and ancient) physics would be unable to move an inch. You can explain to youngsters that the concept of a *universal constant* is every bit as absurd and illogical as *absolute movement*. But as long as they see it confidently used in their textbooks and get the impression that it is an essential tool in the construction of physics they will laugh at your objections and take them as unconvincing philosophical nitpicking. Show them instead that eliminating it from the very structure of science will yield incalculable advantages . . . but first, before young people, it should be demonstrated to scientists and to ourselves, because it has not yet been demonstrated, and it is very complicated to demonstrate. (If you are interested, I could develop the topic further, with examples, etc.).

In short, what you want is to spread among young people the idea of proper scientific thinking, kidding yourself that it is unprejudiced and anti-metaphysical. I think that finalism and a certain form of transcendence today find their main support in the physical sciences.

Otherwise, I am in complete agreement concerning the teaching of medieval humanism in our middle schools. How much more useful it would be, for example, if instead of all those years of Latin and Greek, they were to undertake a serious in-depth study of modern languages and literature! A high school graduate not only doesn't know who Galileo, Newton and Darwin were, but is no better acquainted with Shakespeare and Goethe and Voltaire and Montaigne. (I do recognize that *De rerum natura* is in the program — I myself, for example, studied it at school; but it is not really the text I would recommend to educate the mind for scientific inquiry.)

I agree with the idea of a course in scientific methodology to accompany the course in the elements of natural science. But here the most urgent thing would be to set it up at the universities, where its absence is an absolute disgrace.

RITROSO: Going back to the previous argument, I don't see that it's really necessary to subvert all of science in order to affirm our anti-finalist principles. You could even concede the use of all metaphysical and transcendent concepts, as long as you remained aware that this use was purely conventional and symbolic, and preceded it with an initial disclaimer, an *as if*. Once this preliminary disclaimer is made I don't see any problem with introducing *forces* that explain phenomena, speaking of *universal constants,* etc. Especially since the new subversive theories, as far as I can tell, bring with them such small modifications that they don't in any way change the effective practical scope of the traditional laws. Indeed, I must confess to you that there is something that bothers and irritates me about this iconoclastic frenzy in modern science, all this drum-beating at the appearance of each new theory, as if all the foundations of human knowledge had to be renewed from the ground up. You should recognize that there's a strong dose of charlatanism in all this.

COMMODUS: There is, undoubtedly — and Einstein is certainly one of the biggest promotional windbags of our time. But just smile at it — you don't need to get upset. Looking at the facts, we can see that these theories derive directly from the criticism of first principles formulated by Poincaré. This is not just my opinion; it is a known fact cited in the texts — Poincaré had arrived a bit earlier on the road to relativity, so that many refer to the famous transformations as the "Poincaré-Lorentz-Einstein Transformations." If you really want to follow Poincaré's thinking you have to see it essentially in terms of these developments.

But I don't agree that you can use concepts that are finalistic or animistic or what have you just provided you include a disclaimer that labels them at the outset as useful but arbitrary conventions. There are ideas which, once they are known to be conventions and not *realities,* can never again be used in the sense they had before. This *anti-finalist correction* is not a side issue for science, but deeply affects what science is. Let us look again at the usual example of light, which is the most convenient because it introduces only two variables, while others, generally taken from experiences in which include the concept of force (gravity, etc.), introduce three variables and numerous complications.

The Physicist says, "We observe experimentally that the speed of light is a universal constant. For every observer, and in every direction, it has the value of 300,000 km/sec."

For us this constancy stinks of finalism, earthly harmony, the geometrizing God, etc. We say: there must be a hidden appeal to principle here. The speed of light probably appears to be constant because we unconsciously set up our measuring devices so that the experiment always gives the same result. Isn't light the instrument of our sight? And do we not perhaps measure distances (for example, astronomical) by means of sight — by light, that is? How marvelous then that the speed of light is constant! It is we who, without realizing it, measure it by means of itself! It is like saying that thanks to a supreme miracle of nature, a meter-stick is always one meter long.

The Physicist would answer: "Fine. In the experiments you're talking about, space was measured using platinum bars, time by pendulum clocks. You now want to say that the speed of light is an arbitrary constant — that is, that we arbitrarily assume it as a constant in our measurements. Which is the same as saying that we take the speed of light as a unit of measurement. We can do that — indeed, we often do — but then we are forced to abandon either the platinum bar or the pendulum clock as a unit of measurement. In fact it is true by definition that speed = space / time; therefore when units of measurement have been assumed for two of these quantities (for example space and speed) the unit of measurement for the third is necessarily determined. In this case, the unit of measurement of time will no longer be the period of the pendulum, but the time taken by a light ray to travel the length of the platinum bar that constitutes the spatial unit of measurement. This being the case, I can tell you: concordant experiments show that every pendulum has a constant period. The finalism we chased out the door has come back in through the window. In short, there is undeniably a fixed and constant relationship between platinum bar, pendulum and speed of light. Which of these three quantities you want to consider an experimental constant is not important to me, but one of the three must be, in such a way that you can't transform it into something defined by us. Now this fixed relationship between sensory inputs that are so different from one another is strange and disturbing, and nothing can remove the impression that we have grasped here the linchpin of a regularity which, even if we don't want to attribute it to things but only to our own senses, is a regularity that *we observe* without having looked for it, one that we are passive in front of and that presents itself without regard to what our intellect needs."

What answer can we give? There is an answer, in my view, and it is the only one that can save our anti-metaphysical thesis — but it is an answer we cannot give until it can be supported by a rigorous scientific demonstration. Be that as it may, my anti-finalist convictions are nevertheless so deeply rooted, and in my view stand on such solid logical foundations, that I am absolutely confident that such a scientific demonstration can be found. The answer, in short, is as follows.

The platinum bar, the pendulum and light are in a fixed relation to each other; this means that they are the same thing — that is, that the phenomenon of the pendulum's oscillation is, if undisguised, the same phenomenon as the propagation of light. In other words, and more generally, every time the constancy of a determined phenomenon is observed experimentally, it means that the measured phenomenon was no different from the phenomenon adopted as a measuring device. The thing being measured is, in short, the same as the measuring device. No wonder then that the result is always the same.

Putting it in this second way makes it seem more than plausible, but put the first way it seems like a madman's hallucination. The truth is that this answer is neither unusual nor self-evident. It is not self-evident because physics today is far from attributing the same nature to the phenomena mentioned above. Nor is it crazy, because the problem of universal constants has today reached such a high degree of unification that it allows for the formulation of such a point of view. Eddington's *New Pathways in Science*[2] comes to mind, which has a brief discussion of the problem at the end.

Anyway, what interested me was to show you that if we want to be able to advance the anti-finalist thesis seriously and productively, we cannot avoid showing that whenever physics measures the constancy of a phenomenon, the phenomenon measured and the one measuring it are the same thing. This is something, I repeat, that is far from having been demonstrated; and this is why even the boldest physicists continue today to be finalists. However the essential cases in which this problem arises boil down to very few (probably three). And in any case, until physics takes this step forward, anti-finalism will remain at the level of a mere need, a program, a desire — but one that can always be refuted in the light of experimental data.

Implementing a program of this type would be simply absurd in sciences like biology or economics in which the laws are many and are not reducible to one another. But the science of physics is much simpler than it appears. It deals with three variables: space, time and mass. (Or space, movement and force, or time, movement and energy, or other equivalent triads). The number of essential and primitive laws that give rise to all other phenomena is also three: gravity, electrical charge and electromagnetic phenomena. With these simple primitive data you can account for all the phenomena observed by physics. The search for *finalist inversions* can therefore be limited to these elementary laws, and does not appear to be an unworkable enterprise. I want to give you an example of how this might proceed in the case of electromagnetism.

PHYSICIST: You know that an electrical charge in motion produces a magnetic field — it behaves, that is, like a magnet. This is one of the strangest and most amazing phenomena in nature and gives rise to the most diverse consequences, from the splitting

---

[2]A. Eddington, *New Pathways in Science*, Messenger Lectures, Cambridge UK, 1934.

of atoms to radio waves. Now you try and deny if you can, given this fact, the order and regularity of nature. A magnet and an electrically charged body are located respectively at point A and point B, neither moving. As long as they are like this they take no notice of each other and do not experience any sort of stimulus. Let one of the two move, however, and you now see that forces, stimuli, impulses have been set off between them; it is as if they suddenly recognized each other. And the beauty is that these forces are perfectly calculated and are in a simple and unchanging relationship with the reciprocal movement of the charge and the magnet. Now try and deny that there is order and regularity in nature.

US (a watered-down first anti-finalist objection): You speak a language that is mystical and utterly superfluous. When you say that forces arise — impulses and the like — the way you express the facts is animistic and anthropomorphic. You can express facts without bringing in all these ambiguous concepts. Saying that a body is stimulated by a force or receives an impulse expresses nothing beyond the fact that this body moves along a certain trajectory at a certain speed. Say things in this simple and direct way and you will see that a great part of the wonder disappears.

(This objection doesn't object to anything. And the Physicist is perfectly right to answer):

PHYSICIST: It isn't how it's expressed, it's the fact itself that's wonderful. It amazes me that a body in the presence of another doesn't move if the other doesn't, and moves if it does. Any way you express it, the fact remains strange and disconcerting; and it is not just a question of language.

US (second anti-finalist objection, this one much more concrete): If this is the case, then we may presume that in substance the magnet and the electrically charged body are of the same nature — that is, that the phenomena of magnetism and those of electricity are essentially a single order of phenomena.

(This second objection makes more sense and effectively moves the problem forward a step. But it needs to be demonstrated.) As a matter of fact, today it is almost certain that magnetized bodies and natural magnets contain within them moving electric charges. But this still doesn't completely solve the problem. The physicist can still object that the phenomenon is strange and wonderful even if it happens between electrical charges alone. Two electric charges attract each other with a certain force when they are still. Set them in motion, even keeping the distance between them unchanged, and a new force is added to the primitive one — and we cannot help seeing it as an effect of the movement. We are always in the same place; it is the movement that creates a force. Even if you eliminate the mythical language this fact remains.

We can answer this in a way that eliminates all the wonder from the phenomenon. We recall that modern mechanics (which is based on simply adopting logical and homogeneous definitions and units of measurement without presupposing any experimental fact) applies its particular spatial, temporal, dynamic measurements to any system in motion. If we consider the two moving charges, the measurements we have to take to measure their reciprocal action will not be our measurements, they will be those of observers in motion along with the charges. Hardly a cause for wonder if they come out different from ours — indeed it would be amazing if they came out the same. This magnetic force that appears to be created by the movement thus turns out to be a simple optical illusion, an effect of perspective due to the different measurements by the two observers. And this difference in the measurements is in turn nothing to be amazed at since it is a direct result of the way the measurements themselves were taken.

In this way finalism is totally eliminated from the phenomenon. But for this to be convincing it is absolutely necessary to be able to deduce the laws of electromagnetism from the simple transformations of spatio-temporal and mechanical measurements. Such laws have up to now been framed as the synthesis of a series of experimental facts. Only when the consequences of electromagnetic phenomena can be derived from these simple assumptions based on definitions and measurements — only then will electromagnetic phenomena have lost their aura of mysticism.

RITROSO: And when this has been done, will we be able to say we have really discovered something new? Won't the laws we arrive at be the same as the ones we started with?

COMMODUS: Maybe they will, but it's also possible that they won't. Let's say that following this purely deductive route we arrive at formulas that coincide only approximately with the known formulas

for electromagnetism. In this case some very sophisticated experiments could bring to light the differences between the two formulas, and these new experiments might lead to applications and
discoveries. This might or might not happen. With similar proce-
dures in other fields, it did.

In conclusion: You believe that anti-finalist claims are part of
the high road of classical experimental science and the scientific
positivism of the last century. I believe instead that they are part
of an important deviation from this road which now threatens to
replace the road itself, a deviation started by Poincaré and Mach
(and their precursors) and inspired less by Spencer and Comte
than by Kant.

I also think that if you want to take anti-finalism to its logical consequences and see its concrete results, you have to abandon the standard conception of science as an abstract and symbolic
expression of experimental facts (a conception presupposing that
these facts can always be ascribed to some order and harmony),
and instead develop a view of science as the logical deduction of
consequences implicit in the initial adoption of some definitions
suggested (but not imposed) by experience — that is, by the behavior of our senses in the face of external stimuli. I believe that the
way things are now, it is not far-fetched to believe that this logical
and deductive path can lead us to all the laws that up to now were
thought to have been obtained inductively from experimental data;
and that in addition to the resulting enormous logical clarification,
the method would also result in actual discoveries and applications.

5. Altiero Spinelli: [Ends and Means][1]

SEVERUS: So there is a group of paralytics — philosophers, at least those following in the wake of Kant — who have made a discovery, which is that what is grasped by our sensory organs must adapt to them, and this is not due to some pre-established harmony, but because what does not adapt cannot be grasped. Then there is a group of people — scientists — who, although blind, are very active and do actually grasp, continually and effectively, but being ignorant of the paralytics' discovery, do not realize that certain qualities of known things derive from the hands that have done the grasping. On the contrary, they believe that these qualities are part of what is knowable, and that we simply observe them. Consequently, when something partially escapes them even as they strive to grasp it more completely — to impose its qualities themselves, that is — they all say that this knowable but rebellious element has qualities that are different from the ones they have imposed a priori without realizing it. They think they can discover them, and they call these mysterious and unknown qualities life. Your aim is to tear out the eyes of the useless paralytics and give them to the very useful blind men, who will then no longer go vainly searching for these supposedly knowable qualities, but will work much more coherently at defining what is known, understanding that it can only have certain determined forms.

COMMODUS: Well said; this and only this is what I mean to say and do.

SEVERUS: And these qualities that something known must have a priori would be?

COMMODUS: The short answer is predictability. To grasp, to understand, to use a thing implies knowing that given certain facts, certain others must emerge. It is all too clear that it is only then that

---

[1]Untitled dialogue: August 1941. Checked by Luca Meldolesi on 18.11.2016 against the autograph text kept in the Spinelli Fund at the Archives of the European University Institute at Fiesole (editor's note).

I can use that certain thing, or rather that certain breakthrough. If, given certain facts, there is a possibility that others will come out that I have no idea about in advance, then I won't be able to use them in any way. How can you use a rifle if you don't know whether it will shoot or not, or in what direction? I'm not claiming that everything can be understood and made use of. But it should be acknowledged that we can understand and use only what is reducible, indeed what has been reduced, to this framework. — And this sort of knowing will be perfect when the framework has taken the form of perfect deduction, something we are very close to reaching in physics, and it will remain very imperfect as long as we only have sequences of facts that have been empirically ascertained but cannot yet be deduced — as is generally the case in sciences that have more complicated subject matter than physics has. I think I have made myself clear.

SEVERUS: Very clear, first-rate for a layman. But I would like to ask you for a further explanation. Do you not think that using something means using it for some purpose?

COMMODUS: But of course! Nevertheless, that's not what's important to me here. Purposes can be anything you like, in conformity with the tastes of individuals, eras, civilizations. And I want to point out to you again that one of these purposes is the advancement of science, which is the only purpose I am presently interested in.

SEVERUS: And to achieve these variable purposes, you have to master the means, take them in your hands, understand what they lead to. . . .

COMMODUS: Precisely.

SEVERUS: And science is nothing more than the construction of these means.

COMMODUS: Yes. . . .

SEVERUS: It goes without saying that to build them you have to have the intention (that is, establish the purpose) of building them, and that therefore the progress of science is also a purpose.

COMMODUS: Precisely what I said.

SEVERUS: And I intended only to repeat your words. From which, it seems to me, the following may be deduced: If the activity of the scientist is aimed at the construction of things that can be grasped and used, it seems to me legitimate and not too scandalous to say the same thing a different way. That is that science consists of considering the object of consciousness as a means. And that the ends toward which those means are applied are things that do not concern science. That it provides hypothetical imperatives. (If you want A you must first have B — the same as saying A derives from B). That if there was rhetoric that was out of place it was produced by someone who felt the need to ascribe a "categorical" to the scientist, and to take refuge in the little Gentilian game of science done and science in the making.

COMMODUS: I admitted it, I myself admitted after Catilina's mocking remark, that I was being hyperbolic. But it's your fault for provoking me with your empty bombast. Anyway, I do recognize that the science is in the instrumentalization, and that the ends are foreign to it and immaterial. What I don't like is the use you intend to make of this statement, trying to reintroduce empty entities that I have tried so hard to banish.

SEVERUS: But these people who have put so much effort into these operating tools that in a particular place and time (modern Europe) they have even developed a class of people who work religiously solely on perfecting the construction of these means — these people, I say, when you talk about purposes, are supposed to just shrug their shoulders and not be concerned with them?

COMMODUS: This is not at all what I'm arguing. It's fine if they bear them in mind. But they shouldn't think they are making them part of a science. If science touches them it turns them too into means. You can walk to reach a given point whatever the cost, but if I know your intention and your consequent action I have enfolded you into the framework. Given certain facts, including your intentions, your walk will follow a certain direction. Once this is known, your pompous teleology vanishes like fog in the hot sun. Now I can make use of you, maybe hitching you to a cart that I want moved to the place where you will stop.

SEVERUS: I agree with you. Even purposes can be taken as scientific objects, and will then be transformed into mechanisms (the sense of this word is not pejorative — it refers to the previously mentioned character that science necessarily imposes on its object).

There is one science that has mechanized its goals in grand style — political economy. But if you can, try and understand that my intention is not to set limits on the scientific position by saying that there is *something* that needs to be subtracted from it. Indeed, I acknowledge that it has every right to address everything and bring anything into its framework. The limitation I'm talking about is something else — that in addition to the scientific position there can be others. In our case, in addition to dealing with goals scientifically — that is denying them as goals — there is perhaps also another way of dealing with them where they retain their quality as goals.

COMMODUS: Oh, the great discovery! And all these words — for what?

SEVERUS: It's not a great discovery; it's old, very old. But it's worth talking about here because it could lead to some strange consequences concerning history and perhaps even biology. So allow me to deal with ends as ends, and not using the criteria of science that see them as means.

COMMODUS: I allow it, but against my will. What's the point, if after dealing with them unscientifically we can't make use of them?

SEVERUS: But my dear fellow, just deal with them without worrying too much about how they can be used. Maybe they're not useful for anything. Is it possible that you, who made such a big thing of soft tentacles, should be so afraid of giving in to idleness that you have to question everything you do or think: "What is it for? How can I use it?" Be a little braver. Don't be so afraid that if you do this your soft parts will be offended.

COMMODUS: Well, go on then. I'm stuck here listening to you.

SEVERUS: Do you think that everything, ourselves included, is subordinate to a supreme goal, that there is a providential plan that holds and directs everything, and that we are simply its more or less conscious tools?

COMMODUS: I take great care not to believe that. Anyone who ever professed to think this was in reality doing no more than infinitely inflating his own goals.

SEVERUS: And I don't believe it either. Goals that are worth thinking about are not these mysterious supreme ideas of God but rather those that we ourselves set.

COMMODUS: What I am really asking and don't know how to answer is whether it is so necessary to establish purposes, whether we can't just "get on with it" without chasing *Weltanschauungen*. Whether all that isn't a psychological illness.

SEVERUS: For the sake of easing the discussion I would suggest setting this question aside for the moment. Let us suppose that you (I say you, leaving aside everyone else) were cursed in such a way that you could not help but set goals — not a new goal every second having nothing to do with the previous one — but rather goals in the course of whose achievement the curse makes you modify, amplify or restrict in such a way that every goal is not only something to be fulfilled in the future but is also a goal for you in that it connects with and variously modifies your teleological activity and your teleological achievements from the past.

COMMODUS: For the sake of argument. What follows?

SEVERUS: For the sake of argument! Well, I'll have to be satisfied with that for now: It is clear in any case that if you seriously want to work toward the fulfillment of goals you have to possess and employ some means. Science is therefore a preliminary condition. Every teleological activity presupposes scientific knowledge, but this is cultivated and worth cultivating because there are goals. That is, to put it in a way that will irritate you, it is the purposes that give science its value. Medicine would be pointless if one of its proposed goals was not to save the sick. All modern natural sciences would be pointless if the aims of our civilization did not include controlling so-called natural forces. And there have been, and probably will be, civilizations for which this purpose had or will have minimal importance.

COMMODUS: Agreed.

SEVERUS: So we were talking about goals that you set yourself, like goals connected with previous goals and achievements. So if I set them, if I am aware of them, I must also be aware of my past. This awareness is historiography [(thus far: autobiography)].

COMMODUS: Fine.

SEVERUS: I should point out in passing that you listened so absent-mindedly to what I said the other time that you laughed at my supposed phrase: "historical knowledge containing the future," when I was actually talking about a present containing the past. But it's not important. — When you talk about history here is how your thinking goes: What I try to understand is how such and such facts in the past have produced my present situation. A scientific attitude. The present, and my present goals, appear to me as consequences of past facts and nothing else. If you've been following what we've said up to now you will see that the process of becoming aware of the past, the history we've been talking about, is the reverse: These current goals of mine are the continuation of such and such activity (activity = fulfillment of goals). Becoming aware of this activity, whatever it is (aware of it as activity and not as a product) means becoming aware of my present goals.

COMMODUS: But if I become aware as you say of this past activity, won't I automatically come to determine what my present activity will be — that is, won't I still be doing science in a more or less confused way?

SEVERUS: Dear boy, you understand nothing. What you say would require that my present activity not be the criterion by which I seek to become aware of my activity in the past, but only the occasion that moved me to an awareness of the conditions that generated it. In physics, Michelson's experiment was an opportunity for the construction of the theory of relativity from which that same experiment would then derive as a logical deduction. In history, past work becomes part of the work going on now, not because it has produced the present work (past work has produced only the present situation and not the present work), but because today's work considers the past as still operating, and it is still operating, annoying as it is to repeat it, not thanks to its own merit, but because it is still incorporated (and it could cease to be incorporated) in the present work.

COMMODUS: But all this is true of scientific work as well, which rests on what has come before and seeks to utilize it and continue to modify it.

SEVERUS: Excellent! But even scientific work is work. And even scientific work has a history. That much is self-evident. Becoming aware of scientific endeavor (building the history of it) is something that always occurs (if only when a scientist remembers what happened yesterday in order to continue with it today — which would be impossible otherwise). But this remembering is not scientific work, which consist rather of building tools. In memory the object is the scientific work; in scientific work the object is the construction of usable things. It seems to me there is a slight difference. In memory, what is remembered retains its quality as work, as a process of achieving goals, while in scientific work what is known assumes the aspect of a product of certain circumstances.

COMMODUS: So in short, your historiography is memory! I will admit that I have memories of myself as a being working in various circumstances, and not as a product of various circumstances. But this applies to me exclusively. Others are for me an object of knowledge only insofar as I apply scientific criteria to them — resulting in my seeing them reduced to instruments. This also applies to politics, to give an example close to your heart, which you can work in only because you understand the causes that move people and can therefore reach them.

SEVERUS: Current events are in a certain sense the right nemesis for the wrongheaded politics, both democratic and communist, that functioned "scientifically," — that believed it could take control of people not by jumping into the mix to help them or to overthrow something, but by using the scientific method to act efficaciously in the manipulation of known causes. So even if for other reasons this development might displease me, I am more than satisfied with how everything has turned out. It will free us from the comfortable and lazy "science," security, or whatever you want to call it, of politics. But this is an interlude. Getting back to the topic: The history of my goals and their fulfillment is actually nothing more than memory.

The question that needs to be answered now is this: For what reason do I go beyond *my* goals, which I am, you might say, directly conscious of, and claim to perceive others and to "remember them" — that is to be aware of them historically and not just scientifically? Isn't this an illegitimate procedure? The reason seems not to lie in any particular limitations of the scientific subject matter. Science, as we have seen, is authorized to extend its deadly (I use this word taking it from your vocabulary and with the meaning you give it) tentacles into everything. Just because it can't reach something now doesn't mean it won't get there tomorrow.

Furthermore, even if some object of scientific investigation is motivated on teleological grounds, the scientific nature of the mechanism remains equally valid *once these are known*, since the resulting event is still determined by the set of preconditions, as we saw in the case of the characteristics you attacked a little while ago behind my back. But you were able to use me only because you supposed that at least for a while my goal would stay the same — that the cards in your hand wouldn't change. If I had changed them [my goals], who knows where your cart would have ended up.

COMMODUS: Well then I would have said that you are a living being, to veil my ignorance of your goals and how they vary. What I call a living being is something that does not submit to me, that I cannot use — something that is that I do not know. But as you see, these determinations are essentially negative.

SEVERUS: And how will you act in the face of this enigma that is a living being?

COMMODUS: If dominating you were a purpose of little importance, I would be able to give up knowing you and using you. If, on the other hand, manipulating you motivates me, for whatever reason, then I will go about devising means that will let me get hold of you — that is to say, understand what it is that makes you tick.

SEVERUS: Then there will be a fight between us, because I too, o Zarathustra, have my own goals to achieve, and I am quite willing just to treat you scientifically as an instrument. And I am afraid you will never be able to know my goals well enough to master them because in the course of the fight I will continually change them, keeping in mind, dominant over all the others, one purpose only — to defeat you, to make you my instrument, and even if you come to discover this you will not be able to use it because it is perfectly antithetical to what you want. In fact, you want me to stop having the arrogant desire to use you, and instead you let me do it.

Now, you see, as long as you fight against me without realizing that I want to defeat you, use you, know you, you can go on thinking that my "life" is just a word that indicates your ignorance. But if you should happen to notice that I am something that wants to do with you exactly what you want to do with me, then things are a bit different. My being "alive" would begin to mean something quite positive for you; you would know that it means that I am a center of work, like you. You would be forced against your will to become an anthropomorphist.

COMMODUS: I don't deny the reality of this experience. But what has it got to do with science?

SEVERUS: Nothing, I agree. But didn't I ask you right from the start to follow me into a land that I promised would be something different from science? You went on believing that I asked you this as a joke, that in reality I wanted to build a different kind of science.

Between you and me in this situation we've got ourselves into there are now two alternatives. One is that one of us manages to destroy the other's will to win — and I do mean *destroy* and not simply *understand,* since understanding it serves no purpose as long as it remains inexorably antithetical to the other's desire to win. In that case you have broken up the unit that opposed you and you have its dead pieces at your disposal. You have remained scientific. Right to the end. You have chopped a living dog — one that was not unknown since you knew what it wanted — into two dead but known half-dogs. (The dog in this case would be me. I have temporarily turned into a dog to look ahead to the answer in the field of biology which we will talk about later.) The other alternative is that each of the two adversaries recognizes in the other a hub of activities that achieve purposes, and they make peace. On what basis? Surely on the only basis possible, which is to establish a certain coordination in their purposes. Each recognizes in the other a certain positive rather than simply negative determination, and the word "life" which seemed to indicate the unknown, now indicates a well-known thing, albeit completely different from the thing known to science; it indicates another self.

The coordination of ends and achievements and their progressive modification is what allows historiography to be more than simply my memory, but the memory of the community that has those ends in common. I am not here to repeat the observations already made about how this awareness that is history differs from science, since it seems to me that this is now clear. Non-autobiographical historiography is the result of the failure not of science, I would say, but of the auto-Socratic scientific attitude that held that there were no other ends to be achieved beyond those of science, and that whatever remained was to be seen from the instrumental point of view — asking "what something is for."

COMMODUS: So that, in your view, the winner is what presents itself to us as a center of resistance to our scientific methods — as something not knowable, if knowable means subject to those criteria. But you do understand that basically you've come round to saying the same thing as me. The sphere of life is the sphere of the indomitable. For the primitives, every stone was alive, every river, the sea, the earth and the sky. And rightly so. But for many of these things we have gained the power to grasp them and use them and therefore we no longer consider them alive. Indeed, we have reached the point of abandoning mythological expressions like life and death and using the much more precise known and unknown.

SEVERUS: Resistance to our scientific methods is in no way positive, and can only cause us to question whether it's not only our current incapacity hiding behind that resistance, but perhaps an autonomous center of finalist activity. What I would say ought to be called alive is what has *shown* us that it is such a center by resisting us, fighting us and collaborating with us. And hasn't just shown us once and for all, but continues to show us every time we tend to forget it.

COMMODUS: According to what you say, life should be spoken of only concerning relations among people, and perhaps not even all people. But what can you say about life as biologists speak of it?

SEVERUS: I feel less secure talking about biological life because I am quite ignorant in this field. But I would like to make it clear that at least in relations that concern people, experience requires that we view them, become aware of them and *know them*, if it doesn't upset you too much, as creative centers of goals and their fulfillment; and that by means of the scientific method it is possible to *know them* — that is, to use them, only if it is established *arbitrarily* (even *fundamentally* for some limited purposes) that the goals that move them remain constant or change in ways that we have previously and, I repeat, arbitrarily established. All common political forecasts are trivial (although they can also be quite ingenious) applications of a currently quite crude sort of political science. This can certainly be refined, but it will always sin in the arbitrariness with which it supposes that now and in the near future certain determined goals will be in effect, and that *it cannot in principle know the different ones that will come into being*. — Political economy, much more precise than political science, is the most exhaustive proof of science's inability to predict, not what will happen given certain conditions, which indeed it is fairly good at, but to predict what new conditions people will set. And we can't escape from this situation by desperately hunting for a science of sociology, but instead by intervening and *working* to achieve, with the *aid* of the sciences, the goals we want.

Bearing this in mind, we are able to understand the history of an event — that is, to write not a means of taking action (although this too must be done, but it is a work of political or economic or social science), but a chapter in the project of working out the goal itself, toward which such means will be used.

COMMODUS: I don't understand.

SEVERUS: Okay, suit yourself. But if you want to understand you need to make some effort. If you want it put in terms that have by now become trite between us you have to translate the ones I use. Or do you think you can understand without the translation. Wouldn't that be nice!

COMMODUS: It's okay, but how suffocating you are! Tell me something about biology. Whether there is a qualitative difference between it and physics. Up to now you've been talking about history.

SEVERUS: Like you, I allow that biology is not qualitatively different from physics, even if it is a very empirical science. It tries, that is, to establish certain sequences of facts that are linked in such a way that the later ones can always be derived from the earlier.

There is in its subject matter, however, a strong resistance to being framed by scientific categories, and this resistance leads us to *presume* that there is a center of finalist activity. Too many things present themselves *as if* they were made for some purpose. But the purpose is something no one has yet managed to understand. That's why I say there is only this presumption. I would say that in the experience that allows us to know the "other," we do manage to understand.

And we manage in the case of some of the higher animals (chimpanzee, dogs, horses). In other cases we don't. It may be that marching to the tune of your scientific trumpet we will go down the road of mechanical explanation to its triumphal conclusion and erase any appearance of teleology, just as it has been erased in other fields. In that case life (at least the biological variety) will prove to have been simply an unjustified anthropomorphism. We will be able to determine what that something is that when added to two dead dog halves makes one live dog. As I told you, to be able to speak of living beings in a positive sense, you need an actual experience in which the object rebels at efforts to make a tool of it, and in its turn shows that it too is an exploiter. As long as this battle goes on, and it goes on in biology, there is no a priori affirmation that can tell what the outcome will be. The sequences established in biology up to now are analogous to those in political science: given certain conditions and a certain living being (that is, one that seems to exhibit this apparently finalistic behavior) the result will be such and such. Nobody has anything to say about this *apparently* finalistic behavior. I recognize that this is why when people talk about a life force in biology they don't know what they're talking about, but if the expression is used it is not in reference to some pointless essence, but to indicate a direction for research, to indicate the *suspicion* that perhaps organisms are centers of teleological activity — and in such a case science will be able to construct its frames every time it presupposes the purposes to be such and such, but the actual purposes themselves cannot be known except historically. Perhaps all this will turn out to be simply appearance. But perhaps not. Until we have had the experience in one way or another, I don't see how we can resolve the question a priori by cutting through it with a statement about the necessary form consciousness must take. But if we don't yet know whether this consciousness is historical or scientific, can we in the case of organic beings assume once and for all the despotic scientific attitude that dictates to the known thing the form that it must take, or rather take the collaborative historical attitude that acknowledges the forms that the known thing gives itself?

COMMODUS: In any case, it is important to explain to scientists what their concepts mean and what they can expect from them.

SEVERUS: It will be important — to tell you the truth I don't know how important. It seems to me that even though they often formulate it badly scientists have for some time followed the criterion of constructing the different sciences on the basis of predictability and usefulness. And if in some field like biology it doesn't work, the reason is not in the methods, which they see successfully applied in other sciences, but rather in the persistently enigmatic nature of their subject matter. You can cheer for the scientific efforts of the biologists and scream "*mata la vida*," but until you succeed it is equally possible that you can't destroy life but will instead discover that it is something analogous to us. Why do you insist that it is absolutely impossible to end up identifying (loving in your philosophical language) the animal or vegetable element?

COMMODUS: It is possible but it won't be science; it will be something else.

SEVERUS: That's what I think. Science is knowledge of the means, and instead what we would have here is knowledge (becoming aware) of the other — who remains other and establishes contact with us on the basis of an awareness of the commonality of what we do, and not based on scientifically ignoring the other as other — on not wanting to see anything there but a means. I myself am trying, as you see, to translate what I think into your language.

COMMODUS: When I spoke of the nature of science, it wasn't that I didn't know there was another attitude. But this is a different topic.

SEVERUS: I really admire the way you talk one minute 'in a scientific setting' and the next in some other. You who mock Crocian schematizations! — By now I know very well that when it comes to anything but science you want to be soft, a listener, artistic, carefree, not boxed in, and so on. But you look at all this as divine leisure that you allow yourself. In serious things, in physics and not only, you need security — you need to go into battle well-armored, and the tougher the armor is, the more rigid, secure and forbidding, the safer you feel. You are afraid of getting hurt. All this talk of mine — you can take it as the doubtful head-scratching of someone who doesn't

believe in these sharp divisions, this world where the precise and secure are strictly distinct from the insecure, the sensitive. Probably —
and I hope so for your sake — this artificial toughness of yours will
be very useful in physics, and then everything will be fine and all the
rest will be forgivable.

6. Eugenio Colorni:
On Anthropomorphism in the Sciences[1]

COMMODUS (to Severus): I will suppress the anger that your confused and bombastic talk makes me feel, first of all to point out that you have not even offered the beginning of a discussion of the two main points of our conversation — namely:

1) whether there is a *qualitative* difference between biology and physics; and in particular whether the fact that two half dogs are not equal to one whole might be compared to the fact that two atoms of hydrogen and one of oxygen are not a water molecule.

2) What the characteristics of *historical knowledge* are and whether it has anything to do with scientific-natural knowledge; our having agreed that saying that historical knowledge is *freighted with the future* and the other kind isn't, even if it were true (which it is not), would not be saying nearly enough. But you preferred to take refuge, like Gentile, in the self-creativity of the spirit, and in the process of self-formation; magic words, such that if you try calmly to clarify their meaning you become a science maniac. And *clarifying their meaning* immediately becomes — for the convenience of your argument — *defining tautologically*. And then after another half-dozen of these little games you maintain with utter contempt that this is all an empty discussion. This is the only thing we agree on.

Your method is this: (1) Reduce what I say to trivial paradoxes. (2) Counter them with trivial truths. (3) Nobly profess disgust with both positions. Now I would be prepared to support (1) if you didn't answer me with (2). And the fact that you do shows me that perhaps even (1) wasn't done correctly.

CURIOSUS: Admit that all this ranting is to show that your debating weapons are just as sharp as Severus's.

COMMODUS: I admit it. But this takes nothing away from my arguments, which I stand firmly behind. Anyway, let me get to the point.

---

[1] In *Sigma* I, 2 (1947), pp. 87–106 (editor's note).

I never said that life *doesn't exist*. Nor do I deny that there may be forces that we cannot grasp. I say only that if they cannot be grasped, then we cannot say anything at all, and that we can only say something about them if and to the extent that they can be. And if they can be grasped it means that they fit into our patterns of regularity, prediction and reconstruction. And once they have fit into these patterns, they are in our power. And what is in our power we call *matter or a dead thing*.

SEVERUS: This is the point. Is it really true that for us grasping something only means fitting it into our predictive frameworks, etc? Isn't there a form of knowledge that such frameworks have nothing to do with? Historical knowledge, for example. Now that doesn't consist of banal predictions, but of something much more alive. It is an extension of our personality into humanity's past, to make it reach toward the future. History is not a hypothetical science that considers its subject matter as a means. It is active, full of what is to come.

COMMODUS: Beautiful and holy words, but how much more useful if we were allowed, without incurring anathema, to see them closer up!

SEVERUS: Here's the prisoner of the intellect again.

COMMODUS: Go to hell. Yes, of course, history is our knowledge of ourselves, and so on. But as a living and present activity of the mind, not as a body of notions and facts encoded in books and collected in archives, and classified by statisticians and jurists. In this last sense it is just a collection of facts whose utility, if there is any, is actually hypothetical (if you want this end you must use this means) — that is, consisting of very uncertain predictions based on analogies. Now you cannot deny that *history*, for someone who doesn't work with it currently and actively, *history* as a subject of study in the schools, as an organized body of doctrine, is nothing more than this. Another thing entirely is the case of someone who makes it the center of their own moral and spiritual life, who experiences it as their own past and makes it the basis and starting point for every action and goal (and everyone does this to a greater or lesser extent). But then you can say the same thing for the natural sciences, whose value is instrumental and goal-free only for those who consider them to be a codified and stable body of knowledge. But for someone who experiences science as the central drama of their own research (and here again more or less everyone does) it is something that extends its roots ever further into the surrounding world, always setting itself new goals, something that indeed dictates goals to the researcher, and in its own growth and development finds reasons to grow and develop even more. I believe, incidentally, that even the great Croce reaffirmed that the natural sciences are nothing other than *history*. And he is not a person suspected of sympathy for the sciences.

SEVERUS: You have to recognize, though, that the goals of history are what you might call finalistic, and not so instrumental as those of science. It touches something more intimate in people, more categorical.

COMMODUS: Perhaps, but this has nothing to do with our argument. And then, basically it's a question of taste. There are those who feel a need to expand their own communion with the world around them as actually *categorical* in itself. I would say in fact that this need is one of the essential needs of human beings. Even leaving aside that one of the great purposes that science sets itself is saving humanity from illness.

As I said, however, our argument doesn't touch on this. The fact is that whatever ends any kind of study or knowledge points us toward, the greater the predictive power science provides us with the more precisely we can reach them. And this word *prediction* does not necessarily indicate something mechanical or narrow. It can be viewed as something embodied in the very nature of man; an agility of movement, a control of the situation, a precision of reflexes that makes an action safe and fruitful. But reduced to its most intimate essence, it will still be that faculty of being able to see, to the greatest extent possible, that given certain facts about the present and the past, certain others will occur in the future. (I intentionally did not say *that given certain causes, certain effects will follow*).

SEVERUS: Briefly then, you don't admit that in certain cases, recognizing certain events as they unfold forces us to introduce causes that already potentially contain the effect in themselves, in the form of more or less confused tendencies? Final causes, that is?

COMMODUS: I have never understood the nature of such causes. Nevertheless, I wouldn't be at all averse to admitting it, specifically concerning causes. But I maintain that their level of suitability for contributing knowledge about the future depends on the degree of reliability with which they can predict an effect — that is, on the strength and necessity of the effect's connection to them. The *nature of causes, why* a given cause should produce a given effect is, on close inspection, extraneous to the true interests of science.

In general, the more finalistic and anthropomorphic the causes, the less reliable they are — the less they are *causes,* that is, and the less useful they are to science. But basically there is nothing preventing you from saying that the north pole of a magnet *is attracted* toward the south pole and vice versa, if it is clear that this means that when the two poles are placed in each other's presence, each moves in the direction of the other; or saying that phagocytes *defend themselves* against pathogenic germs by attacking them, if it is clear that a series of exactly predictable and calculable facts lies behind these words. In the economic and historical sciences it is often the very observation of human psychology and the phenomena of will that leads us to conclude that these modes of knowledge can be said to contain the future. But even here we're talking about the aspects of the psyche and will that are permanent, recurrent and predictable; there is always a certain mechanism in these activities, that is, that allows us to stand on them (not too steadily, it's true) in order to proceed further.

CURIOSUS: Okay, and so? You're not telling me anything new. I learned these things by heart from idealism. The static thought is nature, it is death — and so on. Is it really worth all this eloquence and combativeness just to produce this tired truism?

COMMODUS: It's worth it, I think, because the context here is different from idealism. I say these things not because I've deduced them from my philosophical readings, but because I've run into concepts such as life force, internal finalism, etc. in my scientific readings. It's because I need to clarify the nebulous meanings of these terms to myself, it's the suspicion that there is a yawning emptiness within them — this is what led me to the above formulation. And you see that, in the scientific context, these formulations that are so innocuous in a philosophy book take on such a subversive and paradoxical force that a serious scientist apparently cannot even take them into consideration. Severus in fact opposes them not as truisms, but as banal paradoxes. And the fact is that this is where their strength lies, in being the two things together — obvious to the philosopher, paradoxical to the scientist, and irritating to both of them. And this in my opinion shows the lack of seriousness of both scientists and philosophers; one group is careless of the significance of the concepts they use, and the other is content that their discoveries fit harmoniously with their system of doctrines, but trust so little in their actual value that they don't even bother to apply them in the fields they refer to.

CURIOSUS: These attempts of yours to find higher authorities unifying science and philosophy, I find suspect. I believe it to be no coincidence that these two fundamental attitudes of mind have remained separate throughout history. There must be a fundamental autonomy in each of them that does not allow higher unification.

COMMODUS: I agree in opposing the higher unification, but not about the autonomy. Actually, I think autonomy is the main disease of philosophy, and perhaps of the sciences as well. And I do not want to find any *super-logic* or superior authority which, precisely because it is superior, would sanction the autonomy of entities beneath it. I would, if anything, reject autonomy or, more modestly, take seriously discoveries made by thinking. This would mean not testing autonomous entities' value in the easy circularity that they have within themselves, but rather expecting that there should be some activity in the field that they operate in, and if there isn't, abandoning them. Therefore, if I manage to convince myself that the static thought is nature, and that the term *life* as used in the natural sciences has no meaning, my claim will be that this discovery applies to the natural sciences, and not to philosophy. And for the natural sciences it is no longer a truism, but a paradox — that is, it subverts their whole method. And if it does not find any application in the natural sciences nor help them move forward and solve any of their problems, then this alleged discovery will be worth nothing and we should abandon it.

SEVERUS: What I can't stand is your referring to everything that's known as *dead.*

COMMODUS: It's about time! I can't stand it either. But it's just as bad to call everything that isn't known *alive.* Indeed, I would eliminate the two words *dead* and *alive,* and replace them with *known* and *unknown,* or even better — predictable and unpredictable. Basically, this is all I'm asking.

SEVERUS: If all you want is to reform the nomenclature, master.

COMMODUS: But words are evocative. Calling what is known *dead* is the symptom of hypostasis, of entitation; it is relating the set of known things not to a choice made by us as we look for what adapts itself to our grasping organs, but to a supposed body of facts and autonomous laws that stand alone (*physics,* the *sciences,* the *material world*) whose intimate structure is allegedly knowable, predictable. The entitation is all in this transposition of the *known* to the *knowable.* And this brings with it the analogous entitation of the *unknown* into something *unknowable* or *free* or *spontaneous,* etc. All I want to do is this: replace the suffix -*n* with the suffix -*able.* But I believe this simple shift would lead to a fair amount of upheaval in the natural sciences. And it is far from easy to do it seriously.

SEVERUS: [his reply is missing from the manuscript, but its drift is easy to deduce from what Commodus replies.]

COMMODUS: This last objection of yours hits fairly close to home. But really I don't know if I should correct the defect you charge me with and which I surely have. With you it seems to me the moment has come to speak against what has been said up to now; and deep down you yourself feel this need, when you make an apology for *resentment.* Certainly with friends who are open, free and nimble listeners (the ones I like best), I often feel ashamed, limited and petty, selfish, aggressive, and much more *Severus* than *Commodus.* And their ironic smiles and shrugging shoulders affect me deeply, and I feel that they come from a higher world than the one I belong to, a world without *fears, defenses,* and *conquests.* But in spite of this, I often think this meanness is basically necessary if you want to build something. It is the tribute you pay to *getting things done.* People who do things are necessarily more aggressive, less open, less available, and less free than those who do not. They must to a certain extent become deaf and blind to what lies outside what they are doing, which they must love with a love that is exclusive, concentrated, selfish, and mean. Therefore, if at a human level I feel great respect and affection for people who are completely disinterested and friendly, whose spirit is better compensated in living than in doing, I nevertheless cannot help finding the others useful as well. More useful? I don't know, because the former have very great utility as friends, as conversationalists, as leavening. But the latter, in short — we need them. Their work is more conspicuous and this makes them more unpleasant. In the former category I know of only one who has become immortal: Goethe.

But let's get back to us. I want to try and translate what you say into my language.

SEVERUS: I'll help you. What you are doing, if I understand you correctly, is waging a campaign against anthropomorphism. You see it as the number one enemy of science, the primary cause of its failure to progress. To the extent that man is so in love with himself that he sees in himself the supreme purpose of the world, or a world made in his own image and likeness, to that extent science does not progress. And this anthropomorphism is often so subtle and inadvertent that it is difficult to flush out. For now you want to fight it in its expression as life force, internal finalism, etc.

CURIOSUS: On the other hand it seems to me that you are the most ardent of anthropomorphists. Ultimately, all you're trying to say is that everything we know we have reduced to our own image and likeness; and that we are the measure of all things. By the grace of anti-anthropomorphism!

COMMODUS: It's a question of interests. You are both right, but I see myself more in the description of Severus. Curiosus's kind of anthropomorphism exists, of course, but it is something that is experienced, not desired. It is the recognition of a fact — that we are unable to get outside ourselves; for us, knowing can only be in the form of learning — which amounts to reshaping [what we intend to learn] to fit our grasping organs. But this is a necessity, a harsh necessity indeed, which we would gladly do without. It doesn't address any of our needs. . . .

CURIOSUS: *The word is requirements.*

COMMODUS: Any of our *requirements*. And from the time this restriction was discovered, twenty-five centuries ago, human thought has done nothing but struggle to get out of it.

CURIOSUS: *The word is escape from it.*

COMMODUS: I would say, in fact, that in a profound sense efforts to escape from it are themselves anthropomorphic, given that anthropomorphism means attributing a human aspect to things supposedly outside ourselves, but not attributing a human aspect to ourselves. Every time you want to escape from *man as the measure of all things* and try to discover the conformation of the actual *laws of reality*, you can't help but imagine in a more or less sophisticated way that these supposed *laws* include a set of *tendencies, purposes,* and *harmonies,* etc. that come from the world of our own desires and feelings. This is the anthropomorphism that I maintain is damaging to science and, I would say, all knowledge. It shows an irrepressible pride, a self-love that makes us blind to anything that is basically *other,* different. Curiosus's kind of anthropomorphism is actually a correction of this. It shows how this supposed similarity between the external world and us is nothing but an illusory projection of ourselves into the external world. And when we recognize once and for all (with little satisfaction) that there is no getting outside ourselves, and that everything we take in will always be affected by our grasping organs, it may teach us to keep the organs relaxed, soft, without preconceived form, and ready to adapt themselves so as to engulf any stimulus that touches their semi-fluid suckers. It does not exclude an attitude of passivity and receptivity with regard to the data. The basic difference between one sort of anthropomorphism and the other is that one is an observation, or rather a necessity, which up to now we have not been able to escape from, while the other is a requirement. Now I hate requirements. Nor do I have any reason to like necessities, but I see no way of getting free of them except in illusion.

CURIOSUS: A sort of experimental idealism, then.

COMMODUS: If you like. But just speaking these words makes me angry and embarrassed. I only speak of these things to please you and because you dragged me into it. I'm not remotely interested in the initial conception, the method I use, or the system

I am part of. What interests me is what I want to do; and what I want to do is to clarify the meaning of the concepts of life force and finalism within the sciences; and to demonstrate that they are good for precisely nothing, except to satisfy our need to see in the world around us facts similar to those that we find in our own minds.

SEVERUS: There it is. Here's what I've been waiting to tell you: Supposing while not conceding that you could eliminate anthropomorphism in reckoning with the external world, there is at least one field from which you cannot eliminate it — the case where the object of your consideration is a person, or other people. In this case, if you don't want to use anthropomorphic criteria you're a fool.

COMMODUS: And my fear of being taken for a fool is so great that I willingly concede these profound truths. If the object I am studying resembles me to a T, clearly I have to attribute to that object everything I attribute to myself — namely, goals, volition, free will, etc. There are these special and disconcerting objects called other people, in short, that we can't consider only as objects precisely because we know or think we know that they are, for their part, subjects. It's not so much the fact of the battle itself and this going back and forth trying to get the upper hand (something you [*Severus* (Altiero)] are fanatical about) that stops us from subsuming them under scientific categories, but rather the fact that once this subsumption has taken place, you have to recognize that the other person also acts as a subsumer (interesting word) and therefore cannot be studied scientifically without the loss of something very important — just as the fact that when you study your own behavior in establishing scientific categories, you still need to study the behavior of studying the behavior, and so on. In brief, it is exactly this necessary anthropomorphism, this obligation to consider another person on an equal footing with yourself, that stops you from studying the other person; in the same way that you will never be able to study yourself, since the behavior of studying oneself studying can never be studied.

CURIOSUS: See how even you are forced to use idealist formulations. If I had used them this way you would have been all over me.

COMMODUS: Let me be. I will use them when and as I please, without feeling that this means I have to build some system or *Weltan-*

schaunng on them. I was saying that in the case of other people — yes, the only way of studying and knowing them thoroughly is by analogy with ourselves, and that this analogy can never give us a truly complete picture, not because our tools are insufficient, but because of an intrinsic contradiction. Am I right?

SEVERUS: Absolutely.

COMMODUS: Now for these cases, we are equipped with special intake organs, quite different from those that bring scientific knowledge — that predict, that is — but which nevertheless allow us to derive from their use a level of satisfaction at least as great as prediction would provide. They are what I would call, in a word, organs of *loving*. In using this word I mean something very wide-ranging, a generic affective attitude that includes things like hate, fear, hope, desire, pleasure, pain, etc. It is these organs of attachment that we use on objects that resemble ourselves. And this is fundamentally because in the end they are the same basic organs of attachment that we use on ourselves. I don't want to dwell too much on this argument, since I imagine you are familiar enough with what I mean.

SEVERUS: Yes.

COMMODUS: Now it is precisely this attitude, this way of taking hold of things, that makes us set *goals,* these being nothing but rough sketches of acts of will, which themselves are no more than expressions typical of emotional attitudes. I hope this is clear and familiar to you; otherwise it would require a dialogue of its own.

SEVERUS: Go ahead. Don't worry about me accusing you of introducing new categories (love, etc.) in the place of the old.

COMMODUS: What a relief. Now, the way of *love* proceeds along many paths — but if there is one that it is incompatible with and that indeed kills it, it is prediction. Loving in the true and non-degenerate sense of the word means seeing your own object of love as supremely *other* and therefore always new, always a mystery, every time met with surprise as if for the first time — in a word, unforeseen and alive. And this once again is by analogy with ourselves, because what we love best in ourselves, what we consider most intimately ours, is our freedom of will — the intimate and essential possibility in us that we can be different every time from what would have been predictable.

SEVERUS: I'm not saying this is wrong, but it's tendentious. You could probably say very different things, almost the opposite of this, about love that could also claim to be right — to represent, that is, the *true and non-degenerate sense of love.*

COMMODUS: Just grant me one thing — that when we find before us something in which we suppose there is a life-center similar to our own, our mode of attachment is always emotional. Or is there some other possible way of behaving?

SEVERUS: There are no others in plain sight.

COMMODUS: Allow me one other thing — that this emotional mode of grasping exists nowhere except in beings that are or are presumed to be alive — that is, where there is presumed to be a life-center similar to our own.

SEVERUS: This I concede more easily.

COMMODUS: And this leads us to think that the emotional mode of attachment is precisely the transposition to others of feelings that we initially have toward ourselves. Here again the important thing is not to be anthropomorphs, or rather in this case, auto-morphs. For this reason I don't much care for your description of the two men trying to overpower each other and taking turns *using* each other. The way you experience contact with another man as a collision, a struggle, an effort to overwhelm or not to be overwhelmed is to me the worst aspect of everything you do and think. For you a relationship with another hub of life is always in some way a need for self-assertion.

SEVERUS: Don't start again with your preachy tone and your gospel of meekness. I took that example, but I could just as well have taken some other one.

COMMODUS: But to me it's interesting that you took that one. The tongue probes where the tooth is sore. And I think the topic will be very useful to us. The mode of attachment to apply with someone who doesn't want to be used but who wants to use you is, I believe, to give up the fight and let yourself be used.

SEVERUS: Good heavens, where will we end up!

COMMODUS: Never fear, we will end up in another place entirely. What I mean is that the true manner of emotional attachment to other people is to let them exist — not to transform them the way I want, but to enjoy their being different from me. That is what I call loving and understanding another person. Not 'don't do unto others as you wouldn't have them to do unto you' but 'do unto others what others would like done to them.' Not 'to know others look inside yourself'; but 'to know others, look at others.' And notice what they have that is theirs and is peculiar, different from you. Don't look for points of contact, least common denominators, universal categories, etc. Try to learn their language without always using yours as a basis of comparison. And so on with a series of precepts and metaphors, which I will leave you to work out as an exercise.

SEVERUS: Why not? I have nothing against it. Indeed, I was the one, if I'm not mistaken, who spoke first about understanding, giving up preconceptions, letting others live. And I'm the one who practices it most consistently.

COMMODUS: Quite. Although this is the opposite of 'resentment' and not letting yourself be overpowered. But let's move along. The emotional mode of attachment, we have seen, is identified with the attitude that sets goals. On the other hand it necessarily presupposes in its object an anthropomorphic character. This means that in it there is also a kind of *sui generis* prediction. It predicts, that is, that its object will behave in an anthropomorphic and therefore unpredictable way. It foresees the unforeseeable.

SEVERUS: And you get angry at being called paradoxical.

COMMODUS: It's a paradox only in its external formulation. It is an incontestable fact that we expect an object that we consider alive and treat as alive to respond in a way that makes us feel its autonomy, its independence as a center of life endowed with liberty. It is precisely this basic unpredictability that offers the greatest incentive to our emotional grasp. When it is missing, when the response is too regular or mechanical, our affect subsides and we seem to be dealing with something that's dead.

SEVERUS: And so? I wasn't saying anything different.

COMMODUS: I know that. But I want to use this to show that my argument against the *concept of life* was not out of place. I am also prepared to recognize that you are basically right about the instrumental nature of science — as long as you recognize that all science is instrumental, historical science as well as natural; and that there is no room for speaking of two types of science: instrumental and finalist.

SEVERUS: It's a matter of words — of what you want to define as science.

COMMODUS: But for our purposes it's very important to see how we construct our definitions, because it is precisely on the basis of them that we form the basic groupings of intellectual activity — the recognized professions, university faculties, topics of treatises, scientific and historical societies, and philosophical systems. I would say we can label as science any and all activities involving research and knowledge that try to construct, by any means (mechanical, mathematical, statistical, probabilistic, philosophical, etc.), systems of predictability. We can refer to finalistic activities as those in which an emotional element comes in, directed toward other people, ourselves, past and future generations or what have you.

SEVERUS: I wonder if it was worth it to you to get so angry over my initial rebuttal. What you have just said is the best justification of it.

COMMODUS: No. Thanks to the usual graphic way it was expressed, your rebuttal tended to extinguish the discussion — since it exposed the weakness of its logic, which was nothing more than a skillful arrangement of definitions. I would say on the contrary that it is just here that the conversation starts to get interesting — because what it has come down to is determining the boundaries within which a concept like 'life force' makes sense. Depending on how you define history and philosophy, for example, you can think of them as related to the natural sciences or to art or to something else. And to set this or that definition, therefore, is the same as saying that a certain activity must be carried out in this or that way.

SEVERUS: Okay. Having established the definitions the way you have, which I am ready to accept, I don't deny that history falls under the category of behavior you have called finalist. Now if you want to deny that history can be characterized as knowledge, you can do so by defining the concept of knowledge the way you want. But it seems to me that without some kind of construct you will just confuse your ideas.

COMMODUS: I don't think so. One of the results of this discussion might be understanding more clearly what we mean by history.

SEVERUS: You certainly wouldn't be doing anything new. For the last century and a half it's all that's been talked about.

COMMODUS: Well, I don't know anything about it, or else I've forgotten all this research you're talking about. And I haven't read Croce's latest book on *History as Thought and Action*. So I risk either talking nonsense or saying things everyone knows. But at least I would be saying them with a certain naivety, unburdened by traditional frameworks. And it's this that I am most interested in right now — since in any case I'll always have you to correct whatever nonsense I come out with, and for the rest I don't care so much about saying new things, as about saying things that are free of systematic preconceptions.

SEVERUS: But don't you ever get tired of these methodological polemics? Get to the point.

COMMODUS: History, it seems to me, can mean three different things: 1) Analyzing events for the purpose of establishing in them systems of *constants,* laws that repeat, relations of causes and effects that, as they say, *account for* what has taken place. This way of thinking is more or less consciously scientific — aimed, that is, at establishing a system of predictability. Essentially, researching the causes of things that happened always has the aim of predicting things to come whenever these causes appear to be approximately the same. Vico's cycles, the Hegelian dialectic, and historical materialism are after all meant to be keys for understanding history. Whether or not they reach this goal is not what I want to investigate. But it is clear that their interpretation of the past would not make sense if it couldn't also be presented as an investigation aimed at explaining the present and moving into the future. In this sense, and in spite of appearances to the contrary, history is a typical hypothesis-based science of the type you described. Given these conditions, these consequences follow; a given situation of this type will develop in such and such a direction. Now you'll have your say about the link between premises and consequences being animate; that the situation develops due to free and spontaneous acts of will, etc. etc. The fact remains that your historical investigation led you to observe certain *constants*, which you still have the right to call spontaneous and animate only because they are not fully realized and to the extent that they are not. In brief, you use the word animate for something you are unable to get hold of, something that irritates you and disturbs your effort to construct your law. Do you agree?

SEVERUS: For the moment, yes. But I don't think I can concede all of this. Let me think it over; in the meantime, go on.

COMMODUS: This first way of practicing history, though very different from science in appearance, is in many ways related to it. The second is instead very similar to science, but does not identify with it. It is the simple search for the facts that have occurred, and the objective assessment of them. The procedure in this type of history is very similar to that of the experimental sciences — it sets great store by precision and objectivity. But it is missing that push toward the future, the inductive element and the formulation of laws. It is odd that while in the experimental sciences the search for facts is always oriented toward the formulation of laws, in history this doesn't happen. What is more, scholars of the first type of history are quite distinct, as a human type and in their mental attitude, from those of the second type, who could be compared rather to the manufacturers of microscopes and telescopes, to those in short who provide us with tools that broaden, organize and increase the strength of our senses. The former organize our memory, allowing us to *remember*, one might say, even things we have never seen.

SEVERUS: Okay; and the third way?

COMMODUS: The third way, finally, is the good and true and right one, the one in which you bask and revel — true history as experienced, living and working history, in which the past is your past, and precisely for this reason it is articulated toward the future, not as prediction, but as a tendency, a push, a positioning of ends. The history that is Life. . . .

SEVERUS: I don't see what there is to make fun of.

COMMODUS: Neither do I, to tell the truth. But still, I have the urge to make fun of it, maybe because of the obstinacy and violence you put into your love of history, which is to me, as always, a bit suspect. I sense behind it personal ties and grudges; I can see you holding on by inertia to the road once taken, wanting at every turn to convince yourself that it is still the best — the most just and glorious. Anyway, this teasing isn't aimed at the thing itself, but at the way you practice it, which ought to please a noble and disinterested spirit such as yourself.

SEVERUS: And it would, if I didn't suspect that you, deep down, were indeed making fun of the thing itself. And this, I have to tell you, disgusts me. To me it looks like the most petty and selfish thumbing your nose at everything, and delivered with that patronizing, blase tone, that air of being *au dessus de la mêlée*.

COMMODUS: I honestly don't think that's what this is about — especially considering that your accusation doesn't bother me at all. But in any case, this last way of doing history, seeing it as humanity's past, in which our own past is implanted, clearly does not include prediction, but it does to a very large extent include affection (in the broad sense of the word). In short, it is a question of setting goals, of initiating actions dictated by the feelings and relationships that exist between us and ourselves and between us and other people, present and past. History allows us to expand this affection and these relationships, to extend them to what was and to what is to come, to have feelings and sketch out actions in the context of a broader horizon, one which potentially embraces the totality of our fellow beings.

SEVERUS: This is exactly what I meant. Let me repeat, if I may, what I said a while ago: "in relations that concern people, experience (history) requires that we view them, become aware of them and *know them,* if it doesn't upset you too much, as other creators of goals and their fulfillment."

COMMODUS: I'm not too comfortable with the expression *know them,* which might lead to misunderstanding since it's used in the sense of know scientifically, based on prediction, as well as for this emotional knowing, based on attributing finalistic behavior to other people. Go ahead and use the word, if you like, even in this case, as long as it's clear that when *know* means to let finalistic behavior exist in the object, the only way open to us is to apply goal-directed behavior to the object ourselves — that is, to cause the other person to react and pit his goals against ours.

SEVERUS: All right. Now we agree; but it seems to me that we've agreed right from the start and that this discussion hasn't been worth having.

COMMODUS: It's been worthwhile for two reasons: (1) It has been clarified that historical knowing has nothing to do with scientific knowing. (2) It has become clear that the notion of life only exists where goals are set and the setting of goals is presumed; and that in these cases the interpretation of this finalism as a force, an action, a law that can be used in a scientific way — makes no sense precisely because such use involves a predictability that is in open contradiction to finalistic activity. For this reason we can talk about *life,* but not about a *life force,* and we can talk about *finality,* about *end positions,* but not about *final causes.*

SEVERUS: Having got to this point I would have no problem saying you're right. But I don't know objectively whether you are or not. Have you read [Kant's] *Critique of Judgment?*

COMMODUS: I had another look at it for the occasion. But I think it should be rejected — what he wanted was to turn these formulations upside down. We can talk more about it some other time, because it seems to me that the topic runs up against every sort of relationship between natural law and experience. And now, to finish up, we can have a little fun. Write your age on a piece of paper.

SEVERUS: Done.

COMMODUS: Now write the age of your first-born child, the year when you were born, the year of your marriage, and then the number of years between your marriage and the birth of your first child.

SEVERUS: Done.

COMMODUS: Now put all the numbers in a column and add them up.

SEVERUS: Done.

COMMODUS: Is the total 3880?

SEVERUS: How did you know that?

COMMODUS: It's a law of nature that I have recently discovered. Using the statistical sample of all the married men with children in southern Calabria (a region in many ways typical in that its racial composition approaches that of the global average) I found that this law is corroborated 97% of the time, which fits quite easily within the margin of uncertainty due to possible errors of observation. Indeed, I think we find ourselves in the presence of a new universal constant — that is, to echo Max Planck, of one of those mysterious messages that Nature sends us from the heart to reveal to us the intimate structure of its fabric. I'm now extending the research to women.

SEVERUS: And doesn't an observation like this in some way bring you closer to a certain finalism within nature?

COMMODUS: Yes, o worthy one — and indeed I say that faith in internal finalism grows in my soul to the same degree that my wonder grows at the mysterious message Nature has sent us by way of the married men of southern Calabria.

RITROSO (*addressing Severus*): I confess that I cannot fathom how a serious person such as yourself can stay with conversations like this for such a long time. What good do you get from it? This man paints himself as an anti-philosopher, but this is simply a pose, a demagogue's habit. I haven't said much, it's true, but I don't much want to talk to him. One look at his discussion arguments is enough for me — typical philosopher stuff. The presumption of re-examining the principles of all the sciences without ever having practiced them; the self-delusion that he has in his hands the key to every door. . . .

COMMODUS: I believe there is a key that opens lots of doors in the field of the sciences based on reasoning — but this has nothing to do with a philosophic system. It is within everyone's reach and not exclusive to the priesthood of a specific science. It is just common sense and the calm, peaceful, unprejudiced examination of starting points and initial definitions.

RITROSO: And isn't this what you call philosophy?

COMMODUS: No, because the aim of this examination is scientific rather than philosophical. It's not at all a question of justifying these principles before an instance of universal validity, or in relation to a circular or self-sufficient line of reasoning, or a dialectic of the spirit, or what have you. It's a matter of seeing how suitable such principles are for fulfilling the purpose assigned to them in the restricted sphere of each science. The research therefore has a pragmatic character, and can only be justified by success in a scientific field — that is, by some actual discovery and explanation it can carry out within a specific science.

RITROSO: Don't be offended by my question, but how long have you been doing science?

COMMODUS: Around two years.

RITROSO: Then you won't mind if, just to clarify my ideas about scientific principles, I consult people who have been at it a bit longer.

COMMODUS: Of course I don't mind; and I can't compel you to listen to me. But it seems to me, o Ritroso, that you are too attached to professional authority. Are you so sure that going to an official school and reading a lot of papers and having long experience with the tools of the trade are absolutely necessary conditions for understanding something about the basic principles of a science?

RITROSO: Frankly, yes, I do believe it, petty and pedantic as it may seem. I have too much experience with the upheaval and disorder that amateurs and outsiders bring, at least in my science. . . .

COMMODUS: Pareto was an outsider, if I'm not mistaken. But that isn't what I wanted to say. I wanted to make an observation, limiting myself to physics, that I think may be allowed even though I've had only two years experience. And that is that belonging to the professional category of physicist entails such close contact with physics and such direct dealings with the specific moment-by-moment problems of research that there is scant possibility to re-examine initial problems and fundamental principles. These first principles are rooted in the memory of the first years of study; they were, you might say, sucked up like mother's milk in a form that is now stable and accepted. Continually going back over them would be impossible — it would mean disrupting the entire construction of one's knowledge.

RITROSO: But there are physicists who did just that: Mach, Poincaré.

COMMODUS: Mach wasn't a physicist, and Poincaré did it with philosophical intentions at the end of his life, independently of his work in physics. But you will never find a physicist who, faced with an intractable problem, goes back and questions whether the initial definition of mass or force or length or velocity was properly set out. The only one who did this, in his youth, with a certain scandal-mongering and unorthodox zeal — as something of an outsider, that is, was Einstein. And the outcome was that trifling little discovery you may have heard of. But all the others, even the greatest of them, at best limit their revisions to a correction of classical principles, in the face of a new experience that otherwise cannot be justified (Heisenberg, Schrödinger).

RITROSO: Well, if they don't do it there must be good reasons, and I trust them more than I trust you. And besides, in many cases it may be helpful for research purposes to make use of concepts that are not well defined, that serve as a scaffolding, a temporary structure that helps the investigation move forward.

COMMODUS: Agreed. And I wouldn't have any objection either, if I knew that this lack of clarification of principles was the result of a reasoned analysis and that there were valid reasons for deciding to keep some as they are, even if not clearly defined. But this is not the case. You hear vague expressions like the 'idealization of daily experience,' or 'generalization of sensory data.' In other authors, like one that I have in front of me now, you read that 'all sciences have their roots in metaphysics' and therefore first principles are not worth bothering with. Do you know, I couldn't find any book, not even the one by Einstein and his students, that contained a non-puerile definition of a rigid body? Everyone has decided to say: a rigid body is what everyone knows it is. Except that then, after hundreds of pages of abstruse calculations, they declare that in the present state of science we do not know precisely what a rigid body is. And note that the rigid body is the basis of the definition of the meter and of two equal lengths. If you don't believe me I can show you the text.

RITROSO: This may be the case in physics. But in economics?

COMMODUS: In economics, my friend, I'm ready to concede that everything is going as well as it could possibly go.

7. EUGENIO COLORNI:
ON PSYCHOLOGISM IN ECONOMICS[1]

The tendency nowadays is to view economics as a purely deductive science. There is an initial premise: *People use preference scales,* and no determination whatsoever is made concerning the form and content of such scales. And the law of marginal utility and the entire body of laws in economics derive from this simple premise. But at the same time any statement regarding the conformation of such scales of preference — that is, regarding people's tastes — is not considered to belong to the science of economics, but rather to the *psycho-sociological penumbra* that economics is so often surrounded by, and which so often leads to confusion concerning its methods and goals.

Now what ought to be examined is whether the premises (or axioms) that underlie pure economics, and on the basis of which it proceeds purely deductively, are truly free from any sort of psychological elements, and do not implicitly contain statements about people's tastes and preferences. I am speaking of very general psychological statements that are so elementary and probable, at least in collective phenomena, that they can be taken as thoroughly confirmed. But they are psychological statements nonetheless, and not therefore different in nature from other statements belonging to the "penumbra" that pure economists try so carefully to differentiate themselves from.

If this is indeed the case, then the difference between pure economics and psycho-sociological science would be a difference of degree rather than kind.

Robbins[2] considers economic deductions to be due to a purely logical-analytical procedure — an explication of consequences already contained in the premises (cf. mainly p. 110). The procedure applied is thus in no way psychological, and ought to enjoy

---

[1]In *Scritti,* ed. N. Bobbio, Firenze, 1975, pp. 28–304 (editor's note).
[2]*An Essay on the Nature and Significance of Economic Science,* London, 1932.

the same apodicticity or automatism that characterizes the exact sciences. The laws of economics are in this view basically tautological (cf. pp. 81, 82, 110) and this guarantees their validity within the limits of the set premises. Outside these limits (that is, when the premises themselves vary) they obviously no longer claim to be valid. And Robbins considers variation in the premises to be a problem outside the purview of economics, which takes them as given and leaves it to other sciences (psychology, etc.) to study their variation (pp. 115–18).

But in doing so Robbins introduces a new content limitation that sacrifices all the advantages of his beautiful "formal" or "[. . .]" definition of economics. Already on pp. 116 ff. he speaks of endogenous and exogenous changes, excluding the latter from economics. And this distinction reappears at various points in his book (pp. 64–93 ff.). This distinction between "economic material" and "extra-economic material," as I have said, re-introduces "materialistic" or "content-related" definitions of economics.

This distinction derives from the illusion that economic laws have a tautological quality and are thus absolutely certain, while others belong to that "penumbra of psychological and sociological probabilities" (p. 118) that the field of economics is always surrounded by. But does this sharp distinction really exist?

Let us examine these supposedly necessary implications — economic, that is, as opposed to those that are only probable (that is, sociological and psychological) with reference to Robbins's own examples (p. 116,1). Inflation is followed by a drop in the value of the currency (a law of economics — impersonal, analytical, automatic, non-psychological). Instead: a fall in the value of the currency is followed by inflation (probably psycho-sociological rather than an economic law; a change which is exogenous and not necessary, involving an act of will by the government, and by its nature not predictable with certainty).

Now is it true that proposition (1) is analytical, tautological, and certain due to logic rather than psychology? It is not. The proposition "the volume of currency in circulation increases" does not by analytical implication contain the proposition "the value of the currency falls" even if it is assumed that everything else stays the same. To deduce one position from the other it is necessary to make certain assumptions about the human mind and its reaction to certain stimuli. We would have to know that the less scarce a commodity is, the more inclined people are to exchange it for other scarcer goods. Now this is an elementary law of psychology, the same in its nature as the one that predicts that a government will print money when its value diminishes.

But what makes the first law seem so much more sure and necessary than the second? If both are psychological implications derived from the observation of the human mind, why does one appear so obvious as to be tautological while the other doesn't?

The answer, I think, is this: that the first type of prediction is collective and static, while the second is individual. To say that an increase in currency circulation leads to a reduction in the value of money you have to suppose that people behave in a certain way and react in a certain way to altered conditions. But it is an average of these reactions that is considered, an overall result in which all individual differences cancel each other out. On the other hand, saying that a reduction in the value of money leads to inflation, you have to presume that a very limited number of people will behave in a certain way, so that the statistical laws that eliminate individual differences no longer apply. If (an absurd supposition) the printing of money were a matter of private initiative, the second law would be just as necessary as the first.

Thus there is no clear distinction between economic laws (analytical, tautological, necessary) and the "psycho-sociological penumbra" that is assumed to surround such laws. Both involve predicting certain human reactions to certain changes in exterior conditions. It is just that in the second case, since it involves the reaction of one or a few individuals, there is wide latitude for the unexpected; while in the first case such latitude, which still exists for any single individual, is eliminated by the compensation owing to the large number.

The difference between laws that are economic (or endogenous) and extra-economic (or exogenous) is thus not a difference between analytical (tautological) laws and empirical (psychological) laws. It is rather a difference in degree of probability between statistical and individual laws (between macroscopic and microscopic laws). We pass with continuity from one to the other with no clear break.

OBJECTION: Even assuming this to be the case, of what practical importance is this clarification? Isn't this basically just academic nitpicking? The essential thing is that there should still be a very obvious distinction between those laws for which predictability is assured and those in which it is uncertain. Economics concerns itself with the former, not the latter.

RESPONSE: Indeed. But I believe the observation is worth making all the same, for this reason — that economists commonly look upon the "psychological penumbra" with scorn. It is, they say, a field open to easy and arbitrary generalizations, to pseudoscience and a muddying of the waters, which casts a doubtful light even on the surest deductions of the science of economics (cf. Robbins *passim*).

OBJECTION: Well, all right — but isn't what they say perhaps true?

RESPONSE: It is true, but there is something more; from this contempt for arbitrary and random laws which remains at the margins of their own science, economists are led to aim for constitutions and regimes in which the least possible scope is left for the formulation of such laws. The ideal regime for them would be one where everyone behaved according to the iron laws of economics in the restricted sense as defined by them; in which predictions must never be based on psychology but always on analytical logic. They transform their irritation with anything that disturbs the calm and serious proceedings of their own science into a general contempt for humanity — a *Weltanschauung* that their ideologies, moral, social, etc., are made to depend on. Now, while it is true that a state of affairs in which actions and choices proceeded from an aggregate rather than individual will would provide the broadest scope for the formulation of economic laws (and would be catnip for economists like Robbins), there is nothing to indicate it would be a boon for people in general, who normally couldn't care less about living in a world that is accessible to clear and solid generalizations and predictions, but would rather eat well, dress well, have fun, learn things, widen their horizons, etc.

I am saying, in short, that the illusion of a clear and qualitative division between economic and psychological laws promotes feelings and passions that extend beyond the limited field of economics to general moral and social conceptions, leading to confused ideas and countless misunderstandings.

SEVERUS: I am amazed that you, a believer in [. . .] can be satisfied with such external, superficially logical explanations. A simple series of wrong logical steps is for you enough to explain an entire *Weltanschauung* with its infinite implications, moral, psychological etc.

COMMODUS: It's precisely because I believe in [. . .] that I do it. It is exactly to show that this *Weltanschauung*, which seems so serious, imposing and full of struggle and sacrifice, often in large part derives from likes and dislikes learned at school, from attitudes acquired in that dangerous age between 16 and 25, when we are condemned to carve out our future physiognomy and mature opinions once and for all, without any actual opportunity other than to follow whatever teacher we happen to get or some randomly chosen readings.

It is exactly in this period that our scientific opinions are most passionate, infused with love and hate along with academic hubris and contempt. Then these feelings spread into other, non-scientific problems — and what is worse, they leave their mark on us and determine the face we present to the world. Can't you always spot somebody who read Croce at age 18? It's not so much this person's aesthetic and philosophical opinions as it is a whole series of likes and dislikes — this is someone, for example, who will go through life with an unshakable aversion to Bocca publications and an attraction for Laterza and La Nuova Italia.

The transition I tried to describe before is like this, from the distinction between endogenous and exogenous changes to a sort of moral and social attitude. It is an "idolum academiae" that I have tried to identify.

SEVERUS: And you claim to be able to eliminate this "idolum" simply by demonstrating that the distinction between endogenous and exogenous causes doesn't hold up?

COMMODUS: Not in my wildest dreams. There is no logical argument that can extirpate this idol from someone who is attached to it. Indeed, it was seeing this logical incongruity in an otherwise serious and rigorous author like Robbins that led me to conclude that perhaps he also may be counted among the legions devoted to it. Rooting out his feelings of attachment and reverence for it is something I would never be capable of. But the small logical error, the obstacle dodged with such hasty aplomb, is for me a clue that beneath the surface there are problems that logic would rise up against. And it invites me to take the whole argument less than seriously.

I see you going back to Robbins's arguments, and in a sense this is good because it eliminates a certain semblance of agreement which can only lead to misunderstanding. Thus you maintain that propositions such as: "an increase in the currency in circulation leads to a rise in prices" are analytical propositions that contain no supposition that people use a certain scale of relative preferences, and are "valid regardless of what the scales are in reality." These would therefore differ *intrinsically* from propositions like: "City girls prefer silk stockings to wool socks," which contain the psychological observation of a certain order of preferences in a certain group of people.

I would say instead that the two propositions are not *intrinsically* different, since the first implicitly contains other propositions that also come down to the observation that people use certain scales of relative preference and not others. That these scales are of a high degree of generality, stability and certainty is not what I want to contest. If I am able to show you that the first of these two propositions is also based implicitly on two observations about the scales of preference people use, then I will have demonstrated that the two propositions, even though one is much more stable than the other, belong to the same type, the same category.

We shall see. The proposition: "The less scarce a commodity is for an individual, the less sacrifice that person is willing to make to obtain it" doesn't apparently contain any observation about the scales of preference used by the individual in question. It is a purely tautological proposition as long as the concept of scarcity is defined as follows: For an individual, a unit of a commodity is less scarce than a unit of another commodity when said individual will give up the second to obtain the first (I am deliberately not talking about *increments* because, as we shall see, in that case there is the implicit supposition of certain relative preference scales. For this reason the use of the word "scarce" is somewhat peculiar here. "Desirable" would be better).

This proposition is substantially the same as saying: "People regard various possible commodities in terms of their scales of relative importance." I could tell you that even this is a psychological observation, but I won't. It would just be stupid nitpicking and would serve no purpose. I am therefore ready to recognize that in the aforementioned proposition, there is nothing having to do with the use of one scale of preference rather than another. All that matters is the observation that there are preference scales.

But does the law of diminishing marginal utility really derive from this proposition as a corollary, and from it proposition (1), without the introduction of anything new? A detailed examination of this problem would be most instructive and ought to be done, if others haven't already done it. But it would require knowledge that I don't have, so for now I will limit myself to this:

Going from proposition (3) to (1) requires *at least* that the following proposition be considered valid:

(4) a greater quantity of a commodity is more desirable than a smaller quantity.

Now this proposition constitutes the observation of the objective validity of a certain determined scale of preferences. To understand this, compare the two propositions:

"City girls prefer silk stockings to wool socks" (2), or "Every person prefers two lire to one lira" (5), and the character of both as psychological observations jumps out at you. The objection is not valid that (5) derives from the fact that 2 is greater than 1 — this does not authorize us to *conclude* that a person prefers two lire to one lira. To say this we would have to observe an order of preference in the human mind.

Let us deal with the arguments in a more orderly way. There are two things we need to demonstrate:

1: that (4) and (3) are psychological;

2: that (4) is indispensable for going from (3) to (1). Let us first of all define what we mean by "psychological." We mean, following Robbins, something very precise.

We say that a proposition contains psychological statements

if it contains statements about the *conformation* of the preference scales used by one or more or all individuals, and not only the statement that people use preference scales.

Let us now define the term "preference scales." Let us say that:

> A person uses preference scales if the units of each possible commodity (appropriately defined) arrange themselves in a given moment in a series such that the possession of each term in the series is for that person preferable to the possession of the following term, in such a way, that is, that he or she is ready to exchange each term in the series for each of the terms that precede it.

It seems to me that this definition takes account of Robbins's two main concepts (scarcity and alternative uses) and not of others. The scarcity of goods is expressed in the fact that they are desirable (and here scarcity is taken in the broad sense as "not possessed in quantities corresponding to desires and obtainable only through sacrifice"; and is therefore susceptible to "more" and "less," o fussy Ritroso!). That they have alternative uses is shown by the fact that they can be exchanged for other things. Preference scales show only the desirability of any commodity by comparison with others, at any moment.

How shall we now define *goods* — or even better *units of each of these goods*? This is where the issue begins to get complicated. In the first place it is clear that *qualitatively* we should include as "goods" anything that could be desirable to any person — so, objects, services, concrete or abstract enjoyments of any kind, the elimination of evils, etc.

(2) Let us say that a "unit" of some commodity is an indivisible quantity of it, or a quantity that in common use can be considered indivisible (a kilo of coal, 100g of pasta, etc.).

(3) There is a third problem that is much more serious than the others: how to be sure that the definition of the goods themselves does not contain the implicit assumption of some particular scale of preference? An inattentive assumption about the concept of "goods" can easily in fact contain the implicit affirmation that a certain commodity is preferable to another. The concept of "mar-

ginal utility" has eliminated the most serious of these drawbacks, but perhaps has not yet eliminated them all. In short, the idea is to increasingly eliminate any psychological intrusion (in the sense now defined) from the concept of "preference scales."

Let me explain this better. Mathematical analogies can lead us into assumptions not contained in our premises. The statement $a>b$ (the possession of a unit of commodity a is preferred by a certain individual to the possession of a unit of commodity b) does not in any way entail, as it does in mathematics, the statement $2a>2b$. Such an affirmation would be the same as assuming a certain scale of preference. It is therefore *extremely dangerous*, in economics, to say: "We establish certain definitions and premises and then let mathematics do its work." The simple assumption of the fundamental postulates of mathematics can lead to very serious misunderstandings because it means assuming psychological laws that are not necessarily valid. The fact is that even the symbols $>$, $<$, $+$, $-$, etc. are used by simple analogy and do not mean the same thing in economics that they mean in mathematics. We suppose, for example, that we are giving a the meaning "one unit of a certain commodity"; for example, a kilo of meat. Here we cannot even write $a = a$; for in economics this equality means that "the possession of one kilo of meat is just as desirable as the possession of another kilo of meat, under other conditions." This statement already implies the assumption of a certain preference scale and, as we know, this is not valid.

This first observation thus tells us that the elements in our scale cannot be *tout court* the units of each commodity. In fact, each takes a different place on the preference scale, depending on whether its possession is considered starting from one set of conditions or from another. It would therefore be more correct to give the elements on our scale the form $M + a$ where M is an overall state of possession. Then you can actually write $(M + a) - M = (N + a) - N$. This inequality is meaningful precisely because we have established that the symbol a in itself has no meaning, and it is therefore not possible to write $(M + a) - M = a$; and $(M + a) - M = (N + a) - N$ is not true, which it would be in common mathematics.

This observation thus does not limit, nor does it determine the contents of preference scales, but actually makes them broader and more indeterminate. It removes psychological assumptions rather than introducing them.

But now, take the proposition:

"If the price of a certain commodity goes up, demand goes down."

I am told that this is derived by logical implication from the principle of marginal utility, and thus from the simple assumption that people use preference scales, without in any way determining that they use certain scales rather than others. Let's see if this is true.

Suppose that in a certain town a merchant sells toothbrushes at the price of five lire each, and manages to sell ten of them. This means that in this town there are ten people, whom we can call i, for whom the following inequality holds: $M_i < (M_c - 5l) + sp$ (with i varying from 1 to 10). For everybody else, whom we will call K, the opposite inequality holds: $M_k > M_k - 5l + sp$.

Now suppose that the merchant sets the price of his toothbrushes at 6 lire. It is possible that among people i there will be one (the first, for example) or more who never buys another toothbrush. This means that for these people two inequalities hold:

$$M_1 < M_1 - 5l + sp$$
$$M_1 > M_1 - 6l + sp.$$

This buyer obviously disappears from the market. But to say that demand goes down, we have to accept as given that there is *nobody* from group K for whom the following inequalities are true:

$$M_K > M_K - 5l - sp$$
$$M_K < M_K - 6l + sp.$$

Assuming that for some people in group K these two inequalities hold, it cannot in fact be said that demand decreases.

Now obviously it will be unusual to find a rational person for whom these two inequalities are true at the same time — that is, someone who won't buy a toothbrush for 5 lire but will buy one for 6. But in the abstract there's nothing that rules it out. And in any case, saying that such a person doesn't exist means making an assumption about the conformation of people's preference scales — a psychological assumption. This assumption, in its general form, is none other than (4), which is:

A greater quantity of a commodity is preferable to a smaller quantity (4).

RITROSO: I don't deny that this proposition is necessary to the law stipulating contraction of demand with an increase in price. But I'm not sure it's really a psychological proposition in the sense you've defined. It seems to me that it's implicitly included in the concept of "preference scales."

COMMODUS: This is not possible. We can always define a concept however we think best. So then our (7) should be changed to the following:

"An individual uses preference scales if for him the units of each commodity are arranged in a series such that the possession of each term in the scale is preferable to the possession of the following term; *and such that a term consisting of units of a commodity never follows a term consisting of m-1 units of the same commodity.*"

This restriction on the concept of scales is, I repeat, always possible. Only we can never legitimately say:

"Everyone uses preference scales."

Do you admit that it's possible to find exceptional cases where a person or a group of people prefer to possess less rather than more, and spend more rather than less?

RITROSO: Of course: the case was studied by Pantaleoni and Pareto; Wicksteed thoroughly re-examined it; Spatenbräu[3] refuted it; Water Closet worked out the consequences. Compare the 1913 edition of *La Riforma Sociale* [*Social Reform*] . . . (*goes on with a ten-minute soliloquy, incomprehensible to Commodus*).

COMMODUS: All right then — you can clearly see that if we want (8) to be valid, we have to say that the people Pantaleoni and Pareto studied were not people. If we instead endow them with the divine gift of humanity it will no longer be possible to establish any law about the contraction of supply following an increase in prices.

RITROSO: But there are so few of them. . . .

COMMODUS: This is exactly what I was getting at — the fact

---

[3] A famous Munich beer.

that the propositions we have looked at are valid statistically and are therefore not applicable to a limited number of people. Go back to the case of the ten toothbrushes. If by chance in that moment a couple of Pantaleoni and Spatenbräu's inhuman humans should turn up, then the law of supply and demand would no longer be applicable. The economist, however, committed to this law, would say that it had worked perfectly, except that a couple of misfits had bought toothbrushes in defiance of any preference scale, however defined; for which they were banished from the ranks of humanity, thanks to the obvious advantages provided by scientific clarity and the mathematics of economics. So in the end, that extra pair of toothbrushes "were not bought." Their transfer at the price of 6 lire to non-humans who wouldn't buy them at 5 lire can in no way be defined as an act of buying and selling.

Now you're really angry at the pointlessness of this teasing; but this — and I am ready to prove it to you — is the basis of what they mean when they say, whenever economic laws don't work, "exogenous and psychological factors came into play." This means nothing more or less than: "Factors were introduced that stem from a less elementary sort of psychology — something more complicated and unusual than what presides over the formulation of the laws of the market."

What I mean in this criticism is only that if we consider these anomalies to be qualitatively extrinsic to the laws of economics, then our attention will continue to be focused on the laws themselves and on the extremely basic psychology that underpins them. We will get from the laws all the possible consequences they contain; but when we are faced with a fact whose premises do not fit with the definitions of economics (for example, someone who would rather pay 6 than 5) we just won't deal with it at all; we'll just call it extra-economic — psychological — and with that we'll have dispensed with it completely.

RITROSO: Dispensed with it as far as economics is concerned. There's nothing preventing some other discipline from taking it up.

COMMODUS: True; but this would be denying the benefits that might derive from the application of a science as progressive and organized as economics.

If we see, on the other hand, that the initial definitions in economics are marked by extremely elementary psychological principles — manifest and self-evident, but still psychological; if we see that, then when we find ourselves faced with a phenomenon that stems from more complicated psychological factors, we will be tempted to verify it with the tools already in our possession as economists. Or instead, we can modify our tools (that is, our definitions and initial postulates) in the light of the new phenomenon and obtain new laws, perhaps more limited than the previous ones, but such that thanks to them the great calculating machine that we have available in economic science is not simply thrown out. Something similar is happening in physics with the introduction of non-Euclidean geometry, etc. And the benefits are immense. A brand of economics that included the person who pays 6 rather than five would be a similar thing.

RITROSO: This is all very well — but the fact is, this psychology that you call anomalous doesn't lend itself to laws, definitions or generalizations. The deeper we go into it, the more we find ourselves in the field of the arbitrary, the haphazard and unpredictable.

COMMODUS: Agreed, but what I've been trying to do is no more than to point out that the line of demarcation between the field of science and the field of the arbitrary (or between the fields of the predictable and the unpredictable) does not lie, as the economists make out, just beyond the threshold of the lucid mathematical edifice they have constructed. If it is true that inside it everything is scientifically predictable and observable, it is nevertheless not true that as soon as you leave it you enter chaos, a world of randomness, individual willfulness and psychology. The change is gradual.

RITROSO: What does that mean? How can there be a "gradual" move from a mathematical law to a non-mathematical law? Mathematics, as far as I know, doesn't allow for gradualness.

COMMODUS: There can be, because mathematics is not just concerned with organizing the field of predictability, but also with tracing the limits of unpredictability or indeterminacy, and these limits are mobile and imprecise; but it is not beyond the scope of mathematics to clarify them and make them graspable. Think of the immense service rendered to physics by the "Heisenberg relations," which are nothing more than "indeterminacy relations" that determine the limits beyond which a phenomenon is *not* predictable.

It seems to me that though this error concerning the arbitrary and random is common to economists of the most divergent schools, they react to it in different ways and the quality of their output differs as well (I speak here only from hearsay). As we have seen, if economists of the Robbins variety followed their instincts regarding these somewhat messy phenomena that don't fit the definitions, they would close their eyes and say they didn't exist. But since they bump into them at every turn, they say that they don't exist in economics, and that way they can ignore them as economists. And since this still doesn't exempt them from dealing with them as people, they reject them, fighting them and contesting their right to life — which is another, more angry and confused way of saying "they don't exist," and excluding them from the world of moral ends.

Other economists, more consistent in their desire to eliminate the *psychological penumbra* at the margins of their science, actually deny its existence — and they demonstrate this. Every action, they say, is individual only in appearance, and individual people, in their desires and actions, are the unconscious expression of strict economic laws that determine and dominate all their activities. Once these laws are known, it would not be difficult to predict even the single individual's behavior and bring it into the scientific fold.

Now on the surface this looks like a rejection of reality even more pigheaded and obstinate than the previous one. In reality, it is the first major attempt to pin down those laws of indeterminacy we were talking about. The Robbins style of interpretation offers no possibility of grasping anything outside the laws of economics and, as elucidated with our good Ritroso's impeccable coherence, leads to a view of history as a sort of novel, a series of facts and acts and desires that went a certain way but could have been different, in which it would be useless to look for a causal connection that could repeat itself in the future. The other conception, on the other hand, used intelligently, has allowed us to determine the limits of this randomness of individual volition — it has presented the facts of history, apparently determined by the will of the individual, as actually linked to a series of deeper causes of which the individual, having believed himself the master, was in fact the servant; it has made it possible to discern a profound logic in historical facts that at first sight appear unrelated and chaotic; and it has dictated some criteria of interpretation and prediction that everyone today, whether or not they embrace the doctrine, can no longer do without.

RITROSO: Let these developments go. You say the origin of the whole problem is in the fact that a proposition presents itself as analytical, or mathematical or tautological, when in your view it is synthetic, and psychological or empirical, because it comes from observation. In the end it boils down to this. Are you sure you can draw a clear distinction between propositions that are abstract and empirical, analytic and synthetic, or what have you? Don't you think one of them could easily turn into the other? If I say "marble is hard," the proposition is empirical because it derives from an observation I made; but I can make it analytical by defining anything as marble that has the essential characteristic of being hard. Then if I ran into some marble (calcium carbonate) that wasn't hard, I would say it wasn't marble.

COMMODUS: This is a very interesting question, and is the theme of innumerable variations on the question of scientific definitions. Do the definitions that underlie a science derive from experience? Evidently not, since experience is supposed to stand on them. And in any case, can I put together scientific definitions without reference to experience? No, at the risk of building a science whose laws are not applicable to any known fact. I'll give you an example. I cannot experience physics in any way without knowing what a rigid body is. This is what allows me to know what two equal lengths are, etc. Therefore, the definition of a rigid body is absolutely independent of experience and cannot be anything like "a body is rigid when the distances between its points remains invariant." This way we are free to say anything is rigid, whether a piece of platinum or a piece of rubber. So what moves us to choose the piece of platinum? Experience? No. We are moved to choose the piece of platinum by considerations about the use we are going to make of the definition; its content will have to be provided — the objects in the actual world it will be applied to.

If we decided to call a piece of rubber rigid, then every time it was stretched or squeezed, as we usually speak of these things, we would have to say instead that it had stayed the same and that what stretched or shortened were the other objects: the houses, bits of iron and platinum, etc., and introduced forces that explained these changes. Which is possible, but obviously not helpful.

SEVERUS (*to Ritroso*): I advise you not to embark on a discussion on this topic — you won't escape without first being subjected to the whole of special relativity.

COMMODUS: Actually, these statements, though apparently paradoxical, are absolutely exact, and I think it would be worthwhile for anyone to be aware of them at least partially, because they have a significance that far transcends physics.

Returning to economics, I can certainly define the concept of "preference scales" in such a way as to analytically derive the contraction of demand in the case of a price increase. For this purpose I need to impose on the concept of scale at least the limitations of (7). (And perhaps other limitations, which at the moment I don't want to go into). There's nothing stopping me from doing this. Except that I would like also to be able to say:

"All people also use preference scales."

Can I? That is: is (8) compatible with (7)? Certainly, as long as I appropriately define the concept of *person*. And nothing stops me from defining it however I like. Except that lots of ordinary flesh-and-blood people would probably be excluded — precisely those people studied by Spatenbräu and Pareto that we talked about before. For our purposes they will be excluded from humanity. Can I do it? Undoubtedly? Should I? Another matter.

As you see, your conversion of empirical judgments into "analytical judgments" does not avoid psychology. Chased out the door it comes in through the window and installs itself before you can even get started. It means that now, when you run into an *anomalous* or *extra-economic* fact, instead of modifying and extending your laws, you have to modify and extend your definitions. Unless you don't want to modify or extend anything and just act as if the new fact didn't exist, which is what you economists, if I'm not mistaken, are most prone to doing.

Imagine the physicists witnessing the famous Michelson-Morley experiment.

RITROSO: Not again with the physics!

COMMODUS: If you'll allow me. It's a clean, straightforward science — just the kind you like. And it's the one that up to now has been the most productive. I think it has something to teach economists.

So imagine the reaction of the physicists to this experience that didn't fit with some of the known laws. If they had been economists, they would have said that the experiment was "extra-physical," and gone no further with it. And so would the physicists if they had lived two centuries ago. They would have invoked transcendental factors, pointing to experience to demonstrate the existence of God or who knows what.

Today's physicists are more aggressive and have more faith in their science. So two roads were open to them:

(1) Find a new law or invoke a new force that would explain the results of the experiment. This is what Lorentz and Fitzgerald did, with their famous *contraction.* But this procedure was contradictory because its outcome was that under certain conditions a rigid body is not rigid.

(2) Modify the initial definitions themselves of a rigid body, or of time, etc. This is what Einstein did, with the spectacular results that we know. And the importance of his procedure is almost greater from the point of view of methodology than of physics itself — it really opened the eyes of the physicists and may do the same for other scientists.

Now, moving to economics, the first type is the Spatenbräu-Pareto solution: in the light of the known laws of economics, study those "anomalous" — that is, extra-economic — individuals who pay six rather than five. This method, as we have seen, involves a contradiction because it implies the existence of subjects in the market who were excluded from it by the initial definitions — it considers as people (market elements) beings who have been initially denied the attributes of people — that is, market elements.

The second type of solution, which seems to me more consistent and productive, is to revise the original definitions so that they also accommodate these particular anomalous people, even at the cost of causing the collapse of all the most celebrated laws and the most unshakable principles.

But the most foolish and sterile is undoubtedly the Robbins-type solution: not to deal with such people at all, saying that they are not covered by economics.

When I speak of people who buy at 6 rather than 5, I am of course only giving an example. You know about these things and can surely imagine better examples, closer to everyday experience.

CONCLUDING: All the sciences, especially economics, began as experimental sciences. They observed facts, continuities and regularities, and upon them they built laws. Galileo *experimented* with the principle of inertia, which today for us is a definition. Ricardo *experienced* the fact that people buy more when the cost is less.

RITROSO: It wasn't Ricardo.

COMMODUS: It doesn't matter — let's call him Pinco Pallino. In making these observations Galileo thought he had found something constant in the nature of bodies. Pinco Pallino thought he had found something constant in the nature of people — in their psychological makeup. And in doing this neither of them worried about clearly defining the terms of their propositions. In talking about a body at rest, Galileo meant to say something obvious to everyone, without need of further clarification. In using the words "person," "buy," "cost," "more," "less," etc. the primitive economist was claiming that their meaning was clear and unequivocal.

When science had reached a sufficient level of generality, they thought the time had come to transform it from experimental to mathematical, and from empirical to analytical.

This was a way of breaking free of experience and relying totally on pure reason. I could show you that this also happened in physics, even though it still calls itself an experimental science. But it certainly happened in the case of Robbins-style economics. It was irritation with its imprecision that did it, the annoyance of having to take the exceptions into account and view its own laws as statistical approximations not applicable to single individuals. This irritation and the triumph of having eliminated it are clearly visible in Robbins's book. No more "psychological penumbra," no more dependence on misleading observations or on the deceptions of history (see mainly pp. 72 ff.). Now the theory stands on the unshakable foundation of pure analytical reason; it is as applicable to a single individual as to an entire nation; it has been cleansed of exceptions and is valid today just as it was yesterday and always. How was this radical transformation achieved? Very simply — by transforming previously empirical propositions into tautologies, defining their terms in such a way that they are unconditionally valid. Do we want to be sure that people always buy more when the cost is less? Do we want to eliminate the exceptions to this rule? All we have to do is define as people only those who behave this way; that way we can be sure that no exception is going to come along and spoil the party.

The illusion is perfect; whoever wants a quiet life without head-aches has found what they were looking for. But . . . but flesh-and-blood humans go on buying and selling as they see fit. Economics can predict very little, and is increasingly discredited.

RITROSO: If you say that physics has proceeded in this same way, transforming its empirical propositions into tautologies, then I suppose you will criticize it the same way you did economics. If the evil is all in making everything mathematical and in arbitrarily setting definitions, and in transforming empirical propositions into abstract ones, I don't see why you should get excited about physics and look down on economics.

COMMODUS: The evil is not at all in making things mathe-matical nor in arbitrary definitions. Indeed, I would consider the "freedom to define" one of the main conquests of contemporary science. But this freedom has been used differently by physicists and economists. Physicists have always been concerned that their definitions should be such that the reality of experience can be entirely contained in them, and to arrive at definitions that adapt in the most precise way to the essential characteristics of what we see, touch, measure and experience. They are ready to abandon the most stable laws — concepts that had until now been the safest; notions of equality, simultaneity, space, and causality; laws con-cerning the conservation of energy, etc. Indeed, they exhibit a cer-tain arrogance, a sort of iconoclastic ardor that urges them forward even in the face of some conceptual cornerstone, as long as they can fit their science to the concrete reality of the events that take place. Experience no longer serves as an incentive for the creation of a new law. It is instead the starting point for a transformation of all the old definitions, and it matters little if the whole edifice of classical physics crumbles with them — as long as the new edifice under construction is able to take in more of the world. You can in fact see that the only people who argue and oppose this destruction of principles are philosophers. The physicists hardly bother with it — they accept the new formulas (perhaps without understanding them) and use them in the service of wonderful discoveries.

Economics, on the other hand, does exactly the opposite. Its main worry is to save the received laws, come what may in terms of concrete events these laws are meant to apply to. The principle of marginal utility and the law of supply and demand *exist*. If some fact comes along that violates them, it's the fact that doesn't exist. Or, to express it scientifically, it is due to exogenous, psychological, extra-economic causes, but the consequence is always the same — it needn't be bothered with.

And if we ask what these exogenous and extra-economic causes are, the answer we get is that they are causes that contradict the laws of marginal utility, supply and demand, etc. So the proposition takes this wonderful form: "If a fact doesn't come under the laws of supply and demand, this means that it is due to causes that don't allow it to come under the laws of supply and demand."

The difference between physics and economics is the difference between a rash young science, anxious for new discoveries and heedless of stumbling blocks, and an old science, devoid of curiosity or any interest in expanding, and desiring only tranquility, order and tidiness.

Appendix
[*Ernesto Rossi*] *Ritroso to Commodus*

(1) I think this proposition[4] needs to be connected to the one that follows, like this: "doesn't contain any observation etc., as long as it is defined etc." Otherwise, seeing that it doesn't contain any statement about preference scales, the problem you pose would dis-

---

[4]Cf. above, p. 152 ff (editor's note).

appear.

Reading what you wrote in proposing the idea, I thought you were using the word "scarce" in its common meaning of "available in a quantity lower than demand" (demand = a sufficient quantity to fully satisfy need in the unit of time considered). But now I see that you are using it in a way that is "somewhat peculiar." I'll say it's peculiar! No one has ever used an expression like yours: "a unit of a commodity is less scarce than a unit of another for an individual." You admit that maybe it would be better to say "desirable." You are right, but for some time economists have been using the word "preferred" (Pareto's word was "*ofelina*"). When an individual is prepared to give up a unit of A for a unit of B, we don't say that the former is less scarce for that person than the latter, but that it is less preferred. The sense of the word "scarce" that I mentioned allows it to be used with *more* and *less* in reference to the same commodity. When an individual passes from having ten units of a commodity to having only nine, the commodity in the second situation may be said to be *more scarce* if the person's need remains the same.

Quite often in common parlance it is also said that a commodity is more scarce if its quantity diminishes, irrespective of demand considerations; "more scarce" in that case only means "available in a smaller quantity." This meaning alone can lead us astray if it is confused with the previous one. But the most dangerous use of the term "scarce" comes when it refers to different commodities, such as when commodity A is said to be more scarce for an individual than commodity B. For this to make sense it has to be based on a comparison between the ratio of the available quantity of A to the demand for A, and the ratio of the available quantity of B to the demand for B. In any case, even then it could never be inferred that a unit of the scarcer good (with the smaller ratio) has greater utility, and it is a concept that we don't need in economics. When I said that the expression "other scarcer goods" didn't make sense, and that the comparative had to be removed, I wasn't trying to nitpick, o presumptuous Commodus. If you told someone ignorant of physics that you didn't understand the meaning of the expression "rigid body," if they were presumptuous as well as ignorant they would take you for a niggling pedant.

I've spent more time than necessary on this point to try to show you the difficulty of a discussion of the premises of economic science with someone who has never studied it.

(2) That two lire are preferable to one — all other things being equal — is not derived from the fact that 2 is greater than 1 (otherwise two kicks in the teeth would be better than one), but from the fact that every individual prefers greater satisfaction to less (that is, prefers a more complete to a less complete achievement of his or her goals) and two lire give the satisfaction that one alone gives, plus the additional satisfaction of the remaining lira.

And what if the second lira, instead of satisfaction, produced annoyance?

(3) You are such a bumbler. First you define a as the utility of a unit of a commodity, and b as the utility of a unit of another commodity (saying that $a > b$ means that an individual prefers a to b). Then when you write $2\,a > 2\,b$ you have in mind that the quantity (not the utility) of a and b is doubled. If you hold steady the first meaning of a and b a necessary derivative of this is that $2\,a > 2\,b$, because it means that more satisfaction is preferable to less. It is not "extremely dangerous to let mathematics do its work" if you know how to set out the premises. If it were clear to you that the utility of goods is a function of the quantity in which they are available and that all the functions corresponding to various goods are different, it would not even cross your mind to "let mathematics do its work" as if the unitary utilities of the goods were constants. Given $u_a = f$ (α) and $u_b = \varphi/\beta$ (that is, the utility of commodity a is a function of the quantity α of commodity a available, and the utility u_b of commodity b is a different function of the quantity β available of commodity b), if also $f'(3) > \varphi(5)$ no one is going to think that it must be the case that $f'(3 \times 2) > \varphi(5 \times 2)$.

(4) The notations $=, >, <, +, -$ etc. have exactly the same meaning in economics that they have in mathematics — or rather, mathematical economics is an application of the reasoning methods taught by mathematics.

(5) The usual muddle. If a means a kilo of meat "$a = a$" means "a kilo of meat" = a kilo and nothing else. If a on the other hand means the utility of a kilo of meat, then you can't disregard the psy-

chological conditions of the subject and the quantity of meat and other goods available to him. Assuming no variation in time and therefore in the psychological conditions of the subject, then this utility presents itself to us as a function of countless variables f (a, b, c, . . .) but the symbol f (a, b, c, . . .) = f (a, b, c, . . .) has a clear meaning, and it remains true that $\delta f/\delta a = \delta f/\delta a$ — that is, that the marginal utility of commodity a available in a certain quantity is equal to the marginal utility of the same quantity of commodity a, if all the quantities of the other goods remain constant.

(6) Very ingenious, but it is an umbrella that was already discovered some time ago, and in a much handier and more comprehensive form, one that does not lead to the inconvenience you observed of being then forced to use mathematical symbols in a way that is different from how normal math uses them.

(7) This doesn't add or subtract anything. And I don't understand why you went on this long rambling speech, completely off topic.

(8) Often an incompetent buyer takes the price to be an indicator of the quality of the merchandise. It's not hard to imagine a less than rational person who pays six for something they wouldn't pay five for. Other times a high price is "within certain limits" desired as a tool for selecting the group of buyers you want to be part of (think of certain renowned dress designers and milliners, or luxury hotel rooms). These cases, along with others that are more complex, easily fit into the economic models, which from a certain point of view accommodate all practical activity. To explain this in a way that you would understand I would have to write several pages. If the question interests you it would be better if you read Wicksteed; then we can talk again if you still have doubts.

(9) You have to take into account that this statement always implies "other conditions being equal." Robbins points out that, as A. Smith had already shown, a worker may prefer a wage of 10 to one of 15, if the former corresponds to a job that gives greater satisfaction, is healthier, more dignified, etc. Thus, someone who loves the land might prefer an investment that returns 3% rather than 5% because of the satisfaction that comes from land ownership, the prestige it affords, etc. Even though health, prestige, dignity, etc. are not goods sold on the market, their assessment by the interested

parties is part of the data of the economic problem contributing to the determination of the general equilibrium.

(10) For the reasons I gave in n° 2 the highlighted part of the proposition is included in the preceding part.

(11) What you have Ritroso saying is rubbish. It is not at all the case that "there are so few of them" and even if it were true, such an objection would show a total incomprehension of the logical problem.

(12) Economists are not all bunglers ready to switch the cards on the table like Commodus. If Commodus, for example, knew how they dealt with the problem of the rise in the poorest consumers' demand for bread relative to the rise in its price (a result of their need to compensate for the forced reduction in the consumption of meat, fats etc.) perhaps he wouldn't come out with such nonsense.

(13) Not true at all. You can complicate the psychology as much as you want — you just have to keep the premise that people act with a view of reaching their goals, because all of economics derives from this. Exogenous factors can, in my view, be involuntary (an earthquake), or else things that for reasons of convenience we don't include in the study we're doing (for example, if I study the economics of housewives, I take market prices as determined, considering the factors that determine their variations as exogenous; if I study the economics of consumers, entrepreneurs, and productive service providers, I take the legal system as determined, along with the relative cost of violating it, and consider the factors that determine variations in it to be exogenous).

(14) You could have mentioned the "reports" of Water-Closet, Kodak and Pinco Pallino.

(15) I hope you understand the physicists a bit better than you understood Robbins; otherwise you won't make much progress in physics.

(16) For me this is a topic for sociology (not economics) and won't produce anything useful. In addition, the statement that once general laws are known "it would not be difficult to predict even the single individual's behavior" strikes me as pure fantasy. Statistically you can establish a close approximation of how many males will be born for every 100 females, but knowing this doesn't help you in the slightest to predict whether your next child will be male or female.

(17) If you like socio-economic studies, there are those of Loria in Italy which are exemplary. Economists do not claim to describe the whole of reality, nor that their science is sufficient to direct human activity as a whole. They work like other scientists who specialize in a certain category of facts or particular aspects of certain facts. Criticizing economists because they don't provide historians with the tools for interpreting history is about as reasonable as blaming physicists because they don't provide recipes for the best way to cook food.

(18) I read these things some time ago in the books of Poincaré (who wrote forty years ago). Poincaré explained very clearly that you could say that the earth stands still and the whole universe moves around it, but it is more useful to say that the earth moves.

(19) Commodus's pomposity is hilarious. He doesn't take into account that methodological progress never remains within a single science, nor that all sciences are more or less permeated with the same spirit that he considers exclusive to physics. Economics in particular immediately felt the influence of the new developments in physics because its best scholars were and are expert mathematicians.

(20) All these last pages just show what a lightweight Commodus is — spouting sentences on a topic he knows nothing about. It's how I might look if I started holding forth about sinology trying to teach sinologists what they should do and how they should do it.

[Eugenio Colorni] Commodus to Ritroso

I see you haven't had your fill of easy victories. If your aim was to show that you know economics and I don't, you've achieved it in full, to your everlasting glory and satisfaction. But if I wanted to throw back at you these insinuations about my abilities in the sciences I deal with, I would have to say that with all your wizardry, you haven't even managed to clear up my doubts. I won't say it because I'm sure you would have got there quite easily yourself if you had let my mistakes and inaccuracies lead you to what I was trying to say, instead of just venting your spleen.

If a dilettante or beginner in scientific theory comes to me and talks about a "rigid body" in a sense that is mistaken and different from how physicists use the term, I would try and understand what concept is being obfuscated behind the improper use of it; and I would try not to yield to the petty satisfaction of catching him out over every word. No offense, but that would be what in Italian they call pedantry.

I don't want to take this way of arguing you have seriously — it's probably just a reaction to my aggressiveness and a reflexive anger left over from other discussions. And I still haven't given up the hope that you will be an open and expert guide to the problems of economics rather than a jealous and small-minded priest of the temple of science.

This method of mine — you're right — is supremely presumptuous and irritating; but for me it's very useful, since it allows me, among other things, to take in fundamental concepts with greater awareness, without having them imposed on me, and without losing that certain detachment with respect to the sciences that is still necessary for the critic and the methodologist. An idea takes shape much more firmly in my mind when it has successfully resisted my repeated attacks than when I have had to learn it from the pages of a manual.

I don't know if this passes in your eyes as a justification. You mustn't think this method of mine is something I consciously seek. I realize this now for the first time, trying to work out why your accusations affect me and at the same time don't affect me.

Concerning your observations, I have certainly taken on board the lesson on mathematics; I had no other intention except to re-invent that umbrella on my own; and of course the way I invented it was uglier and more clumsy and confused than what was already there.

The only point I'm still not clear about is the one indicated in the enclosed leaflet.[5] If you just answer in monosyllables I don't think it will take you more than a quarter of an hour.

[*Eugenio Colorni: Recantation*[6]] *Commodus to Ritroso*

At first I got myself into a serious rage and wrote you an insolent letter in reply. But then, re-reading everything in a calmer frame of mind I saw that you were perfectly right after all. But since your

---

[5]Cf. below, pp. 174–75 (editor's note).
[6]Disavowal of what has been claimed previously (editor's note).

accusations affect me only in a certain special way, I want to explain some things to you purely as a clarification at a personal level:

It is right to expect that someone approaching an unfamiliar science should do so with his mind "on bended knee," ready to learn, that is, rather than criticize. He observes, and quite rightly, a long and silent apprenticeship, and it is only at the end of this that he can grant himself a place in the conversation.

All this is right (and I say it without the slightest irony). But the outcome is that a person usually does only one of these apprenticeships and then remains stuck there for the rest of his life. You specialize in a subject and never leave it, except for amateur excursions taken out of curiosity.

This is not allowed to me at the moment, since my most specific interests are directed toward the methodology of the sciences. And since it would appall me to apply a top-down solution to the problem, devising a couple of philosophical criteria and treating them as keys that would open all doors, I am forced to approach each science not seeking to learn about it generically, but committed rather to observing its internal mechanisms with a critical eye and drawing conclusions that are not philosophical generalizations, but can actually help the science itself move forward. If I want to do this, it's clear that I can't expect to escape the most demanding apprenticeship in each of the sciences I approach. And I wouldn't dream of escaping. But I can try and make the experience more enjoyable. The method I have unconsciously arrived at is this:

Rather than approaching ponderous treatises passively, content to settle in and just absorb the material the way it's presented, I start out with my lance at the ready, full of wrongheaded, confused ideas, breaking down doors at every turn, inventing defenses, eager for clashes and battles. I emerge from every one of these engagements bruised and battered (as in this case with you) but with clearer ideas. Every knockout takes me a step closer to understanding the science. I don't avoid studying, of course, and I do read the treatises, but I get more enjoyment taking them on as impassioned fighters rather than loving pedagogues. With the understanding, of course, that there will be no tantrums; one must be ready to recognize defeat.

[Eugenio Colorni] "Fight, but Listen!"[7]

Transcribing your note (2)

"That two lire are preferable to one — *all other things being equal* — is . . . derived from the fact that every individual prefers greater satisfaction to less (that is, a more complete to a less complete achievement of his or her goals) and two lire give the satisfaction that one alone gives, plus the additional satisfaction of the remaining lira."

I am not questioning whether this proposition is or isn't implicitly contained in the other one: "People use preference scales."

I am asking: Do you think the proposition in your note (2) is necessary to establish the law stipulating contraction of demand with an increase in prices? That is, that such a law wouldn't be valid unless your proposition was?

2nd Question: Do you think it theoretically conceivable that there could be people for whom the possession of one lira is, other things being equal, preferable to the possession of two, in the sense that the second lira, added to the first, forms a single whole that is unpleasant to possess — so that the possession of two lire is for such a person something different from "one lira + one lira," and is instead something unitary: the state of "possession of two lire," different and not preferable to the state of "possession of one lira." Do you think the existence of such a person is theoretically conceivable? Other things being equal, of course.

3rd Question: Assuming you respond in the affirmative to the first two questions, do you think that in a market where the people described above were participants, the law about the contraction of demand with an increase in price would cease to operate? All I need is answers like Yes or No.

[Ernesto Rossi] Ritroso's Answers

1st) Yes

2nd) To me it doesn't seem conceivable. The "greed for gold" is

---

[7]This is the "enclosed leaflet" mentioned above in the second fragment (editor's note).

justified in a monetary economy by the desire to obtain the greatest possible cooperation of other people and the greatest possible availability of material means for the achievement of one's ends, whether selfish or altruistic, ascetic or epicurean.

If you give the expression "other things being equal" the meaning it should be given, I believe you will be convinced. Even imagining individuals so extravagant as to prefer an object at the price of two lire rather than the same object for one only because they liked hearing the seller say "two lire" more than "one lira," we should say that in addition to the object they were also buying the satisfaction of hearing these words.

3rd) Having answered that I can't conceive of them, the third question evaporates. Just for curiosity's sake I can tell you that Pantaleoni, in *Principi di Economia Pura* [*Pure Economics*], after having erroneously placed the hedonistic principle at the basis of all economic analysis, wonders what would happen if he started instead by recognizing a force opposite to the usual one, writing (on page 10) "altruism . . . would, if universal and isolated, *produce the same effects as egoism*," so that "it would probably be convenient to work out the problems relating to it in terms of egoism, just as it is sometimes convenient to invert the signs in an equation in order to solve it." If you're interested you can also read in the text the examples he gives in the notes, examples that as far as I'm concerned show what a simplistic concept he had of "egoism" and "altruism." (The "altruist" doesn't try to do the maximum good for whoever he's conducting business with, whoever it is, but always discriminates to get the best result, given the limited means available, according to his own concept of the world — that is, according to his own goals.) If you are able to conceive of your hypothetical person not as a general type, but as an exceptional type valid within certain limits (for example, preferring to pay two lire to paying one, but not paying 1000 lire to paying two) you could perhaps keep all the results of the economic analysis without going back to the individual curves, contenting yourself with the equilibrium positions resulting from the collective curves (curves expressing the overall quantities supplied and demanded on the market at all possible prices from 0 to infinity).

Just for the sake of simplification, economists generally admit for the hypothesis that 1st) the judgment on the utility of an object does not vary during the negotiation.

2nd) The individual we are dealing with should be considered only as a means, and it is not in any way assumed that his goals are the same as ours.

To make the analysis easier it helps in short to imagine each of us in front of automatic vending machines; by putting goods and services in some of them we get money, and putting money in others we get goods and services. This simplification makes the meaning clearer of "other things being equal" and highlights the absurdity of imagining an individual who prefers paying two lire to one lira.

8. Eugenio Colorni, Altiero Spinelli, and Giuliana Pozzi: On Action[1]

[Writer: Colorni]

SEVERUS (*to Genevieve, walking excitedly along a lush, tree-lined avenue*): You know, if I'm being honest I have to tell you I really get irritated with speeches like the one Commodus made the other night when he was talking about next year as if he were going to be in this place forever. I see behind this such a level of resignation, of sloth. You should know that all that shines is not gold — nine tenths of these martyrs you see around you are people for whom internment is actually an excellent arrangement. People who wouldn't know what to do with themselves if they went home — they would end up married and unable to put their lives back together. For these people this peaceful and monotonous life, these little acquired habits, this honorable company and the illusion that the sacrifice they're making is admired by the whole world — all this has turned into something not only tolerable, but comfortable and pleasant. Their conscience is always clear, they don't have to work, make choices or act. Everything is decided for us; we have no responsibilities. I know some who were terrified at the prospect of not having their term renewed at the end of the first five years. Now I'm not saying that Commodus is one of these — quite the contrary. But still, this going on of his about the long term bothers me. He takes things too calmly, with too little desire to live life seriously. In a moment like this. . . .

COMMODUS (*coming up behind them*): I heard everything you said. You should know, dear Genevieve, that for several months now all he's done is taunt me every chance he gets for the mediocrity of my feelings. When I was an adolescent, I had three older cousins who made it their task to remind me at every turn how far I was from the ideal of virtue and morality that they perfectly

[1]Checked by Nicoletta Stame on 29.11.2016 against the autograph text by Eugenio Colrni, Altiero Spinelli, and Giuliana Pozzi kept in the Spinelli Fund at the Archives of the European University Institute at Fiesole (editor's note).

represented. I feel now as if I've returned to that time; only there is just one cousin now, but doing the work of three. And with this difference as well: at that time I felt guilty all the time and took my cousins' admonitions very seriously; now I couldn't care less. But I won't bother defending myself, which right now is of no interest; I just want to say about this criticism of these "professional internees" that I am in perfect agreement with Severus.

As far as his attitude goes, I will say that for the last year and a half he's been jumping around on hot coals with one foot always off the ground, set to leave at a moment's notice. I don't know if he's got his bags packed. Certainly, he doesn't study any more, or work; I think you could count the books he's read in this period on the fingers of one hand. All he does is rehash reprimands and re-criminations — dragging us all into endless discussions, which just between you and me are perfectly useless, since we already know each other's arguments. He overdoes it a bit, don't you think?

SEVERUS (silent, glowering)

COMMODUS: Now the harm isn't so much in his doing this — it's in the consequences, and the effect it has on his friends. He was once the only person in this place who was able to listen to others. In choosing his friends, he did not require that they agree with him. He asked only that they be alive and have something to say. Once, he was the opposite of a moralist: we waged a struggle together against these people whose whole life consists of strutting about with a dig-nified, or disdainful, or decorous, or impetuous attitude — against people afraid of contaminating themselves with unclean contacts, and whose only concern is keeping their conscience and reputation immaculate.

SEVERUS: Yes, yes, that's all well and good. Those were fine things for quiet times; Huxley-style amusements. Today I couldn't care less about this stuff. Now we've come to the crunch.

COMMODUS: There — it's precisely this obsession with be-ing at the crunch, when in actual fact there's nothing concrete that can be done. It wrecks the nerves. You have now become the most exclusive of exclusivists, the most moralistic of moralists. You once said "*chacun tue ses puces à sa façon.*" Today, if someone kills his fleas in his own way, you might at the most let him be your ally —

but not your friend. To be your friend, he would have to kill them exactly the way you do — that is, with the same reactions and the same idiosyncrasies, with the same disdain, the same passions and the same impatience. He would also have to have one foot off the ground and his bags packed. If by chance he thought in the meantime that he might sit down for a while and pick up a mathematics book, you would get irritated and upset; you would despise him. His feelings are mediocre. His passion doesn't burn with sufficient heat. But I tell you, I'll always have my mathematics book with me wherever I go. And if it bothers you it's not my problem.

Perhaps all this is necessary. Perhaps an organizer, a politician can't be any other way. But it could also be that this shrinking and closing yourself off does real harm to the politician as such; and that a more capacious humanity, an eye that is more attentive and benevolent toward what is different from itself, might be an actual condition for success. What do you say, Genevieve?

GENEVIEVE: I say that this speech amazes me. I wasn't aware of any of this.

COMMODUS: Yes — in fact, for the last few days things have been a bit different. Otherwise I wouldn't even have had the courage to write these lines. It took you women to make our relations a little more human; they had threatened to shrink into a series of traded opinions and mutual incompatibilities.

[Writer: Spinelli]

GENEVIEVE: It would appear that we women are only able to achieve such results on behalf of others. I haven't been able to establish a more human relationship with Severus. I've offered my friendship and . . . well, I won't say he refused it — but pretty close. He treats me with malicious condescension, he welcomes me one day at a time, and if from one day to the next he were deprived of my company he would remain perfectly unruffled and go on sneering, ready to turn his squalid arrogance on others.

SEVERUS: Here I am, brought down like in the ending of the *Calzolaio di Messina* [*The Shoemaker of Messina*].[2] Behind the two

---

[2]Play by Alessandro de Stèfani, 1925.

of you I see other ghosts rising with other, or I should say, always the same reproaches: indifferent, without mercy, mind of a ruler, willing to understand only those who revolve around me, and so on. And since one memory leads to another, a long line of ghosts from the past rise before me with the same words on their lips. I confess that I didn't sleep well last night mulling it over and cursing Commodus because he was right.

COMMODUS: So if you recognize that I was right, my counterattack was a success.

SEVERUS: A great success indeed. – But tell me, commodious Commodus, have you ever been drunk?

COMMODUS: No.

SEVERUS: And you, Genevieve?

GENEVIEVE: Oh! What do you take me for? And what's it got to do with what we're talking about?

SEVERUS: You should get drunk sometimes, you who don't know the intoxicating feeling of action, to get an idea of it from the similar feeling wine produces. For the drunk, everything vanishes except the act he is about to perform, and he rushes to it, oblivious, not realizing how limited and senseless what he's doing is. That's how it is with action. – It isn't true that I'm always ready to leave, anxiously waiting for what tomorrow will bring. Yes, it's true that I sometimes feel like Orpheus, a monkey in the Rome zoo that would suddenly fling himself against the bars, seize them with all four hands and feet and shake them frantically. But these are only momentary bursts of madness, and they're not even that frequent anymore — I've known for ages how pointless they are. The shrinking that Commodus reproaches me for doesn't come from them; it is due to a wave of activity that has gripped me for the last few months and is now coming to an end.

And taking action always involves finding yourself in a state of exhilaration in which you neglect and forget the Apollonian quiet of friendship.

COMMODUS: But all this is very animalistic and unbalanced. You have to know how to maintain the necessary detachment from your work, to keep yourself for yourself, and for your friends.

SEVERUS: Yes, it is fairly animalistic. But do you think it's so easy being human? It hasn't been for me. It's been like discovering an unknown land that I was led to reluctantly by a woman's hand. I'm like a drunkard led to sobriety by the Salvation Army. Show a little understanding and let me occasionally fall totally back into my old vice.

COMMODUS: But you'll end up not being able to get free of it and also not achieving that success you're looking for.

SEVERUS (in a low voice): Beast! You think what matters is success! (out loud) – I hope not, but it's possible my thin veneer of humanity will go by the board and all that's left will be the animal of action. What to do?

The memory that kept coming back to me the other night, because it summed up the whole matter in a few strokes, was this.

Imagine me at 18 years old — almost your age, Genevieve — sitting in a university classroom. The professor was delivering his lesson. I was daydreaming and contemplating an attractive classmate I had something of a crush on. Suddenly, one of the usual political quarrels of the time heats up in the courtyard. I get up to go out. It was almost perfectly pointless going out there and I would have preferred the lesson of that pair of eyes. I felt no duty ordering me to go and challenge the bullies. I just wanted to be a bully myself — possibly more than they did. The girl, who returned my feelings in a general sort of way, grabs my hand and with her lips and eyes begs me to stay. I had never before received such a show of interest from her. For a few moments I explored the sweet idea of sitting back down, of seeing her smile triumphantly and of enjoying my surrender to her. But I was no good at being so human. I smiled at her, let go of her hand and went outside. And still now I call myself a beast.

Your rebuke and invitation is of the same kind. But now I am a little less of a beast and I am able to sit back down at the desk of humanity and understanding, making an act of submission, even if I can't guarantee that I'll stay seated forever. Not everyone can have your happy nature.

COMMODUS: But it's something you have to acquire. It was a painful acquisition for me as well — as you well know.

SEVERUS: No. For you, all you had to do was get yourself free from an ideological superstructure that imposed action on you as an imperative. For you it was going back to what you naturally were. For me it's exactly the opposite. If I free myself from what I have acquired — or rather, what has been given to me — and go back to my own nature, I'll be going back to the pure animal state.

COMMODUS: Rubbish.

GENEVIEVE: But my dear Commodus, if I'm not mistaken it seems that now the exclusivist who wants everyone to be like him isn't Severus — it's you. You've switched sides.

SEVERUS: Dear Genevieve, this is how it always happens. The cards on the table change all the time. And if you dig a little deeper you'll see them change again.

This whole tirade of Commodus's is basically nothing but the irritation of a friend afraid of losing a friend and annoyed at the pain it would cause him — he was being egocentric, seeking appreciation and love, and angry at seeing himself neglected and mistreated.

I myself — I will confess — have had the same fears and irritations, but if he hadn't said something I would certainly have let him go without lifting a finger.

GENEVIEVE: But why? You were saying just yesterday that your friendship was what you cared most about and was the reason you were happy to have come to Ventotene.

SEVERUS: The reason would take a long time to explain and would probably lead to the next switching of the cards on the table that I mentioned earlier.

What people are at heart is always something different from what you see, and anyway, no one knows if that heart is the real one — or if another, darker one lies concealed within it.

Commodus is deprived of what I call a Dionysiac sense of life — that is, a sense of communion with the rest of the world. He therefore cultivates all his ties with others as carefully as he can, because if he does not look after them, others would remain strangers and he would be left alone. He is like a spider with its web stretched out in all directions. This is his humanity.

I, as I told you, am much more of an animal and my humanity lies in detaching, not attaching myself. Detachment, however, means that you end up accepting life — the original communion — with something approaching contempt. Come or go or conform as you wish.

GENEVIEVE: I don't understand any of this.

SEVERUS: I no longer understand much of what I'm saying, either.

[*Writer: Colorni*]

COMMODUS: Now I'm the one who is starting to feel bad, and not sleep at night, and acknowledge my guilt. And seeing myself described in this way I hate and despise myself deeply. And yet I'm sure that if I got up a head of steam I could change the cards yet again and make my situation a little more presentable. I'm not going to for obvious reasons of taste. Now I think the real reason two types as different as you and me can be friends is this ability we both have to despise ourselves deeply and sincerely, and still basically be more than satisfied to be the way we are. If you were a pure Dionysiac animal, simply drunk on action, you would be much less interesting. Think how many of them there are among our enemies!

The curse is that we are stuck here elbow to elbow. How often I've cursed this chicken-coop lately and longed for six months or a year without having you underfoot. You know how happy we'd be to see each other again? And as for you, Genevieve, don't take his self-possessed posing too seriously. All men, when there's a woman around. . . .

SEVERUS (*enraged*): Will you stop? We can do without your advice and your marital experience.

PS (*Question for Severus*): I wish you would write a little chapter on "Being and Doing." In my opinion you, after all, are on the side of Being, even though you think you're for Doing. You are essentially in favor of "Doing as a way of being." And everything written here shows it.

Appendix

SEVERUS: This whole tirade of Commodus's is basically nothing but the irritation of a friend afraid of losing a friend and annoyed at the pain it would cause him — he was being egocentric, seeking appreciation and love, and angry at seeing himself neglected and mistreated. . . .

COMMODUS: True. But this ill-treatment you inflict on me, what is it but the irritation of the friend who would be the most devoted, faithful and blind participant in your struggle, the most unstinting in his dedication and support? I remember one day you were gently scolding me because, just out of friendship, I was about to do something that went against my own convictions. I didn't do it, and now you're scolding me again, and not gently this time, for not doing it.

SEVERUS: Me?! I am very careful not to expect anything like this from you.

COMMODUS: Let's avoid the stupid compliments. I don't believe, like Kant, that marriage is a pure contract. But my position is a bit like that of the father who, before giving his daughter to her hot-blooded lover, would like to make sure he isn't just interested in satisfying his raging passion, but has the will and ability to establish a healthy and solid home. Now, at my every attempt to investigate this, you answer only that your love is strong and that for the moment that's all you care about. Indeed, when it comes to a healthy and stable home you affect a certain contempt. For my part, since I know you are a serious and intelligent person, I would very much like to entrust my daughter to you even without any guarantee. But you understand that I have to keep my eyes open because, if as a friend I want your happiness, as a father I want the best for my daughter and for the well-being of the whole family, not to mention a large and robust bloodline.

[*Writer: Pozzi*][3]
Genevieve and Commodus (placidly sitting under one of the trees of the verdant avenue, head to head, under the irate gaze of M. Champagne).

GENEVIEVE (*following your line of thought*): My dear Commodus, I am not surprised at all by this denunciation, since on that famous evening when I added my words to his, I too noticed a sign of irritation on Severus's face (a face that I have begun to know) and

---

[3]The part of the dialogue that follows is written on two sheets of notebook paper, folded as if they were a letter, and written on the outside, apparently addressed to Eugenio Colorni is the phrase: "To the Professor with condescension (on his part)."

therefore what you've actually done is express my own confused thoughts. Concerning the criticism of the "professional internees," I wouldn't generalize too much — in spite of all the advantages of their position the attraction of life is too strong, and I think that nine tenths, not one tenth, would want to escape, even considering the hardship they would have to face and the uncertainty of having to remake their lives. As for that one tenth — they make do with what they've got not so much because the present position gives them material and spiritual comfort, but because they are so lazy and inert that they would be satisfied with even less comfortable conditions just as long as they didn't have to make any effort to get out of them and look for something else. In short, it's not especially that the conditions of political confinement are good enough for them, but that any conditions would be.

But this accusation of sloth (which indirectly affects me too, because, if you remember, I agreed with you) — I would change it to an accusation of wisdom, because it is the wise person who doesn't bring events to a head but awaits them calmly (perhaps with a book of mathematics), ready to move when the thing is so close that it can be caught by the hair — rather than anxiously preparing programs and making proposals that perhaps when the time comes either are not needed or can't be used. Of course, this sort of impatience generates a continually irritated and irritating mood, and I agree on the emptiness of it. It prevents you from listening and therefore from understanding other people's feelings and attitudes — something that might modify and perhaps improve your own.

But about this, and confident of your intelligent understanding, I want to bring to your attention a passage from a brief conversation that took place between me and Severus.

Genevieve and Severus (languidly lying in the arena, in the shade of a rich and coveted umbrella, at a suitable distance from each other — unfortunately — under the evil gaze of a few soldiers and many internees).

SEVERUS (*going on with what he was saying*): . . . I am really happy to have found friends such as Colorni; thanks to *them* alone I'm happy to have left Ponza with all its advantages (including a washerwoman). They are living people, who continually inspire in you a variety of ideas or help you explain others that were bouncing around confusedly in your head (see Severus's first diary page). This is why Colorni is a true friend, even though he is sometimes or often irritating when he speaks (Genevieve nods) with that tone that doesn't admit reply, or that he thinks doesn't, trying almost to impose on others judgments about facts and people that are exclusively his own, perhaps even trying to impose them with the power of his voice, weakening his argument in the process (*the conversation between G. and S. continues in another direction*).

GENEVIEVE: At this point, if I were Phaedrus (the only moralizing storyteller I know) I would plainly spell out the moral of the story, but following my confidence in human understanding, I will leave the conclusion to be drawn by whoever is interested.

9. Eugenio Colorni and Altiero Spinelli: On Success[1]

[*Writer: Colorni*]

COMMODUS: Another point where I am doomed to look bad is this business of success. "Beast, you think what matters is success!" In other words, even here I am petty and mediocre.

All right, then. I believe you're perfectly sincere when you say you don't care about success. The explanation you gave is utterly comprehensive. What matters to you is action for its own sake, living, doing, fighting. Succeeding is secondary. If you get the chance, this is how you'll enjoy life, channeling your energy in this way, and nothing else will worry you. If success comes, so much the better. But it's not why you jumped into the fray.

Great. Wonderful. But for somebody who was somehow counting on you, and who wanted to offer you certain philosophical ideas and attitudes they had no personal use for; you should understand that it matters very little whether or not you are having a good time, or have found your own way of blowing off steam. For someone like that the essential thing is that you think and behave in such a way as to actually accomplish what you set out to do.

Now the company of such people is something you crave, something you seek and need. You can do without the Apollonian joys of friendship, but you absolutely can't do without a certain number of people who have faith in you. This is part of your original communion with life, what you call your animal nature. Now I think that if these people were mere companions at an orgy, crazy for action the same as you, in a very short time you would be disgusted with them and with yourself. And I think this is the underlying reason you've chosen the path you have and not the other.

The fact is, the main reason I sometimes find it impossible to

---

[1]Checked by Nicoletta Stame on 29.11.2016 against the autograph text by Eugenio Colrni and Altiero Spinelli kept in the Spinelli Fund at the Archives of the European University Institute at Fiesole (editor's note).

sympathize with you is precisely this need of yours to blow off steam, this restlessness as an end in itself, this going around *"quaerens quem devoret."*[2] It's something I admire and which fascinates me in a way, but I can't help but feel that behind it all there's something that's cranking away but not getting any traction. If you should one day find yourself involved in serious action, I wouldn't want to be too close to you — we would be squabbling forever. But I would love to run into you every now and again and clap you on the back. You would tell me to go to hell, but maybe you would avoid some pratfall.

SEVERUS: I can't fault what you've said in any way. But if I were to answer you honestly I would say that the only way to avoid the pratfall is not to worry about it. I don't know why, but I have an almost mystical belief that success comes to those who don't look for it, who act *ex abundantia cordis,*[3] for the joy of the action, without schemes or cheap tricks or subterfuge. I once started writing you a letter about "command." I don't expect you to have faith in me; but if you do, then follow me without too many ifs and buts, without too much clapping on the back.

COMMODUS (a little discouraged) – It's true, yes, it's true . . . . I don't know — I would like you to experience what happened to me with that poet; I wish someone would just ask you point-blank: Why do you concern yourself with politics? And you would get sick of it for months, and be forced not to worry about it anymore. I can't explain it. . . . It seems to me that you love that "blond beast" inside you too much to actually be a blond beast yourself.

[*Writer: Spinelli*]

SEVERUS: I concern myself because I think I have something to say that others aren't saying (the hell with modesty!). There have been whole years when I have been involved only externally, applying a kind of "interim morality." Sometimes — but can I say this? and you won't misunderstand? — I hope things in the world turn out in such a way that I can't take part any longer. But whether or not I do doesn't seem like something that's entirely up to me, but

---

[2]"Looking for someone to devour."
[3]Out of the abundance of the heart.

comes from my strong connection with others, from my having or not having something to say to them. I accept the possibility of being chucked aside like a squeezed lemon. I don't want to be let off the hook at any cost. In the end, maybe I'm doomed. In the same way, I happily accept having to die, and sometimes I hope it happens soon.

If I were to ask you why you love a woman, do you think you would have an answer? All the reasons you could think up would only amount to the simple reassertion of the fact that you love her.

Politics also has a nonsensical quality similar to love, at least in politicians of great stature who feel they need people and that people need them. Caesar, Wallenstein, Bismarck, Cavour, Hitler are made of this fabric.

It would be a very mediocre lover who got so upset that his love dissolved when he discovered that instead of arising from a pure source of energy, it came from something passive in him, from a need for communion with the other person. A good lover, observing his captivity, rejoices that the other person and not himself is the origin of the call he has answered.

COMMODUS: All this is true and what I have always preached. But it has nothing to do with political activity, which is just an abstract relationship with other people deriving from the necessity of satisfying certain concrete social needs. There's nothing about it that's similar to love.

SEVERUS: This is as stupid as when Kant, who obviously knew nothing about love, talked about marriage as a pure contract.

Social needs and political institutions are the necessary framework, but they're not the living flesh and blood of politics. If you can't understand that, just admit that you haven't understood anything we've been talking about.

COMMODUS: Also, I'm not exactly a novice on the subject.

SEVERUS: That doesn't matter. Almost everybody loves or has loved. Yet how few there are who know what love actually consists of.

And they don't know because they are either incapable of sobering up from it, or else they periodically sink back into it with the same hollow obtuseness we see when drinkers go back to their wine after a long abstinence, to forget everything — but without maintaining any detachment in their drunkenness. These are people with no sense of irony. But Caesar and Wallenstein were not just leaders of men; they didn't just lead wars and revolutions and develop grandiose plans; they were also epicureans able to view their own work with a clear and unclouded eye.

Now looking at your work with an unclouded eye is the surest way to see it dry up and to come to hate it, when you have been going back to it to somehow as a safe refuge — that is, when it has sprung from a very superficial source. But if the source is deep an ironic eye won't dry it up — it won't be able to.

Your poet embarrassed you because philosophy was something that for you was a defense against yourself. But what if it hadn't been? If thanks to philosophy you had not felt healthy but sick, if for you it had been not just an activity but an experience of love, do you believe that you would have so easily detached yourself from it? His question would only have led you, if you had not yet noticed it on your own, to making you see how irrational it was and you would have accepted being rationally irrational.

And you are right to say that the mere company of fellow orgy participants is disgusting, and that this disgust has been one of the main reasons for my separation from them. In fact, even though I know how to drink, I normally don't. Anyone in a continual orgy is in it to dull the senses. Instead *you have to know how to get drunk when the table is all laid out and when the glass arrives at your lips on its own.* Then you can happily give in because you are sure you won't get lost, and you can smile serenely at the poor teetotaler shaking his head in disapproval at your fall and explaining to you that there are other, wiser ways of balancing and enriching your soul.

COMMODUS: I still say it seems like the wheels are getting no traction.

Your enthusiasm for the happiness of the blond beast conceals an attitude of disgust and sadness. You can't deny it, since you've had no hesitation in showing it on various occasions, even in this same dialogue.

SEVERUS: As far as I can tell, I would say that sadness is a necessary aspect of detachment, one that comes after the feeling of panic. It's not that its function is to suffocate it, but sadness is the clear eye of contemplation — the daughter of loneliness that must be overcome.

COMMODUS: Anyway, who knows precisely what comes before and what after?

SEVERUS: Truly. Who knows? But right now it really seems to me that this is how things are.

[Writer: Colorni]

COMMODUS: I've underlined a sentence of yours on the previous page. I would like you to adopt it as a motto. I ask nothing else. But you are like the person who does nothing during lent but dream of luncheons and banquets; and, hearing that over at the neighbors' there's a dinner party going on, runs down to the restaurant and gets drunk by himself, fantasizing about being at the party. The effect of this sort of moral masturbation is squalid and shriveling, and gives the impression of wheels spinning in a void.

SEVERUS: Perhaps. In any case, you might have a little pity for a poor wretch who for the last fourteen years. . . .

COMMODUS: I have very little in the way of pity. In these same fourteen years, if you had been on the outside you would have become a habitual drunk, a slave of wine, unable even to enjoy it anymore. You can thank fate, which has saved you in spite of yourself, and kept you sober and fresh for the final drink.

10. Altiero Spinelli and Eugenio Colorni: On detachment and death[1]

Diese Rede ist niemand gesagt, denn
der sie schon sein nennt als eigenes
Leben, oder sie wenigstens besitzt als
Sehnsucht seines Herzens
— Meister Eckhart[2]

SEVERUS: I don't ask for success, as strong as my need for it is. I accept rejection, failure, being cast aside like a squeezed lemon. The same way I accept having to die, much as I need to live.

COMMODUS: This I absolutely cannot abide. And nor do I appreciate this dismissive attitude. There was a time when I surely would have admired the strength of someone who could say: "Sint ut sunt, aut non sint."[3] Now it no longer seems like strength. It's a demonstration of weakness, this not knowing how to be different from what you are. "Accept me as I am" is your motto. Don't you realize how deeply you are affected by that pharisaic moralism that you mock at every opportunity? The attitude of a strong person is another thing entirely. He doesn't accept rejection — he needs to succeed, to be chosen, he actually wants it. Therefore he does not set conditions for his being selected, but takes pains to grasp it in whatever form it may come to him. His ear is not tuned only to a single note, but to any voice that might resonate.

---

[1] Dialogue checked by Luca Meldolesi on 18.11.2016 against the typescript and autograph text by Spinelli kept in the Spinelli Fund at the Archives of the European University Institute at Fiesole (editor's note).

"This dialogue actually unfolded in a very unusual environment. The first part was written by the interlocutor called *Severus* [Altiero, at Ventotene], the second by *Commodus* [Eugenio, at Melfi]. This explains the different accentuation that the various arguments take on during the discussion, and also explains some personal references, which we did not presume to remove [at the time of the subsequent collation of the two texts — Note on the original]."

[2] "This speech has never been spoken, because he already calls it his own life, or at least keeps it as the longing of his heart."

[3] "Let them be as they are, or not be at all."

He alone has truly freed himself from weakness, from the vanity that might lead him to march in a certain direction just because he wants to, even though the necessary direction may be different. Take the scientist — the best model of the type that I can give you. He doesn't accept failure. What he gives up is the idea that scientific discovery has to be done the way he himself has predetermined it. He gives up knowing in advance what he will discover. He gives up all but one thing: successful discovery. And only by completely refusing to make a fetish of the science that's already been done will he be able to discover something. It's like this in any field you name. The essential thing isn't wanting this or wanting that. This and that "will come to us." The essential thing is being among the elect, or in plainer words, contributing to doing the this and that that need doing. Then there is no danger of ever being rejected and condemned. Something, surely, will always succeed.

SEVERUS: Is succeeding, being chosen, really so absolutely essential?

COMMODUS: I don't know if it's important or not. I'm not interested in these value judgments. Being chosen, the way I mean it, is synonymous with living, and whatever the importance of living might be — it's something we experience. Your declaration of indifference about death is just posturing. The fact is, you're not going to kill yourself. You will go on living — succeeding at something, even if it's radically different from what you arrogantly but stupidly would have liked to succeed at. For example, having these conversations rather than leading disruptions.

SEVERUS: As a preacher, you're not bad, the way you shut your opponent's mouth so definitively. Faust could have arrogantly replied to Mephistopheles' objections: "Allein ich will."[4] But in that case it was rhetoric against rhetoric. In this case, after such a clear invitation to sobriety, any impetuous answer of the sort that inevitably comes out in the heat of a discussion would seem ridiculous and artificial even to the one who pronounced it. The words die on my lips, and I will therefore limit myself to telling you that your arguments are not unreasonable, but show that you don't have the

---

[4] "I alone desire."

slightest clue about what is really going on here.

COMMODUS: Well then, explain it better. But I don't believe it could be about anything other than what I've said. Now you're going to embark on a series of considerations whose only purpose will be to conceal the unpleasant side of yourself that I have exposed.

SEVERUS: I will try to make you understand, if I can. I hope you don't expect me to lay out a line of reasoning that forces you to give your assent. I'm just going to try and give you an idea of how I see things. To do this I first have to describe how you see them, to get you to see that looking at things differently doesn't necessarily mean seeing them in a way that's false and incomplete compared to your perfect and correct way. And I would like you to believe me when I say that in doing this I'm not trying to preach to you the way you do with me; I'm not trying to steer you away from a false path and put you on the right one. I accept you as you are. I just wish you were able to understand two things instead of just one.

You are a seeker.

COMMODUS: Oh. The great discovery! And who isn't a seeker?

SEVERUS: Perhaps a lot of people are. And you're also of a breed educated for millennia to seek. Seeking means not having and needing to have. There are endless things you can look for. But it's not for us here to specify what they are. What matters to me is the fact of expectantly stretching out your tentacles in every direction trying to grasp them. – How to do it in the best possible way? If you examine all your work of spiritual catharsis, you immediately see that it all comes down to answering this question. For a while you pursued the idea that what you needed was to be thoroughly armored, to deploy safe and rigid tools, capable of grasping anything. You soon realized that this way you couldn't get hold of anything, that if you wore a steel glove, objects did not adhere to the skin of your hand, and that all you were left with was the measurements of the angles that the components of the glove formed when its fingers closed around the object. So you threw off the glove and in this way achieved the desired bond. You discovered then something that was inaccessible before — that the way your fingers held it, the pressure on the epidermis, came from the object itself. You discovered that in order to get something you didn't need to be domineering, but rather to model yourself on the thing you wanted to embrace, to accept it as it is, welcome it into yourself, be thankful for it as for a gift when it allowed itself to be accepted. This need for passivity was your great discovery and it is certainly very important, since it is the only true path to success. But it wasn't a subversion of the soul — it was only a subversion of the methods that the soul used. This passivity, this softness is only a much more clever and productive method of satisfying the primordial and permanent need to have. And since it is a trick, an intelligent, well thought-out device, it is never meant to be applied spontaneously. The first spontaneous gesture of those who want to get something is to reach out and take it. Only by thinking can you see that you have to wait. But waiting also means ceding the choice of what you can have, and being ready for whatever comes to you. And since something always does come, you end up infinitely richer than if you had been frantically slaving away, determining what to take and how to take it, and thus missing out on a thousand things that maybe just wanted to be taken, but not in the way you had pre-established.

This renunciation, this detachment, this profession of poverty is thus the source of richness. By no longer asking for anything we get everything, since anything that comes our way is a free gift and not the result of a bitter struggle. Not having become hardened in your work, when you finally do possess something you don't run the risk of only enjoying the arid pleasure of the victory achieved, but you know how to relax and savor the thing you have come to possess. Experiencing such happiness it is very natural for you to go around preaching to everyone this simple method necessary to achieve it. My Chinese friend calls it old-fashioned knavery and preaches the same sermon.

COMMODUS: You've described it pretty well. And what do you object to in this method?

SEVERUS: Nothing; nothing at all. I myself am a fan of this detached attitude — concerning anything to do with the desire for possession.

COMMODUS: A year ago I would have been more inclined to believe you. Now though, I can clearly see that deep down you are absolutely immune to it. You are fiercely attached to what you want to possess.

SEVERUS: You need to persuade yourself, if you can, that another kind of detachment is possible, not only separating the desire to have from the objects to be had and the way of obtaining them, but detachment from the very desire to have, from searching itself.

COMMODUS: This seems a bit much to me. Giving up searching means accepting the renunciation of life itself.

SEVERUS: That's exactly what I'm saying.

COMMODUS: What is the point of this monkish detachment? I don't see it leading to anything but perfect imbecility.

SEVERUS: In Mann's *Zauberberg* [*The Magic Mountain*] there is an odd character, quite ridiculous, for whom I felt an unpleasant affinity. It's that big guest of the Magic Mountain who turns up in the second half of the book, the Russian's lover, who ends up taking poison. He can't even produce a complete sentence. His observations are trivial and half-baked. But for the people around him he's like a mysterious source of heat. A mass you can lean on. Not because of anything he does (he doesn't do anything — no one does anything in *The Magic Mountain*). It's just that among all these people who want to take, he's the only one who gives, and therein lies the mystery of his influence. This guy, whose name I don't remember — you can take him as an artistic representation of the attitude of the giver in his grossest animal form.

Now, you see, the problem of giving is very different from that of receiving, even though there is a certain harmonic correspondence. Graciousness, in obtaining something, lies in being ready to welcome whatever comes, in not wanting to prescribe what will be taken. In giving, instead, one must be ready to give without prescribing what will be given. But just as in the first case there is detachment from everything except receiving, so also in this second case there can be detachment from everything except giving. The man who wants to receive something initially feels poor, and gradually gets richer. The man who wants to give, on the other hand, feels rich and gradually gets poorer. He may have the grace to unexpectedly discover new riches in himself, but he cannot seriously believe that he has accumulated them himself through a patient effort of acquisition. What he acquires may or may not be valuable in making him a more productive person, but he knows nothing of this. Therefore the acquisition is accomplished not thanks to an ultimate goal but through detachment.

Someone who wants to acquire something may face death and even be resigned to it, but it will always seem to him like a senseless curtailment of his development. He feels he has a certain right to immortality.

The person who wants to give sees that he will go on as long as he has something to give, and he therefore accepts death as natural when the vein of giving is exhausted. It isn't an act of resignation and renunciation because he has no need of immortality — that is, to keep giving forever. The great acquirers, like Goethe, wanted immortality even if they didn't believe in it. Great givers like Paul called for death even if they didn't believe in it.

People who want to acquire, and have been able to break their chains like you did, can no longer understand what it means to fail. In any case they will always acquire, since wealth comes from outside, and outside there is always plenty to be had.

Those who want to give, however, always know that they can't give anything other than what they have and they therefore understand and accept the possibility of being rejected. And in this there is no bitterness, if it includes the virtue of detachment, since there was no merit in the giving — what they give they never really acquired. The reasoning behind the words that irritated you and moved you to preach against my supposed moralism is therefore, as you see, a little different from what you believe it to be.

COMMODUS: And yet, even someone who is like this, this way that you describe, if he isn't too much in love with himself, ought to be open to changing. Haven't you yourself admitted that such a person has to be ready to give, but not to prescribe what is to be given?

SEVERUS: Yes, you must be willing to accept that the wealth that you want to give can increase or diminish, change or run out. Such wealth is nothing more than a set of relationships with others, relationships that present themselves as a complex of others' problems that you want to solve. (This, in plain words, is what on other occasions I have called the sense of panic toward life; it is, in fact, throwing yourself into a task, not caring about yourself). Therefore you have to know how to listen to others. If you couldn't do that, this richness wouldn't exist — it would be an illusion. But listening doesn't mean accepting what they say and ask for. Listening means trying to understand what they need, which is something that will only be understood, if it is understood at all, by the one who gives and not the one who receives.

COMMODUS: The hell with modesty!

SEVERUS: But this is the way things are with or without modesty. We have seen that those who receive don't really know what it is they need to receive, and that if they are wise they will know how to accept what is given to them.

In the giver, therefore, the attitude of listening must at some point yield to that of being heard, which is, if you like, from the point of view of the acquiring temperament, an impoverishment, precisely insofar as it is giving — moving toward death.

Being heard doesn't mean being a moral model, saying: "Accept me as I am," but rather saying: "Do it like this" (and knowing how to get it done). Saying this is always a risk, because it means getting into a fight whose outcome is not predetermined. Giving does not always mean giving victory, it can lead to ruin.

COMMODUS: What a stupid crazy world.

And yet, since there's no stepping aside from this stupid dance... you dance — I admit it. But without commitment, and all the while seriously dedicating yourself to something else — your own improvement. The realm of happiness is in the attitude of receiving, not giving.

You could also try looking more deeply into the psychology of the giver. You're likely to turn up something abnormal.

What we aspire to is what we don't have, and if we observe that pure giving is giving others a center around which they can move in harmonious rhythm, then there must be a strong suspicion that the giver himself is missing that harmony, that capacity for spontaneous dedication, and that this is why he wants to create it for others; because only in a rhythm he himself has constructed can he find such harmony, and his secret hope is precisely to be able finally to let go of himself. Therefore the donor too, whatever he might claim to the contrary, is an acquirer, even though a failed one. So then what happens to all that wealth he was boasting about?

It seems to me that in the end he is infinitely poorer than the acquirer, but anxious to conceal this irremediable poverty from himself and others.

This is an inability to live wisely and normally.

SEVERUS: Which is much less important than you think, o recovered ex-invalid, o model of perfect health. We are healthy or unhealthy with respect to a certain way of living, not in an absolute sense. – And aspiring to be healthy, having a phobia about illness, is an important need only for the acquirer, who wants properly functioning organs of taste to better savor his acquisitions.

The receiver is a microcosm, the center of harmonization of the gifts he receives, and it is natural that the giver seems to him abnormal. The giver is not a microcosm, a monad; he is part of the cosmos, and his work is directed towards it to make it richer. Now this cannot happen unless he feels lovingly connected by a basic sense of communion with all things. He needs to be sensitive to the harmony of everything — without concern for harmony of his own, indifference toward which is the same as indifference toward what you call his illness.

September 1941

[Drafted by E.C. at M.][5]

COMMODUS: You come back frequently in what you say to the theme of death; and very often it goes together with the theme of fear. You are pleased not to be afraid — to be steadfast. You calmly accept death, just as you accept becoming useless. "We must be ready for every sort of detachment. I believe I can confidently say that I can be ready, that I am not afraid, that I will not waver.."

Why do you force me to say in every letter what I think but would prefer to keep quiet about — that all this is beautiful, one of the most beautiful things I have seen since I've been able to think at all?

SEVERUS: Force you? That's some role you've given me! It seems to me you're the one who sets yourself up as a model...

COMMODUS: This is exactly how you force me. I think it's

---

[5]This is the beginning of the second part of the dialogue, drafted by Eugenio Colorni at Melfi (editor's note).

time to stop with this refrain about me being a preacher, the dispenser of true virtue and the elixir of happiness. I am someone who, having made a psychological observation on his own behalf and at his own expense, argued in support of it for a certain time. But it's a while now that I've stopped doing it. And for a long time I have been specifically working to understand how you are put together, having realized that you are made differently, but in a way that is at least equally human. For quite a while now, as between the two of us, it's you, not me, who's been the model of virtue. And I'm not complaining; indeed I'm glad, since this is the topic we're now discussing.

SEVERUS: Do you see how you are always the same? You're trying to understand how I'm put together — in order to acquire, to enrich yourself, like a miser accumulating treasure. You will never be capable of true generosity.

COMMODUS: That's a different matter. I am made in my own way. Whether I can change and whether it is good that I try to, is a separate issue. I'm just saying it's ridiculous that you continually accuse me of not letting you exist.

SEVERUS: I make the accusation for the sake of the argument. I find it convenient to set you up against me in order to understand myself better.

COMMODUS: And I specifically want to take this polemical device away from you. Find another one. You can easily contrast our two ways of being without continually making this vapid accusation. To show you how far I am now from this preachy attitude about "receiving," I can tell you that I recently read a book by Huxley,[6] and it disgusted me.

SEVERUS: Look, let's get back to where we left off. You were saying, about the fear of death?

COMMODUS: I was saying that's where everything ends and what everything boils down to for all of us, you and me included. You don't fear death; on the contrary, you've actually found a way of life and a spiritual attitude whose natural consequence is this calm in the face of annihilation. But your tone of complacency and triumph when you announce your conquest makes me suspect that

---

[6]Cf., above, p. 178 (editor's note).

it is in fact a conquest; that the indifference you've achieved has its long and painful past of nightmares and terrors. I think you were one of those children for whom "being afraid" was considered the height of humiliation, something that could never be admitted at any cost; and "not being afraid" was the supreme ideal of perfection and virility. It has often occurred to me that many of your attitudes are dictated by a concern not to show fear. Is it any wonder then that you've established being ready to die as the culmination and capstone of what you see as the most right and desirable way of being?

SEVERUS: You really make me angry with your posing as the psychoanalyst. Your versions of things are too simple to be right. I am supposedly, in your opinion, dominated by fear; and this would explain my entire way of being. It seems to me, though, that your diagnosis is too generic and could be made to fit any attitude at all. This is why it doesn't affect me. It is probably true that the fear of death is a primordial underlying feeling in humans, and for this reason it's hardly surprising that a certain amount of this feeling will be a component of any emotional or spiritual reaction. But the point is, it's a fallacy to resort to this feeling to explain a certain specific way of being. I'm saying that if your diagnosis is right for me, then it's right for anyone — you, for example.

COMMODUS: But of course, yes, for me as well. What interests me is the different ways there are of reacting to this fear. Objectively, it would annoy me to die because there are still so many things I would like to do. And thinking about no longer being around is something I almost never do, so I don't know how I would react if I were actually faced with the prospect. But I can tell you one thing. I had a scientist friend who had made a scientific discovery. He told me that during the period when his idea was coming together and he felt he had actually put his hands on a new truth, he went through weeks of actual intoxication that were dominated by the thought: "Now I can die." His imagination had taken this fantasy so far that he said to his wife: "If I should die, my discovery is in this notebook." And it seemed to him that with this he had conquered death. Well, I feel a real kinship with that friend; and in comparing his attitude with yours I realize more and more what my struggles with science mean to me, and my desire to have children, and a lot of other things about myself. Every one of them is a struggle against death, against the unendurable thought of "non-being." They represent the frantic construction of surrogate selves, of things that exist independently of me but are mine and will survive me. For me these surrogates are the only things that can ease the tension and make the thought of dying bearable and a friend.

I say this because it isn't contained in your analysis of me. It is true that in our discussions I have always highlighted the idea of "receiving." Which is, after all, my essential attitude. But at least equally essential for me is conquering death through "doing." Not "giving" nor "receiving," but "doing." This is my inescapable need, and without satisfying it I could never find the calm to freely receive. And by "doing" I mean creating something that stands on its own and is at the same time an extension of myself — something that belongs to me and in which I recognize myself, but whose continued existence doesn't require my presence. This is why I have so often found myself disagreeing with you about the problem of "being" or "doing." For you men of action, paradoxical as it may seem, "being" is everything. What's important for you is "how" and "by whom" a thing is done. What interests you is how you selectively focus your attention and the process of doing a thing and making your action count. Once completed, the thing no longer holds any interest for you. For me, when a thing is completed it holds the ultimate interest of being there, of existing, so that I can then die in peace — or rather, I can live without the fear of dying.

I don't know if you understand me, and if you appreciate for once that I am not remotely claiming that my way is the best way. Indeed, I recognize that the person who is perhaps most seriously ill is the one who has managed to bypass rather than overcome an illness. Your method meets things head on, and is in a certain sense, more courageous. You talk of "detachment from the desire to possess," and you recognize that this detachment means "accepting the renunciation of life itself." Well, let me tell you that this detachment, this renunciation is nothing more than a way of outsmarting death. You know how it works with the guy who is so modest that he strips naked? Or the one who for fear that his secret will get out, reveals it first himself? The psychological process is always the same — the thing you're afraid of, when it is openly desired and spontaneously grasped, loses all its dreadfulness. That's the way it is with death. I try to run away from it by creating a substitute personal life, something that lives in my place, and which I can delude myself that I continue to live in. You want to escape not from death, but from the fear of it, by wanting it in advance, by artificially embracing it yourself, erasing yourself, viewing yourself as a fragment of the cosmos and living a general, universal life, of which your individual self is nothing more than one insignificant contingency. The whole, the cosmos (or, more modestly, society) cannot die. If you can manage to merge with it, to become an integral part of its pulsating life, then you won't die either, whatever might happen to you personally — or rather, you will already be dead as an individual person the moment you dive into that universal communion. From that moment on, nothing terrible or frightening can any longer happen to you. And then you can declare proudly, "I'm not afraid; I'm ready for any sort of detachment that comes along."

That this is true is actually demonstrated by this last phrase, which in a certain sense gives you away. It's the mystical nature (in a positive sense) of your attitude that shows it. It's no accident that you refer to Paul and to Eckhart. No one who wants this kind of detachment, this identification with the whole, is a humble and passive soul capable of living only in relation to others; on the contrary, he is a strong personality who stakes out for himself an important part in this communion, and who wants to identify himself with others only in order to understand them better than they understand themselves, and to guide them in the direction where they, even without knowing it, are destined to go. Forgetting yourself like this is your true way of asserting yourself, of enhancing your strength and your abilities. I don't deny, I repeat, that this is beautiful. And it is of no importance if it originates from an illness. Every one of our moral and spiritual attitudes in some way comes from an illness; and a healthy person, in this sense, would be the emptiest and most amorphous being you could ever imagine. I wanted to analyze these things because it seems good to be aware of them, not because I think they ought to change.

ULPIA (U.H.)[7]: Word of honor, this makes me laugh. Here are two gentlemen, both dominated by the fear of dying, who are doing their best to pretend that death doesn't exist. One sweats and struggles to construct something that will allow him to say: "Non omnis moriar"[8]; the other creates a moral attitude, a personality, whose essence is the satisfaction of not trembling.

And might there not be a third solution — to embrace it, the fear? Not to construct fictitious superstructures, but to look reality in the face just as it is — and if this reality is called death, then call it by its name; and if death is ugly and terrible and fearful, then go ahead and fear it, without pretense and sophistication. For my part, I have known the terror of death for a long time, and I can say that all my childhood, indeed my whole life, has been interwoven with it. But it has never crossed my mind to escape from it, deny it, overcome it, or hide it in some way. I have it and I keep hold of it; and in a way I have made it my friend. I know it by now — it's an old companion from my melancholy days and nights. Listening to you claiming to have defeated it and eradicated it, and then arguing about it the way you are today, you really disgust me a little; and I almost think I'm braver than you. At least, if I may say, more sincere.

COMMODUS: Of course. And especially, healthier. You women, when you are truly women and not being hysterical moralists, are healthier and simpler than we are. This is why you do us good spiritually, and if we want to save ourselves we must look to you. For us, being simple is the most complicated thing there is. But in particular this healthy simplicity of yours, this taking things as they come without fighting, rebelling or "conquering," this is perhaps the secret key to why most of the products of civilization are the work of men. Because civilization, culture, intelligence, action, morality — in short, everything — comes from discontent, or from fear or shame or a sense of guilt that we want to hide or overcome. It doesn't require psychoanalysis to see this — or today's philosopher of the moment, putting "Hingeworfensein zum Tode"[9] at the

---

[7]Ursula Hirschmann (editor's note).
[8]"Not everything dies."
[9]"being cast out to die."

center of being. The fact that we have to die is what gives concrete and finite meaning to what we do; it is what allows us to measure time and to spend it as a treasure that is not boundless; it is what gets us moving, acting, filling this time we have available, creating value, looking forward to the future. There is surely something very healthy and balanced, courageous even, in your acceptance of fear as a constitutional fact, ineluctably tied to your life. But allow the two of us to remain attached to our illnesses — they are so beautiful and amusing, and they so passionately fill our thoughts.

MODESTO (M. R. D.)[10]: I have listened to you so far with some amazement. I'm not used to this sort of introspection; and I don't even know if it is truly useful. What interests me is the concrete side of problems. And here I find myself facing these two fundamental attitudes: "giving" and "receiving." Now I don't want to judge which of the two is healthier or sicker; nor do I want to evaluate them morally. I know that both are justified, each in its own sphere, and that both can lead to optimal results. But in my field of interest, that of practical action, I know that one of them, Severus's, is the one that makes sense and holds value. Not that I despise the other. But the other is the attitude of a scientist, or rather an epicurean of the mind, busy with his own improvement, whose interest in action is basically due to simple intellectual snobbery; it is an individualistic and egotistical (or moralistic) need not to be a stranger to anything, a greedy and mean-spirited "nihil humani a me alienum puto."[11] What drives you to action, o Commodus, is not a true interest in action itself, an emotion, a deep and sincere need to take part in the lives of others. It is instead a sense of duty, a need to be above reproach, to be at peace with your conscience, presentable before any entity of judgment; and a concern that you have to know everything, try everything, and experience everything that might enrich your spirit and widen your mind. Now these things are in the end your own personal business. No one apart from you yourself cares whether or not you go to heaven and save your soul; nobody is troubling about whether your spiritual pleasures are or are not a

---

[10]Manlio Rossi-Doria (editor's note).
[11]"Nothing human is alien to me."

degree closer to perfection. But I can tell you that when you undertake any action and communion with other people with a mind so utterly wrapped up in itself, the result can only be stunted and paralytic, devoid of the breadth and generosity and indifference to its own success that are required for a solid and sweeping achievement. Therefore, the spectacle of a man like Severus, for whom action is neither a duty or an expedient, but a need and a passion, even an illness; a man who struggles not to force himself into action but to hold back from it; who becomes so involved that he forgets himself and almost forgets the aims of the action itself, all so as to be able to immerse himself entirely in the community and mutual understanding of his fellow creatures — a spectacle like this, I have to say, moves and inspires me; and it makes me think that here and nowhere else, certainly not in labored intellectual moralism, is where the truest and most profound way of living is to be sought. Call it an illness if you like, but it's an illness that brings enormous health benefits.

COMMODUS: You're not saying anything I don't believe myself, and my appreciation of Severus's attitude isn't rhetorical but deeply felt. Perhaps it's because I know myself too well, but the fact is that these days it is the attitude opposite to mine that is by far the more attractive. Nor am I hiding the fact that my interest in action is in some ways fictitious and secondary, and due more to reasoning than to instinct. But this recognition doesn't of humiliate me in any sense, nor lead me to conclude that I have to change and try to be different from who I am. This is the grain I'm made of; and with any grain, when you know how to work with it you can make excellent bread.

With this the problem is solved. It's clear that the attitude of "giving" is the only one conceivable for a man of action and the only one that will make his action effective. It is clear that the "receiving" attitude is characteristic of the thinker, and action for him is simply an accessory instrument. It is also clear that you, Severus, are the man for "giving" and that I am for "receiving." But I am still not quite content. I feel I need to add that precisely because I am a "receiver," I have something I can perhaps offer you "givers" something you might find useful, if you care to listen.

Not that I want to take your place. But I would like to accompany you to make sure you don't end up listening only to yourselves. You are the people who, with care, perspicacity, and disinterest, undertake to clarify what needs to be done. This is the first task you face in your work of communing with the world and interpreting its needs. But once it's been decided what needs to be done, it seems absolutely obvious to you that the people who do it have to be you yourselves. If this weren't the case, your communion with the world, your "giving" wouldn't amount to anything. Now I might totally agree with you about what needs to be done; but I am obviously much less tied to the idea that you have to be the ones who do it. I told you that I'm a receiver, but I'm also a man who has a supreme interest in things "existing" in themselves. We have had occasion to see what the psychological process is that this derives from. But I think that as regards yourselves, this process might somehow express the view of people in general, who are essentially interested in things getting done, and are much less interested in the "by whom" of it than you are.

SEVERUS and MODESTO: But don't you see that the "by whom" is everything? And that if the thing is done by others it's no longer the same thing?

COMMODUS: I get it, I get it. But I just want to say, your interest is too passionate and personal, and leads you to work too hard preparing to do things yourselves, and not hard enough on seeing to it that they get done at all. I, on the other hand, precisely because my interest is more lukewarm and reactive, don't dwell so much on action aimed at creating a certain state of affairs, as on the state of affairs itself; I am so well aware of the difficulties that I am ready to accept that the thing will come about through the work and the efforts of someone else. This is, I recognize, the attitude more of a spectator than an actor; but actors perform for spectators, after all, and it is not a bad idea that they should sometimes listen to their audience's opinions.

Appendix: Note of Altiero's on the First Part of the Dialogue (October 1941)

This sketch of a dialogue, which I jotted down last month following your observation at the beginning and then didn't go on to finish, I give to you to read as is. It ran aground because of what almost always happens with me — after a few pages I'm no longer satisfied and I start over. I'm giving it to you to read all the same because there is a certain symbolism I want to pay homage to, meaningless as it is. Our friendship began with a dialogue. Now its initial period is ending with a second dialogue. And it is a dialogue on detachment, on the *Abgeschiedenleit*, the idea Meister Eckehardt met me halfway with a long time ago, and what made me want to meet him.

We are in a moment today when we must be ready for every sort of detachment, in a way that is perhaps much more radical than anyone ever thought.

I believe I can confidently say that I can be ready, that I am not afraid, that I will not waver.

The need to act may burst forth suddenly and tumultuously. In this case we will need to forget, to detach ourselves from all the old grudges and the old bonds, and to focus on what needs to be done. I see myself in this state. It isn't especially admirable. In action there is a kind of mysterious meeting of the needs of the individual with those of the world. It is a coming together in which individuals abandon their idiosyncrasies, and the world turns away from the hard and unyielding features that made it seem to reject individuals and condemn them to solitude. In reality what has happened is that what I have rejected as sterile, the world is also emptying of all content. The way will be vastly clearer than I could reasonably have hoped.

But it may also be that none of this will happen, that no background work is required, and that it is the foundations laid down now that will be applied in the future. A few months ago, or rather even in the previous dialogue that mentioned this hypothesis, I did not hesitate to say that I would leave. Now, on reflection, I see that I had involuntarily submitted to the Manichean idea of the irreconcilable contrast between good and evil, and that in case of victory of the latter there would no longer be any possibility of life for a good person — I mean, very arrogantly speaking, for myself. Now, however, I suddenly realize that even in this case there would be something to do, albeit in a way radically different from the first case. We wouldn't be talking about the collapse of European civilization, but about carrying on with it on the foundation of a German military conquest. It would be the beginning of a long and difficult process of amalgamation, until what was initially a military conquest became civil coexistence. It would basically be the same identical task, but in the first our two cases it would happen very rapidly, in a generation (ours), while in the second it would be spread out over several generations. Should we turn away just because it's going to take so much time? No, the only thing that makes sense is to abandon the restricted field of politics, the organizational field of the existing powers. When the republics were definitively replaced by the rule of lords, a new path opened up for the republican Machiavelli — he was no longer the Florentine secretary, but became a scholar of what had happened and was still going on. And the task was neither easy nor trivial, since it meant opening people's eyes to a new world, one which they already lived in but didn't yet understand. Tomorrow, in the same way, explaining the profound significance of what has happened will be an important part of moving toward the achievement of a European civilization. And to do this, we need neither the stupid and exultant mindset of the winner, nor the frustrated and resentful soul of the loser, but the untroubled heart of the "libertine," who is on a different level from the other two, but one they will need to reach once they have exhausted their arrogance and resentment.

Thinking of all these things now, however, at a moment when everything is still undecided, it seems to me pointless to proclaim them out loud, but in our hearts we need to be ready to accept either one or the other, not as victory or defeat, but as alternative tasks aimed in one direction or another.

And it may therefore be said that only by accepting rejection can one truly manage to escape it. Several months ago I accepted being rejected, in the literal sense of the word — that is, being told by the world: go, you are no longer of any use. — Now I understand that the world may yet meet me halfway, saying: come on then, you still serve a purpose.

This kind of thinking (if I look inside myself) is what comes to me most naturally. But natural thinking isn't easy. You need to overcome a huge number of artificial obstacles, both within yourself and in your environment. Recognizing therefore how much I owe to my friendship with you in helping me think like this, I offer my most wholehearted declaration of gratitude for the two years when we were together every day.

11. ALTIERO SPINELLI: IS WHAT THE GODS WANT SACRED OR DO THE GODS WANT WHAT IS SACRED? (SOCRATES)[1]

(Fragment) Dialogue between Jacolo (Alberto Jacometti) and Sancho (myself), May 1943

JACOLO: I'm sure we'll end up finding that we agree, as soon as you take back your absurd claim that you don't do good, but that whatever you do is good. I absolutely cannot believe this is what you think. If you did think it, you would be a fairly dangerous being, a being I would feel it my duty to kill. But in reality you're a bad boy trying to sound scandalous.

SANCHO: Thanks for sparing my life, at least for the moment. But shall we take a closer look at the whole issue? Do you have the courage?

JACOLO: Courage? Why should I be afraid? I don't shy away from the risks reasoning entails nor the doubts it gives rise to. I am not a coward and I can face up to danger. I will confess to you that I have at times seriously thought about what life's highest values — goodness, I'm talking about — mean to me. And I did not tremble when I said to myself: if these were to collapse around my soul I would kill myself. Please believe me when I assure you there has never been the slightest hint of empty rhetoric in this thought.

SANCHO: I do believe you — Sometimes I feel as if I've been around for millennia — and that I no longer have experiences I haven't had before. And my old soul now smiles at your childishness. But your courage is not enough for our purposes. Indeed, it looks an awful lot like fear. You live, one might say, in an oasis that provides you with food, fresh air, and friends. You assure me that you have pushed yourself to the brink and looked out over the desert and said to yourself: If I were out in the middle of this desert I would die. And you returned with renewed love to the shade and

---

[1]Transcribed by Luca Meldolesi on 18.11. 2016 from the autograph text kept in the Spinelli Fund at the Archives of the European University Institute at Fiesole (editor's note).

the streams of the oasis.

And what is this if not the cold chill of fear and anguish? In one sweeping glance you took in all the powerful beneficial forces that support you and bring you security and tranquility, and you wondered in horror: what would become of me if I detached myself from this?

The courage I ask of you is another thing entirely — I'm asking you not to think about yourself, not to think about what would happen to you out in the desert, but to cross the edge of the oasis and go out into the sands.

JACOLO: What is the purpose of setting out on this arid trek? There are two possibilities. Either you find nothing and you perish by the wayside — at least morally — or, more plausibly, you find another oasis. Here's the thing — if you could offer me even a glimmer of hope that this second oasis was there, and that it was better than the first, I would head off without hesitation, and I wouldn't even ask for any guarantee of getting there. Because I think searching is better than finding. But what you ask is meaningless — you ask me to set out on a journey without knowing where I'm going or why.

SANCHO: (listens without answering)

JACOLO: See? You're embarrassed to answer.

SANCHO: Yes, terribly embarrassed. Because if I were to tell you now the reason for setting out, my answer would seem either presumptuous or banal, and you would drag me into a thicket of useless talk. — I asked if you had the courage for detachment. And on second thought it was a fairly stupid question, since I'm asking you for something you don't know about and therefore you can't know if you have it or not. For this reason I'd like to see if I can at least get you started on this business of detachment, so you can get a taste of it.

JACOLO: At your service.

SANCHO: From what you have told me, it seems that certain supreme values or ends must exist that give meaning to life. They comprise the idea of good, and this is what we'll call them from now on.

JACOLO: Yes, the idea of good exists. All I have to do is observe the history of humanity, its progressive ascent toward ever higher stages, to realize it exists. Time and again it has been reformulated in different and ever higher ways. I don't claim that the idea of good has been laid down once and for all. In the case of good, as with everything, progress is continuous. But always, again and again, there is good that can be achieved, once the lower stages have been passed through as a necessary condition for ascending to the higher ones.

SANCHO: What you say is excellent. But it isn't sufficient, when it comes to good, simply to observe that it's there.

JACOLO: And what else do you need?

SANCHO: Well, it's possible that in this case, as in a thousand other aspects of normal life, you've got it wrong, you've observed something nonexistent, mistaken fireflies for lanterns.

JACOLO: Stop right there! Yes, okay, it's possible that when it comes down to the details — good is this, good is that, it's made this way or that way — that I've got it wrong; but this doesn't in any way rule out the existence of good. It just means that I don't yet understand it. The possibility that I'm wrong implies that I have a duty to keep looking for it, and not to relax when I seem to have reached it, but to remain alert, to sift, to meditate, to be sure that what I've got is the wheat and not the chaff.

SANCHO: This is exactly what I meant when I said that to be sure that good exists, observing its existence is insufficient. We try to observe it and determine what it consists of only because we already know it exists and that we need to look for it. Good doesn't simply exist, it has to exist. And if we don't yet know what it is, or if we see we've misunderstood it, we have to go on looking for it because without a doubt it is there. The idea of good is for us inescapable, don't you think?

JACOLO: Yes.

SANCHO: So then at this point we can stop worrying about actually observing it. Even if we found out exactly what good was, we would always have this doubt that maybe we had simply found a nonexistent chimera. And if it was a chimera, we might be tempted to abandon the search. No one has ever found a unicorn, and since it wasn't in fact necessary that it should exist, today nobody goes looking for it. In the case of looking for good, on the other hand, there is always this secret coiled spring, always under tension, pushing us to keep looking for it.

JACOLO: Absolutely right. And that's precisely why searching is better than finding. The value of what you find is always provisional and uncertain. The value of the search is absolute. You undoubtedly know Lessing's old saying: "You choose. In my right hand I hold the truth and in my left the eternal search for truth," I would say "Father, keep the truth for yourself and give me the eternal search."

SANCHO: (to himself) Calm down, old soul. I won't let anyone hear you laughing at the story of the seeker. Yes, I also know the story of the fox and the grapes. But now hush, otherwise you'll frighten good Jacolo, who isn't yet able to hear the note of delight in your laughter, just the diabolical cackle. (aloud, to Jacolo) So having dispensed with actually observing it, it seems to me that we need to ask ourselves what it is that convinces us that good still exists.

JACOLO: But I've already said it, and more than once. Good has to exist because it's what justifies life. Without it, what would be the purpose of living?

SANCHO: If I'm following correctly, what your statement means is: you love living very much, but you are afraid in some way that you don't deserve it, and therefore you feel you need to provide your life with a justification.

JACOLO: Absolutely not. You surreptitiously attribute a level of hypocrisy to me that is not in my nature at all.

SANCHO: Don't get worked up, o most noble one. Don't be afraid. It's the first step into the desert. In your opinion, do you think taming horses is necessary?

JACOLO: What a question! Of course it's necessary if you want to ride in a carriage, or on horseback.

SANCHO: And if you didn't want to ride in a carriage or on horseback?

JACOLO: In that case it wouldn't be necessary at all.

SANCHO: But if you understand so easily that the need to tame horses is necessary and inescapable only if you accept as a premise the desire to ride in a carriage or on horseback, you can't then refuse to admit that the necessity and inevitability of the idea of good depends utterly on the need to justify life.

JACOLO: This is true, but it has nothing to do with the self-righteous hypocrisy you accused me of a moment ago.

SANCHO: What does "the need to justify your life" mean?

JACOLO: It means that to deserve to live I have to establish a higher purpose for myself, such that if someone asked "why do you live and not kill yourself?" the reason I would give is that I must achieve that purpose. I am ready to die for it. For other purposes I am more reserved.

SANCHO: You remember the thing about taming horses?

JACOLO: Yes.

SANCHO: But you wouldn't feel this need at all if you simply, calmly and without worry just lived, like an animal — or like a god, if you like. The fact that you feel the need to be worthy means that there is some basic uncertainty in you. It's as if you knew you had been given something not as an outright gift, but as a conditional grant, which could be snatched away from you at any moment.

If you were indifferent about this conditional grant it would hardly matter to you if you deserved it or not. The fact that you have this concern instead shows that you care about living, that you love yourself very much. But there's something more. For some mysterious reason you feel that it's not good to love yourself. If you didn't have this fear and this love you wouldn't feel that you needed to deserve to live and therefore you wouldn't need to justify your life. And finally — consequently — you wouldn't need to have good as an ideal.

JACOLO: There's nothing in this reasoning to object to. But I am somewhat horrified at the double abyss that yawns in front of me right from the first steps you make me take in the desert. On one hand, if it weren't for the pole star of good, any crime would for me be lawful! And on the other, what is this formless and immoral love and fear directed toward ourselves that we have found at the bottom of our souls? On this path you want to lead me down everything is uncertain and equivocal.

SANCHO: And you feel instead that you need to be safe in a tower that won't fall down when the wind blows, right?

JACOLO: Leave the jokes out of it, I want to know for sure what I have to do.

SANCHO: I'm not joking. I am noting the discovery that's been made. Morality, the duty to know good and to stick to it arises from a certain deep anguish, from the sense one feels at a certain moment of having been abandoned, of being on one's own in the world. Of these two abysses you're afraid of, the one that apparently worries you most is the one that seems to erase the distinction between good and evil. But this is actually the least important of the two. It wouldn't be difficult to get to the bottom of it. Much more interesting is the nightmarish void right behind us. It has a thousand different names. It is original sin for the religious, the ego — the dark despot — for mystics, arrogance for moralists, disobedience for legislators, the spirit of revolt for the governed, heresy for the churches... And each of them has its own myth of the origin of the abyss, of the evil that weighs like a curse on the shoulders of mankind.

JACOLO: And you who claim to be unprejudiced are interested in these fairy tales? They are stupid stories from primitive minds that haven't yet learned what a human being actually is.

SANCHO: These myths you call stupid are among the most profound things man has managed to fathom. Those who became aware of the abyss have thrown up a bridge for us. Then along come people like you who stroll calmly across the bridge yet believe that the abyss is a fairy tale. . . .

INDEX OF NAMES

INDEX OF SUBJECTS